INSIDE THE WORLD OF MINIATURES & DOLLHOUSES

INSIDE THE WORLD OF MINIATURES & DOLLHOUSES

A comprehensive guide to collecting and creating

Bernard Rosner and Jay Beckerman

David McKay Company, Inc.
New York

Library of Congress Cataloging in Publication Data
Rosner, Bernard.
    Inside the world of miniatures & dollhouses.
    Bibliography: p.
    Includes index.
    1. Doll-houses. 2. Doll furniture. 3. Miniature
objects. I. Beckerman, Jay, joint author. II. Title.
NK4893.R67   745.59′23   76-16458
ISBN 0-679-50617-9
ISBN 0-679-50620-9 pbk.

10 9 8 7 6 5 4 3 2
MANUFACTURED IN THE UNITED STATES OF AMERICA

To Ethel and Binnie

CONTENTS

ACKNOWLEDGMENTS — ix

INTRODUCTION — xi

1 THE FASCINATION OF SMALLNESS — 1

2 A HIDDEN HOBBY SURFACES — 8

3 SCALE: THE RULES OF THE GAME — 12

4 AN INTRODUCTION TO MINIATURES — 26

5 OUTSTANDING MINIATURE-MAKERS — 38

6 POPULAR MINIATURE FURNITURE AND ACCESSORIES — 64

7 AN INTRODUCTION TO DOLLHOUSES — 72

8 SHOPPING FOR A DOLLHOUSE — 82

9 THE CUSTOM-MADE DOLLHOUSE — 100

10 ANTIQUE MINIATURES — 106

11 TOOLS AND SUPPLIES FOR MAKING MINIATURES AND DOLLHOUSES — 120

12 MAKING MINIATURE FURNITURE YOURSELF — 140

13 BUILDING YOUR OWN DOLLHOUSE—SEVERAL APPROACHES — 152

14 COMPLETE DOLLHOUSE PLANS — 162

15 GETTING DEEPER INTO THE HOBBY — 190

16 MUSEUMS AND EXHIBITS — 198

17 GOING INTO THE MINIATURE BUSINESS — 210

18 RESOURCES — 218

INDEX — 233

ACKNOWLEDGMENTS

This book owes its existence to the many craftspeople, collectors, and dealers who, concurring with us that a work such as this was greatly needed, did their best to help us document the explosively growing hobby of miniature collecting. Many of these people gave time they could scarcely afford to part with, burdened, as they were, by heavy backlogs of orders for their work. To these wonderfully generous miniaturists goes our deep appreciation. We hope that our book justifies their confidence and interest.

Among those in the miniature field who helped us were a number of people who went so far out of their way that we wish to acknowledge them individually. Our special thanks to Iris Brown, Mary Dudley Cowles, Robert Dankanics, Kathryn Falk, Robert Milne, John Noble, Jean Schramm, Constance Simone, and John Thomas III.

In addition, we owe a considerable debt to Aaron Priest, who had faith in the book's possibilities; to David Currier, for his intelligent guidance and painstakingly thorough editing; to Donna Bass, who made us look literate; to Arnold Beckerman, for his outstanding photography; to Joe Robleto, for his many patient hours in the darkroom; to Herb Kolb, for lending us his considerable model-making skills; to Bill Wolf of Bill Way Studio, and Kon Schera and Bob Hutter of Lukon Studio, for their retouching talents.

Thank you all.

INTRODUCTION

A few years ago my daughter was given some dollhouse furniture for her birthday, and she appealed to me to build her a dollhouse. Since I had never undertaken a project like this before, I stalled for time, half hoping that her interest would fade and that the request would be forgotten. But the reverse happened: Her interest and her collection grew. And when a friend received a handsome turn-of-the-century dollhouse as a gift, I knew I was about to become a mini-builder.

So my daughter and I sat down together—architect and client—and plotted the basic design of the house. Realizing what was in store for me and seeking to get off easy, I checked out the local toy and hobby shops to see if I could find a ready-made dollhouse that would serve the purpose. What I found at that time, however, was a disappointing lot of poorly constructed houses at prices that were far from miniature. I had no choice but to build the house myself.

The library seemed like a likely place to get advice. But that, too, turned out to be disappointing. What the subject seemed to need was a good book.

Then, fortunately, Jay Beckerman, an antique-collector friend of mine, recommended the dollhouse collection at the Museum of the City of New York. There, in a glass case, was exactly the kind of house I had had in mind, displaying a quality of workmanship that was both intimidating and exhilarating. I was inspired. To match this became my goal, no matter how great the effort involved.

Before construction began, I heard about a wonderful little shop in Lebanon, New Jersey, called The Dollhouse Factory. Jay and I drove out for a visit, and I was surprised to find that I could actually buy many of the things I needed ready-made—miniature shingles, precisely scaled moldings of all kinds, tiny bricks, wallpaper with miniature patterns, in addition to everything I would need to electrify a house, including bulbs half the size of a pencil eraser. What Jay and I had stumbled into was not just an isolated shop but the world of miniatures.

It turned out that there were many thousands of collectors of miniatures scattered throughout the country and that a growing legion of craftspeople were providing them with every conceivable article of furniture and furnishing, from elaborate highboys to tiny fly swatters. I learned that a collector could obtain virtually anything in miniature if he or she knew where to find it. I sent for every catalog and price list I came across, and for a while I was spending more time sleuthing than building.

It was while gathering information on mini resources that the idea for this book occurred to Jay and me. Why, we reasoned, should anyone with an interest in miniatures have to go through what I did in order to track down information and sources of supply when all this material could be brought together in one place by someone who's been through it already? The result is this book—a convenient manual for getting into the hobby, a useful sourcebook that distills for the reader a large body of helpful information that was gathered the hard way.

Our purpose is to provide a guided tour through the world of miniatures in such a way that readers can embark or disembark wherever they wish, depending on the extent of their knowledge and interest.

The problem in writing a book of this sort is where to stop: The subject of miniatures is so rich in material that one is tempted to go on and on *ad gargantuam.* Consequently, in order to offer the most manageable and useful book possible, Jay and I set our sights very carefully and ordered our priorities.

The opening chapter traces the hobby from its earliest beginnings to its recent dramatic growth. Next the reader is introduced to the wealth of dollhouses and miniatures that are available today. Because our purpose is to help the reader participate in the hobby, we have emphasized availability in the materials depicted. There are other books on miniatures crammed with photos of wonderful collections, but the pieces shown are not for sale. Throughout this book, however, a large percentage of the miniatures and dollhouses pictured is readily obtainable by the hobbyist.

To help foster an appreciation for quality, we have chosen to reveal the world of miniatures through the work of outstanding contemporary craftspeople. Here is work of a caliber not usually seen by most collectors, as well as interesting insights furnished by the craftspeople themselves, who comment on their own work and on the hobby of miniature collecting in general.

The more familiar miniatures that are produced in quantity are also shown here; but because these pieces can readily be seen at shops and shows, they are given secondary emphasis.

We have treated dollhouses in the same way, giving primary attention to the outstanding dollhouse-makers of today whose work can be purchased by the miniaturist.

Next, since many hobbyists enjoy making things themselves, we encourage the reader to attempt a few miniature-making projects—but only after having read our comprehensive discussion of tools and supplies.

For the reader interested in building a dollhouse, we have provided the most thorough plans and instructions of any book on the subject in order that future dollhouse-builders will not have to face the experience unaided, as did the author. By following the plans in this book, the reader can construct a spectacular Williamsburg Colonial-style dollhouse; and because people vary in their degree of skill and patience, we have provided two approaches to the project—one simplified; and the other, more highly detailed.

Once the reader has become acquainted with miniatures and dollhouses from the standpoints of both collecting and creating, we proceed deeper into the hobby with a discussion of publications, clubs, shows, museum exhibits—even how to get started in your own miniatures business.

In the final chapter we have provided an extensive list of resources for the miniaturist, and have indicated whether catalogs are available and how they can be obtained.

All in all, we have tried to make our book informative, useful, and, in the case of projects, accomplishable. And while this book is intended to be of value to even the most experienced miniaturist, we most envy the newcomer, for whom many wonderful surprises are in store.

Bernard Rosner and Jay Beckerman
New York City

1976

INSIDE THE WORLD OF MINIATURES & DOLLHOUSES

Terracotta model house, an Egyptian funerary object, Dynasty XII (2000–1788 B.C.). From Hierakonpolis. The object at the rear, resembling a fireplace, is the house itself. To escape the excessive indoor heat, the Egyptians spent much of their time on their roofs, this one accessible by the staircase to the right. In the center are various vegetable offerings—food for the soul. The scale can be ascertained by the indentations to the left, which are the imprints of the craftsman's fingers. (The Metropolitan Museum of Art, museum excavations, 1934–35. Rogers Fund, 1935.)

CHAPTER 1

THE FASCINATION OF SMALLNESS

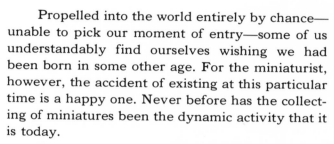

Propelled into the world entirely by chance—unable to pick our moment of entry—some of us understandably find ourselves wishing we had been born in some other age. For the miniaturist, however, the accident of existing at this particular time is a happy one. Never before has the collecting of miniatures been the dynamic activity that it is today.

We can imagine the surprise of future archaeologists excavating twentieth-century sites and finding the level belonging to the 1970s littered with household objects of diminutive size. As they probed for the beginnings of this widespread interest in things small, they would necessarily make detours through many cultures, eventually arriving at the Egypt of the Twelfth Dynasty. Here, in a place called Hierakonpolis, a forgotten craftsman gathered into his hands a lifeless mound of clay, out of which, with a few crude strokes, he molded a rude dwelling—one of the first miniature houses.

At around this same time, in Thebes, Egyptian woodcarvers were called upon to fashion an elaborate and realistic group of miniature figures and objects, which have managed to survive in a remarkable state of preservation. Luxurious Nile pleasure boats parade before us, their retinues of servants rowing, fishing, and preparing food. All the details are there for our inspection.

Other models, in the form of room settings complete with walls, hinged doors, and staircases, provide a revealing look at Theban daily life. In a stable we can see oxen and cattle being cared for by stablemen. A granary model shows clerks busily writing on tablets and women measuring grain before depositing it in bins. Another setting presents a brewery and bakery side by side. In the bakery we can actually follow each of the steps of making bread, from bruising the grain with pestles to shaping it into loaves.

For all their charm, these marvelous miniatures were not made to be played with by some fortunate child of forty centuries ago. Nor were they created for the pleasure of some collector of that period. In fact, they were not intended to be viewed at all, but to be sealed away in a tomb for use in another life, for these were the burial figures of Meket Re, a powerful Egyptian official of the Eleventh Dynasty.

To the Egyptians of that time, death was an extension of life, for which burial objects helped set the stage. The figures were supposed to become life-sized stand-ins for the deceased in the forced labor that the dead were required to perform. As far as Meket Re was concerned, these remarkable miniatures existed only to enable him to take his comfortable lifestyle with him into the next world.

The Meket Re figures bring to life a period of history far more vividly than any other form of documentation could have done. The creators of these extraordinary models could well have said of their work—as did the authors of a later miniature masterpiece—"It is a serious attempt to express our age, and to show forth in dwarf proportions the limbs of our present world." (From *The Book of the Queen's Dolls' House* by A. C. Benson. See Bibliography for complete publishing information on this and other books mentioned throughout the text.)

Many cultures throughout history have produced miniature works of one form or another, sometimes as ritual objects, often as toys, and occasionally as articles purely aesthetic in nature. One thing we learn very early upon being exposed to miniatures is that smallness of size does not prevent bigness of impression. Anyone who has seen the intricate and mysterious Mayan pottery figures of Jaina Island is aware of the imposing presence that small things can be made to have. And anyone familiar with the wonderfully imaginative and whimsical goldweights of the African Ashantis recognizes the personality with which small things can be infused.

The word "miniature" covers a wide range of artifacts, most of which lie outside the realm of this book. For our purpose a more narrow definition is required. Here "miniature" refers to small-scale reproductions of household objects—primarily the contents of dollhouses. As so defined, the hobby of collecting miniatures can be traced back to mid-sixteenth-century Europe, where we find its beginnings in the elaborate curio cabinets that became the rage of royalty and the rich of that time. In these cabinets miniature objects of all kinds—notably dolls, furniture, and household articles—were collected and displayed.

The first actual dollhouse that we know of was constructed for the Duke of Bavaria in 1558. The Duke originally commissioned this elaborate house for his little daughter, but the house turned out to be much more than a toy and found its way into the Duke's own art collection instead. This seems to have started a fashion among the aristocracy for collecting dollhouses—one that continues to this day.

The pinnacle of this trend was reached in 1924, when Queen Mary of England was presented by her loyal subjects with what must surely be the most fabulous house of its kind ever conceived and built. The Queen's Dolls' House was the collective work of a legion of outstanding contributors. Many of the most illustrious firms in England enthusiastically accepted the challenge of producing flawless facsimiles of their products 1/12 their actual size. Under the guiding eye of the famous English architect Sir Edward Lutyens, the entire project took four years to plan and build.

An inventory of the contents would require an entire book and, in fact, is the subject of two large volumes, both by A. C. Benson: *The Book of the Queen's Dolls' House* and *The Library of the Queen's Dolls' House*. The reader is recommended to these handsomely illustrated and charmingly written volumes, which, more than any other source, give an insight into the vast dimensions of this project.

The house, a representation of a "Family mansion belonging to a monarch who seeks relief from cares of state in a quiet family life and a comfortable rather than luxurious routine," measures more than eight feet in length and five in depth. The outer walls are raised and lowered electrically, giving access to the rooms of the house on all four sides. A drawer underneath houses a royal garage complete with a fleet of limousines, while another drawer ingeniously contains a garden with collapsible trees.

Notable among the wonders that abound here is a library containing two hundred leather-bound volumes, each written in longhand by a famous English author or poet. Represented are such luminaries as Hilaire Belloc, G. K. Chesterton, Walter de la Mare, A. E. Housman, Thomas Hardy, Rudyard Kipling, Max Beerbohm, Joseph Conrad, Conan Doyle, John Galsworthy, and Hugh Walpole.

Model of a granary from the tomb of Meket-Re, Thebes, Dynasty XI (c. 2000 B.C.), complete with multiple rooms, stairway, and movable door. (The Metropolitan Museum of Art, museum excavations, 1919–1920; Rogers Fund, supplemented by contributions of Edward S. Harkness.)

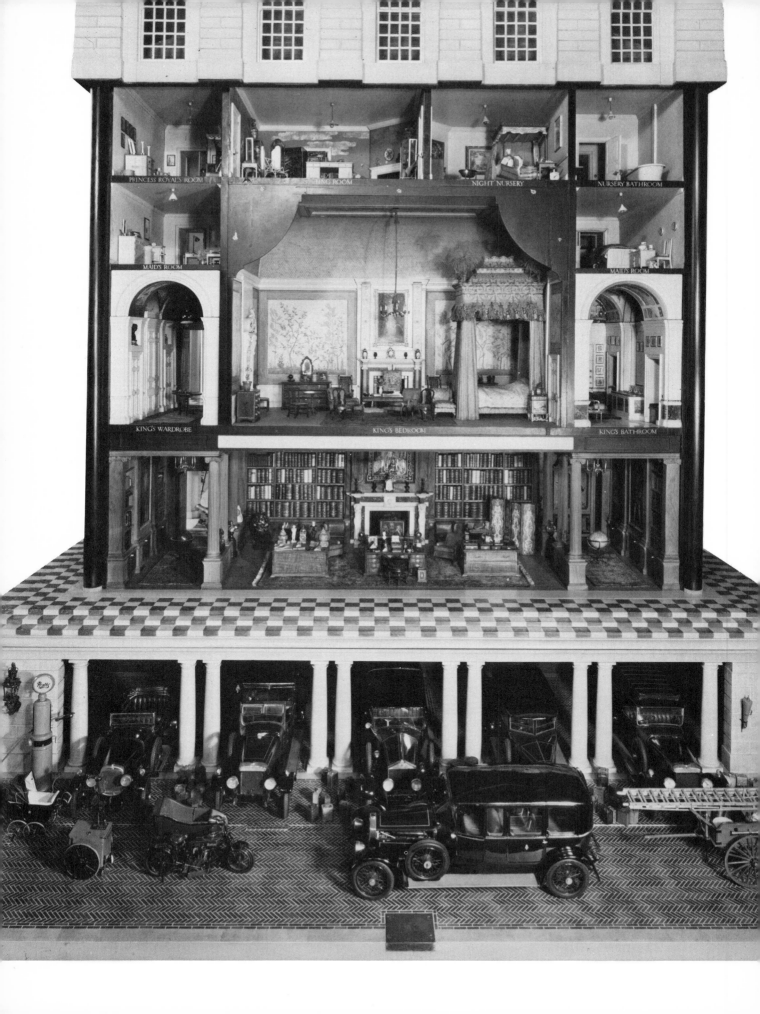

PRINCESS ROYAL'S ROOM   ...ESSING ROOM   NIGHT NURSERY   NURSERY BATHROOM

MAID'S ROOM   MAID'S ROOM

KING'S WARDROBE   KING'S BEDROOM   KING'S BATHROOM

Similarly the paintings hanging throughout the house are the work of famous English painters of the day—David Muirhead, Adrian Stokes, Russell Flint, Sir Frank Short, Edmund Dulac, Albert Rutherston, Sir William Nicholson, John Nash, and others.

In the Queen's bathroom the silver taps of the bathtub provide both hot and cold running water. Two pianos in the salon can actually be played. All one needs are fingers small enough to fit the keys. The diminutive bottles in the wine cellar contain actual vintage champagne, burgundy, sherry, whiskeys, and liqueurs. There are kegs of beer as well.

The fact that so great an effort on the part of so many talented people could have been mustered for the task of building a dollhouse is testimony to the fascination that miniatures hold.

Small versions of large objects have a special appeal, partly because they're "cute," but largely because they're "manageable." The model industry owes its existence to this appeal of small-scale replicas. Model railroad fans have been intrigued by smaller and smaller train sets, until today's "N-gauge" trains have working locomotives only a few inches long. Part of the attraction of stamp collecting can be traced to the fact that stamps are actually miniature prints, with details so fine that it often takes a magnifying glass to appreciate them.

The appeal of smallness is such that, in recent times, entire villages have been built in miniature, serving as tourist attractions. We know of three such villages in Europe. One is in England in the ancient Cotswold hamlet of Bourton-on-the-Water. As Samuel Chamberlain describes it in his travel book, *British Bouquet:* "You will encounter a genuine curiosity if you visit the Old New Inn, built in 1718, at the Southern end of the village. Here is a miniature model of Bourton-on-the-Water, at

View of Queen Mary's Dolls' House, with the exterior raised to reveal all the rooms of the west front, including the fabulous library, King's bedroom, and maids' rooms. A drawer in the base of the house cleverly converts into the garage, with its fleet of limousines. (Courtesy of The Lord Chamberlain, St. James Palace, London. Copyright reserved.)

dolls' house scale. You feel like a Gulliver wandering through this Lilliputian stone village, which was designed by the hotel proprietor and built by local craftsmen. Shops and manor houses are built in perfect scale, together with the library, village hall, war memorial, and the churches, with organ music floating out of their doors. The river is there, of course, and measures about a yard wide."

A second such attraction can be found in Switzerland, three miles south of Lugano, at Melide. This is the Swissminiatur, a village built to 1/25 its actual size, where you can stroll like a giant past Swiss landmarks and examples of the architectural styles of the various cantons. Geneva's St. Pierre Cathedral is represented, as is the fabulous castle of Chillon.

The third of these scaled-down villages is the most remarkable of all—the wondrous Madurodam, in The Hague, Holland. This monumental miniature sprawls over four full acres, is linked by two and one-quarter miles of railway track, is illuminated at night by forty-six thousand lights, and requires a two-mile walk to see it all. Also built to 1/25 its actual size, Madurodam is a replica of a typical Dutch town—a complete community with churches and castles, shops and houses, canals, even an airport and docks. Madurodam is a major tourist attraction, visited annually by more than a million people.

Beyond the universal and age-old affection for things small, the fascination with miniatures seems to have a special significance for us today. The modern world is bewildering in its complexity and fraught with dangers, which the news media confront us with daily. At times, too, our society seems grossly insensitive to its heritage, paving over the past with scarcely a glance backward. It's the kind of world—unsentimental and beyond our power to influence—that we take pleasure in escaping from occasionally. Miniatures provide the perfect retreat. They take the rough edges off of reality. They allow us to preserve the past by re-creating it. And they give us control over a tiny world of our own making where everything is just the way we want it, with ugliness and inconvenience walled out. In our miniature world, roofs never leak, rugs never fall victim to cigarette burns, beds never need making, food never spoils. As one collector put it: "The only perfect thing in my life is my dollhouse. It's there. It's controllable. It's security."

Miniatures also open up the realm of the possible. Through miniatures we can live in any century, adopt any lifestyle, re-create room settings of any period, and people them in any way we choose. Miniatures enable us to act out some of our fantasies, thereby letting us have things pretty much our way.

Collecting miniatures has some other advantages. Because a dollhouse requires relatively little space, a considerable collection of miniatures can be housed in rather small quarters. In addition, a collection of miniatures is always in a state of display, unlike stamp or coin collections, which are usually tucked away out of sight or kept under lock and key. Therefore miniaturists are able to enjoy the satisfaction of having their collections seen and admired.

Small replicas of life-size things have held a fascination, and even a cultural function, for people since the earliest civilizations. We have suggested some of the reasons for this and also for the surge of interest in miniatures today. Perhaps future archaeologists, psychologists, and other culture-watchers will discover reasons of which we are not even vaguely aware. For now, we can note what may turn out to be the strongest motivation of all—the pursuit of pleasure.

*Wine Cellar of Queen Mary's Dolls'
House. The inch-high bottles contain
actual vintage wines and fine liqueurs.
Beer reposes in casks. Everything is so
flawlessly in scale that only the full-size
brass screws in the foreground betray
the actual dimensions of this setting.
(Courtesy of The Lord Chamberlain,
St. James Palace, London.
Copyright reserved.)*

CHAPTER 2

A HIDDEN HOBBY SURFACES

Although miniature collecting as a hobby dates back many years, its widespread popularity in this country is a very current phenomenon. Until a few years ago, the hobby had a relatively small following among adults. Dollhouses were primarily thought of as toys for little girls. A mother might indulge her adult fascination with this tiny world through her daughter's dollhouse in much the same way that a father played with his son's electric trains. But until recently, few adults would have seriously entertained the notion of owning and furnishing a dollhouse of their own, quite likely for fear of being thought of as eccentric or of having entered their second childhood.

Most of the tiny furniture that existed up until the late 1960s fell into the category of toys—either the antique toys left over from Victorian times, when dollhouses were extremely popular, or the mass-produced toys of today.

True "miniatures," however, were not entirely unknown. During the 1930s and early 1940s Mrs. James Ward Thorne, miniature collector, furniture historian, and philanthropist, commissioned a remarkable series of miniature period rooms as a survey of the development of interior design. They were put on display at the Chicago World's Fair "Century of Progress" Exposition, at the San Francisco and New York World's Fairs, and at The Art Institute of Chicago, where sixty-eight of these rooms permanently reside. (Additional Thorne Rooms are in the permanent collections of the Phoenix Art Museum in Arizona and the Dulin Gallery of Art in Knoxville, Tennessee.) The surprising thing is that Mrs. Thorne's widely celebrated rooms—seen by hundreds of thousands of awed spectators—did not stimulate an epidemic of miniature collecting among adults at that time.

Some adult miniature collectors had existed all along, but in very small numbers. They were supplied by a handful of craftspeople who were widely scattered and unknown to all but the most knowledgeable collectors.

In this way the hobby went quietly about its business, attracting little attention and gaining few new recruits.

Then, in the early seventies—virtually overnight, as it were—everything changed. Miniature collecting expanded dramatically, attracting new converts at such a rapid rate that in 1976 this hobby ranks as one of the most popular.

What ignited this explosion of interest? Where did all the new enthusiasts come from?

People have always been fascinated by smallness. The potential for popularity had been there all along. It was simply lying dormant for lack of organization and communication. All that had to happen was for enough people to become aware that miniature collecting was indeed a hobby, and for miniatures to become more readily available.

It was the contact and organization on the part of collectors and craftspeople that provided the main impetus for bringing the hobby out of the woodwork. Miniature enthusiasts gradually became aware that others like themselves existed, and they began to seek one another out. What had been largely a solitary hobby now entered a new period of shared interest. The National Association of Miniature Enthusiasts (N.A.M.E.), formed under the guidance of Allegra Mott, a well-known collector, helped give structure to this formerly fragmented group of hobbyists. Concurrently, min-

iaturist clubs began sprouting up from coast to coast. Shows and conventions brought collectors and suppliers together, and the hobby was off and running.

At about the same time, a large number of women, through their interest in decoupage, were already well primed to respond to miniatures. As their decoupage efforts expanded into three-dimensional forms such as vignettes, shadow boxes, and ecology boxes, the stage was set for miniature collecting, the next logical evolutionary step.

In addition, new suppliers began appearing in record numbers, partly impelled by the crafts movement that had reached boom proportions in the country. A great many of these people were looking for ways to put their newfound skills to work to supplement their income. In miniature making they found the perfect cottage industry—one that required little investment and that could be carried on from a small corner of the home.

Another impetus, and a major one, was the coincident appearance of a number of new and excellent publications catering to miniaturists. *The Miniature Gazette, Nutshell News, Dollhouse and Miniature News, Mott's Miniature Workshop News,* and other periodicals helped spread the enjoyment of the hobby and gave collectors and craftspeople new opportunities for communicating with one another.

The hobby was gaining momentum. There were now hundreds of miniature-makers advertising and selling their work, and offering catalogs of every description. Suddenly the country was dotted with new shops catering to miniaturists.

Manufacturers of tools and supplies, aware of the needs of this new market, were encouraged to bring out new products aimed at miniaturists, and the advertising of these products served to attract still more miniaturists.

All of this activity did not go unnoticed by the press. Illustrated articles about the hobby began cropping up in local newspapers and national magazines, popularizing the hobby even more.

The hobby was no longer miniature.

John Stover, founder of the well-known miniatures firm of Grandmother Stover's, sheds some additional light on what turned miniature collecting into a major adult hobby. Mr. Stover began producing miniature accessories for children back in 1940 and had built a successful business. Then, in 1950, the business, as well as the entire toy industry, took an abrupt downward turn. "Because of television, dollhouse play ended in 1950," reports the Grandmother Stover's catalog.

Block House, a major distributor of miniatures and toys, reports the same thing. "All indoor toys and games—the whole category—took a nose-dive in those early years of television when everyone was glued to their sets twenty-four hours a day."

Looking for a new market for their miniatures, Grandmother Stover's turned to adults. "We were confident miniatures also appealed to adults. We packaged them as party favors and tie-ons for gifts. Adults who had never seen them in toy stores now found them in gift and stationery stores, and consumer acceptance was immediate and enthusiastic." So starting in 1950, many adults were exposed to miniatures for the first time.

Television's hold on children began to weaken in time, and in 1962 Grandmother Stover's was

once again providing dollhouse accessories to small homemakers. In their 1975 catalog, Grandmother Stover's was able to report that they were now selling to a combined audience of children and adults. "Now in our 35th year, a new generation of little girls has returned to dollhouse play . . . and their mothers and grandmothers are buying our miniatures from craft stores for shadow boxes, rooms, shops, and ecology and memorabilia boxes." As an indication of the size of this combined audience, Grandmother Stover's miniatures are today sold in ten thousand stores throughout the country.

The growing interest in antiques over the past fifteen or so years has undoubtedly helped fuel the miniature boom by fostering an awareness and appreciation of the past. This may explain the curious fact that while in other times dollhouses were largely furnished in the style of the same era, today's dollhouses are furnished in the styles of earlier periods. Miniature furniture of contemporary design is virtually nonexistent; most of the emphasis is on re-creating the past. And since we desire to reproduce things to which we attach importance, it may well be that the past is more important to us today than ever before. A glimpse into the average American home would tend to confirm this by revealing a large percentage of furnishings of period design.

Who collects miniatures today? Men, women, and children of all ages. Bob Dankanics of The Dollhouse Factory in Lebanon, New Jersey, observed that his customers vary in age from two and a half to eighty-nine years. "It's a new enough hobby so that many people don't declare themselves. They come in here under the guise of a parent or grandparent, and you don't know what's going on until later, when you get to know the customer. I made one mistake at the very beginning that I've made sure never to repeat. This couple came in and asked me to build a house. And as we got into it there were just so many things she wanted to do with it that I finally asked her, 'How old is the child?' She got a strange look on her face and said, 'It's for me.' I almost lost the sale. That was four years ago, and at that time I was geared to think like everyone else—that dollhouses were for kids. After that I made a little sign that hangs in the shop. It says: 'If you're an adult, please don't be self-conscious about enjoying yourself here. Half my customers are adult miniature and dollhouse enthusiasts. Personally, since I've been playing around with these dollhouses, I've stopped sucking my thumb.' "

The majority of today's collectors are women, largely because the hobby still retains some of the old stigma of being unmasculine. This view is changing, however, as the hobby receives more and more exposure, and the rapidity with which boys and men are becoming involved suggests that in time the hobby will have a large percentage of male participants. Building model houses is, after all, only a short step away from building model railroad layouts, a traditionally male activity.

Frequently an entire family will get involved together. The scenario goes like this. The mother becomes fascinated with miniatures and acquires a few pieces. The next thing the father knows, he's being maneuvered into building a dollhouse, at first reluctantly, then with increasing interest. The children of the family all want to participate, particularly when they see their parents having such a

good time, and they make their own contribution to the extent of their abilities.

The hobby has also encouraged women to want to learn how to build things for themselves, and more and more women are turning up in shop classes these days. As a result, tool companies are beginning to view women as a large new market. The Dremel Company, whose power tools have long been standard equipment for serious model-makers, saw fit to introduce two new power tools—a small lathe and a scroll saw—with the female miniaturist in mind.

Miniature collectors are fond of exchanging ideas and information with one another. Those miniaturists who have contributed to this book have been exceedingly generous with their time and eager to share their experiences. They enjoy talking about miniatures and seem to find it an endless source of pleasure. One excellent crafts-woman, buried under a six-month backlog of or-ders, nonetheless found time to correspond with us, writing lengthy letters that must have con-sumed hours of her time. Many other busy crafts-people were only too willing to halt their work in order to help us take you inside the world of minia-tures.

These characteristics also show up in the friendly approach that miniaturists have to doing business. The miniatures business is unique. It consists mainly of individual craftspeople working out of their homes. Everything is handmade one at a time, just the way the original cabinetmakers and artisans worked. There are no assembly lines; production is limited; and in today's thriving minia-tures market, there seems to be plenty of room for everyone. The better craftspeople have more or-ders than they can possibly handle. Such an atmos-phere of high demand coupled with the person-ality of the people involved results in low-pressure selling and an almost total absence of competitive-ness.

Much of the business of miniatures is con-ducted through mail order, and there is a vast difference among the catalogs and price lists of-fered by the various suppliers. Some are no more than a single, poorly typed list, although others are beautiful and expensively made booklets, com-plete with color photographs. But there is not al-ways a direct correlation between the simplicity of a brochure and the quality of the merchandise offered. Some of the finest craftspeople don't really need anything more than a simple list—they can sell more than they can possibly make as it is. Moreover, the simplicity of these lists and bro-chures suggests a lack of sophistication among the makers about promoting their wares, which is part of their charm.

Of the richly produced catalogs, none is more inviting than the beautiful offering from Chestnut Hill Studio. You'll also enjoy the large and in-teresting catalog of The Miniature Mart in San Francisco—well worth sending for. And don't miss the highly original and thoroughly entertaining catalog produced by Al Atkins—*The Village Smithy*. There are many others you'll want to own. An extensive list, with addresses, is included in Chapter 18 ("Resources").

Dancing figure reduced to 1/12 its size to illustrate the relationship of a full-size object to its miniature counterpart when working in one-inch-to-one-foot scale. (Photo by Arnold Beckerman.)

CHAPTER 3

SCALE: THE RULES OF THE GAME

The activity of collecting miniatures centers around creating realistic-looking room settings in the widely accepted scale of one inch to one foot. An understanding of scale is necessary in order to achieve the desired realism.

Scale is the relationship in size between the original and the model. A change of scale can also change the impression that an object conveys. For example, a full-size locomotive gives us the feeling of massive power, a feeling entirely lost in the scale model. But the model rewards us with something else—it shows us the entire mechanism at a single glance, which helps us to understand how the component parts relate to one another.

Similarly, we experience a full-size house room by room, and only after we've assembled all these "pieces" in our mind do we develop a feeling about the house as a whole. But a dollhouse can be taken in at one glance, giving us a much more immediate impression of the period, the mood of the house, and the "lifestyle" of the occupants.

Scale is a concept of great interest to collectors. The question thus raised is how much importance to place on *exactness* of scale. Many articles have been written on the subject, each author promoting his or her point of view with great vigor. But the discussion really boils down to the distinction between "miniatures" and "toys." Children's dollhouses and their furnishings are toys. The success of a child's dollhouse is judged by the pleasure it gives the child, and, as such, the discussion of scale has little importance. Miniatures, on the other hand, are scale models. Their success is determined by how closely they duplicate the original. Here scale is all important.

Many of the early dollhouses that were built and furnished for children took only rough notice of scale. These dollhouses were intended to teach young girls, through play, how to run a proper household. So as long as the dollhouse and its contents were a reasonable facsimile of a household, it served its purpose.

Most of these early dollhouses were architecturally out of proportion. They were stylized designs invented by the dollhouse builders, who were usually the fathers or grandfathers of little girls. Among their inaccuracies, these houses contained ceilings that were quite high in relation to the room

Authenticity in a miniature is a function of faithful adherence to scale overall. This miniature highboy, a charming and inexpensive piece for the young collector to acquire, represents a simulation rather than a duplication of an actual highboy. Compare the thickness of the wood, the scrollwork, the turnings, and the hardware with that of the highboy shown opposite. From the collection of Valerie Rosner. (Photo by Arnold Beckerman.)

dimensions in order to make the houses more accessible to their owners. In many cases, the insides of the houses didn't relate to the outsides; for example, a fireplace might appear on a different wall than the location of the chimney would suggest. The Museum of the City of New York has several fine examples of such stylized dollhouses and their original furnishings. For contrast, it also has a dollhouse that was built perfectly in scale—"Mr. Briggs' Dream House."

Mr. Briggs was a model-maker who worked at the museum creating dioramas. His skill was considerable, and over the course of the years he constructed his dream house in miniature. The house is architecturally accurate and contains such details as metal flashing around the dormers, gutters and leaders, and a handsome bay window. The interior and its furnishings were also created by Mr. Briggs in realistic detail, right down to the tiny working tools in the attic workshop. In Mr. Briggs's house, which was not intended to be a child's plaything, scale is an important ingredient.

One of the most interesting views on the subject of scale is that held by John Noble, curator of toys at the Museum of the City of New York and a well-known toy historian and lecturer. Mr. Noble takes great exception to what he terms "the dictates of scale."

"The only place where scale is important is if you are actually concerned with a scale model," explains Mr. Noble. "The prime example of this is Mrs. Thorne's Rooms. They were intended to illustrate the different periods of furnishings, as a history of the decorative arts. They were absolutely

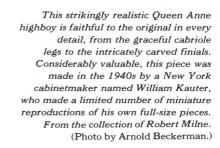

This strikingly realistic Queen Anne highboy is faithful to the original in every detail, from the graceful cabriole legs to the intricately carved finials. Considerably valuable, this piece was made in the 1940s by a New York cabinetmaker named William Kauter, who made a limited number of miniature reproductions of his own full-size pieces. From the collection of Robert Milne. (Photo by Arnold Beckerman.)

Detail of the cabriole leg of an actual Queen Anne side chair showing its size as compared with several of the popular scales of miniature furniture.

This is the size the chair would appear in 2-inch scale. While pleasing in terms of a few pieces, this size becomes unwieldy in terms of an entire dollhouse.

in scale and were deliberately intended to be. The Thorne Rooms are the perfect miniatures—the miniature collector's ideal. Scale, in this case, is extremely important. If anything was even slightly wrong, then the illusion fails. You can look at photographs of Mrs. Thorne's Rooms, and unless you are told that they are in miniature you'd believe them to be the real thing. And this is perfectly valid if you're concerned with miniatures. But there are two things—there's the collecting and assembling of miniature rooms, such as Mrs. Thorne did, and then there are old playthings, which is something totally different.

"Among the really wonderful early dollhouses were the 17th- and 18th-century cabinets which were made at enormous costs—Dutch merchants would spend their whole fortunes on their dollhouses—and their cabinets were very realistic. The tapestry would be real tapestry. The woven carpet might easily be woven in the carpet factory. And the embroidered things, the silver things, the china, the porcelain—all were extremely realistic. But the scale has a surprising discrepancy. The overall realism is not there. You have a house in a cabinet, with no façade, and you have two rooms with no possible way of getting from one to the other—there will be no doorway. And if you follow the chimney system, it isn't logical. And if there is a staircase, it very often doesn't go anywhere.

"The same thing happens in the fine 18th-century English dolls' houses—called "babies'" houses—which were not made for children but were a rich adult's plaything just as the cabinets were. One of these babies' houses is absolutely staggering. The fourposter beds are covered with damask and brocade. The Chippendale chairs were made by Chippendale himself. And yet the house has a staircase which runs straight up into the ceiling and disappears. Its logic is not right, and to me this is an intensely important part of it. It's the creative element, which is missing in miniature collecting. A dollhouse is a toy, and that's the creativity and fun of it. To me the best houses are the ones with an element of fantasy.

"Miniatures are not thought of as play because we're afraid to play. Our culture has done that. One doesn't play anymore. One watches football on TV rather than going out and playing it.

This is the popular 1-inch scale—small enough to be "magical," large enough to be manageable. The 1-inch scale has become the standard among today's collectors and creators of miniatures.

The same chair in 1/2-inch scale. Its size, while fascinating, makes it more difficult to manage. Steady hands and good eyesight are a must. (Photo by Arnold Beckerman.)

"The 18th-century people played. Children play. Cats and dogs and other animals play. It's a natural need. One has the capacity for play. That's why these hobbies are enormously attractive to today's adults. It allows them to play."

Robert Milne, a prominent dealer in antique miniatures, also makes a clear distinction between toys and miniatures. While Mr. Milne collects both, he admits to a passion for exactness and a fondness for reproducing the milieu of a particular period. He favors miniatures that are precisely made in order that his period rooms look as realistic as possible. Among his personal collection of more than fifty thousand pieces, assembled over thirty years of collecting, are many period rooms created with antique miniatures of precise scale. Some of these extraordinary pieces are shown in Chapter 10.

While today's hobby of making and collecting miniatures is based on a scale of one inch to one foot, within this basic equation lies considerable room for interpretation.

The objective of some miniaturists is to achieve photographic realism, and scale is the most important component of such realism. If everything in a room shrinks to the same size, the room will look realistic. Anything out of scale will look noticeably wrong. Take a piece of real carpeting, however thin, and place it in a miniature room setting, and it will look as grossly out of place as a carpet with a six-inch pile would look in a life-size setting. The important thing about scale isn't so much what the scale is (that is, how much smaller than real life it is), but that everything be in the same scale.

If it makes you happy to collect or make miniatures in a scale smaller or larger than one inch to one foot, then by all means do so. There are miniatures available in a scale of one-half inch to the foot, which require a great deal of dexterity and good eyesight to handle. Another popular scale is two inches to the foot—sometimes referred to as "Barbi" size, after the popular doll of the same name. You can create houses and rooms in either of these scales, as well as any other scale you might choose, and your settings will look just as realistic as any one-inch-scale room—as long as you keep everything in the same proportion.

The hobby has centered around the one-inch scale for both practical and aesthetic reasons. It

Thorne Room—Louis XVI Dining
Room (1774–1793). One of the famous
Chateaux of Fontainebleau served as the
source for this elegant dining room.
Among the difficult details that Mrs.
Thorne has managed to capture in
miniature are the numerous ornaments
and tableware. The two Thorne Rooms
shown here, as well as all the other
Thorne Rooms housed in both the
Phoenix Art Museum and The Art
Institute of Chicago, are valued for
insurance purposes at $7,500 each. In the
permanent collection of the Phoenix Art
Museum, Phoenix, Arizona.

Thorne Room—Louis XV Salon, French
(1715–1774). Mrs. James Ward Thorne's
rooms are masterpieces of the miniaturist
art. Every element has been carefully
considered in order to accurately re-
create the style of the period. In this
rococo setting, the walls and all the
woodwork have been hand carved. The
books on the shelves are all bound in real
leather. Walnut and oak were used to
create the handsome parquet floor. The
fireplace has been carved from rose
marble. Everything in the room is in
perfect one-inch-to-one-foot scale. In the
permanent collection of the Phoenix Art
Museum, Phoenix, Arizona.

had to adopt a standard of size to provide a common ground for both collectors and craftspeople. The one-inch scale is convenient to work with. It simply means that anything that measures one foot in actual size will measure one inch in miniature. A room with an 8-foot ceiling would have an 8-inch ceiling in a one-inch-scale dollhouse. Similarly, a room measuring 15′ × 20′ would measure 15″ × 20″ in miniature. Everything gets divided by twelve. The division becomes a bit more complex when dealing with furniture and furnishings, which naturally involves fractional ratios. Thus, a table whose top measures 1½ inches in thickness converts to ⅛ inch thick in miniature. Fortunately, woods can be obtained in whatever sizes you desire, starting from as fine as 1/32 inch in thickness. One-inch-to-one-foot conversion rulers are available. Check with your local supplier.

The difficulties of radical adherence to scale are pointed out with perception and wit by the authors of *The Book of the Queen's Dolls' House:* "A mere change of scale, an apparently inconsequential diminution of size, will bring into play a different arrangement of physical consequences. Properties like the viscosity and capillarity of liquids, the stiffness of fabrics, and weight in proportion to size, gain new importance. No amount of skill or inventiveness can avoid some changes which are thus introduced."

According to Colonel Mervyn O'Gorman, aeronautical engineer, who contributed a chapter entitled "The Effect of Size on the Equipment of the Queen's Dolls' House," "Certain properties of matter do not scale down comfortably when size is altered; thus the stiffness of a steel rope would not be diminished sufficiently to work round the small pulleys of the lift. So also we shall find that the clothes, the linen table-cloths, the bed-sheets, etc. . . . though exquisitely made, of the very finest known materials, are liable to behave as if they had been slightly starched."

O'Gorman went so far as to speculate on the unusual characteristics of the miniature inhabitants—dubbed "Dollomites"—of this 1/12-scale world. According to the Colonel, the Dollomites, if real, would possess enormous strength. "They will move a gilded chair, a lacquer table or a pianoforte as easily as we pass a tumbler of water, a decanter or a footstool. . . . After dinner, when the men return upstairs to join the ladies in the drawing

Victorian dollhouse (c. 1860), a gift of Miss Jane Watson to the Museum of the City of New York. A classic example of a stylized dollhouse, it derives much of its appeal from its mixed scales. Note the size of the bed in the upper right-hand bedroom—so high that one would need a running jump to mount it. The chandelier in the music room is so low that even the shortest pianist would undoubtedly bump his head on it. The chairs in the dining room reach halfway to the ceiling. The furniture in the little room at the lower right, however, seems to belong to another dollhouse entirely. (Courtesy of the Museum of the City of New York.)

room, we see quite elderly persons jump twelve steps at a time."

Where does all this remarkable strength come from? Shouldn't the Dollomites' strength simply be 1/12 of ours, in keeping with everything else in this miniature world? Otherwise, what magic ingredient does miniaturization possess that could account for such a vast increase in the Dollomites' strength? The Colonel offers the following explanation: "Muscular strength depends upon the cross-sectional area of the muscle; and a being who has shrunk to one-twelfth our size has muscles which are, each for each, only 1/144th as strong. That is to say, the cross section of a muscle varies as the square of any linear dimension. But the weight of a body varies as the cube of any linear dimension, so that the midget who is one-twelfth our size weighs only 1/1,728th as much." The Colonel concludes that while the Dollomite possesses only 1/144 of our strength, he "has only 1/1,728th of our weight to move—which makes him, in proportion, twelve times as strong as we are."

Other peculiarities inhabit the Dollomites' world, defying true miniaturization. The viscosity of liquids, for example, prevents the Dollomites from being able to drink their wine in a normal fashion. Instead, they have to suck the wine from the glass. Thick soups cling so tenaciously to the bowl that the bowl has to be held firmly down with one hand while the contents are spooned out with the other.

The Colonel goes on to tell us why 1/12-scale illumination would be far in excess of what Dollomites would find to be a comfortable level of light. He speculates about the pitch of the Dollomites' voices—too high to be heard by human ears. And he leaves us with a curious picture of the Dollomites' sense of time—"the day would appear twice as long—[the Dollomite] will be quite likely to want six meals a day."

Considering these surprising characteristics of the Dollomites, it would appear that if we started out with miniature inhabitants in mind, the dollhouse we would build for them would be very different from the dollhouse we would build for our own amusement.

Aside from any academic discussion of scale is the question of just how far *you* want to go to achieve realism. Are acetate windows with sten-

*Antique Victorian room from the last
quarter of the 19th century. The fireplace
and pier mirror are built in.* (Courtesy of
The Enchanted Dollhouse, Wilmington,
Vermont.)

A Chippendale settee of extraordinary delicacy, elaborately hand carved by the legendary Eric Pearson in the late 1940s. Mr. Pearson was originally a famous cabinetmaker, and began to make miniatures during the 1930s and 1940s. He made many of the pieces in the Thorne Rooms at the Art Institute of Chicago. (Photo by Arnold Beckerman.)

ciled panes sufficient for your dollhouse, or must you have accurately dimensioned working windows? For many hobbyists, a simple shadow box becomes a room, which affords ample pleasure. For others, only an entire house will do. Some dollhouse owners are quite content to settle for a painted plywood roof and other simplified features. Some are happy with nothing less than a roof consisting of hundreds (even thousands) of perfect little cedar-shake shingles, painstakingly applied one by one.

Between these extremes lies a wide range of alternatives. What one collector considers to be a necessary degree of realism, another collector may consider to be an eccentricity not worth the time or expense required to achieve it.

The same holds true for furniture and accessories. Every conceivable degree of perfection is available—at a price. The most basic examples of this furniture are mass-produced, largely in the Orient, where labor is still fairly cheap. Many of these pieces are quite pleasing to the beginning collector or youngster, and well worth the price.

At the other end of the spectrum are hand-crafted miniatures of museum quality: a Queen Anne highboy made with over one hundred individual pieces of wood, specially dimensioned in thickness to convey the impression of absolute realism; a flawless wing chair upholstered in glove leather; china and tinware that give no trace of being less than full size. Examples of these and other notable miniatures can be found in Chapter 5—"Outstanding Miniature-makers."

It isn't necessary to decide at the outset just how far you want to go in assembling your miniature collection. Start at a level comfortable to your pocketbook, and upgrade your collection as your means allow and your growing appreciation dictates. The sources listed in Chapter 18 represent all different qualities and prices. To get a sense of what's available at what price, select a cross section of these resources and send away for their catalogs or price lists. Visit whatever miniature shops are nearby. It won't take long to get a feeling for the range of quality and fidelity to scale found in the world of miniatures.

Not to mention a vast historical scope, to which we now direct your attention.

CHAPTER 4

AN INTRODUCTION TO MINIATURES

In the world of miniatures as it exists today, nearly every household object you could want, from every popular period, is available to you. Confronted by such enormous abundance, the fledgling collector is well advised to go slowly.

The fascination and charm of miniatures are such that the new enthusiast is tempted to buy everything in sight. A more realistic approach is to put yourself through an orientation period—see what's around, explore your own feelings, and decide more specifically what you want to collect.

If, after doing your homework, you find yourself inclined toward a particular period, you'll then be able to concentrate your searching and your spending.

Another decision to be made is whether to buy a dollhouse right away. Our advice is to hold off for a while and start by first developing your collection of miniatures. You can house this budding collection in something inexpensive, such as a shadow box or miniature room (see Chapter 7). As your collection grows, your ideas and feelings about the kind of house you want will begin to evolve from the collection itself. This is the route that most of us follow in real life. It's rare that anyone starts right out by acquiring his or her dream house. That comes in time, after we've had

a chance to do some dreaming. By then our taste is usually reliable and well-formed, and we've acquired sufficient cherished possessions to have something with which to furnish the house.

The one exception to this advice concerns antique dollhouses. Good examples are so rare that if you come across one—and this is your area of interest—by all means buy it. Even if you find a more suitable house later, you can always sell the first one, and probably at a profit.

An introduction to the world of miniatures should include an orientation to the various periods of furniture. To start you off, we'll take you on a brief tour of the more popular periods of collecting—American furnishings from the late 1600s to the early 1900s. Among the major furniture styles during this four-hundred-year span were William and Mary (1688–1730), Queen Anne (1720–1755), Chippendale (1750–1800), Hepplewhite and Sheraton (1785–1815), Empire (1800—1840), Shaker (mid-1800s), and Victorian (1820–1900). Very often several of these periods overlapped and influences were combined.

The Thorne Rooms that follow capture the flavor of the various times represented in room settings that combine furniture, accessories, and architectural features.

Living Room and Kitchen, Typical Early Massachusetts House, 1675—1700

After getting settled in the new world, the Pilgrims began to build homes reminiscent of the ones they left behind in England. Most of the family activity in these homes centered around the kitchen, which also served as dining room and living room. A large fireplace, used for both heating and cooking, was the focal point of the room. Stools and benches were the most common forms of seating, the chair being rare. The two fine examples shown here are based on chairs belonging to leaders of the community. With most of the furniture pieces, function determined form. A good example is the popular settle, its high back providing protection from drafts. In general, the colonial homes of this period tended to be sparsely furnished with pieces of simple design. *(From the American Rooms in Miniature by Mrs. James Ward Thorne. Courtesy of The Art Institute of Chicago.)*

Dining Room, Salem, Massachusetts, Early 18th Century

Salem was the center of the shipbuilding industry during the early years of the colonies, and many of the homes of Salem's prosperous citizens were built by workmen trained in shipbuilding techniques. The high standards of their workmanship can be seen in this handsomely paneled room with its built-in cupboards. The furniture reflects the interpretation by American craftsmen of the William and Mary style, which replaced the heavy oak Jacobean furniture of the late 1600s and early 1700s. The walnut gate-leg table and highboy are familiar pieces of this period, as are bannister-back chairs with pierced scrollwork and deep carvings. A typical design feature was the "inverted cup" turnings of the legs of the side table and highboy. *(From the American Rooms in Miniature by Mrs. James Ward Thorne. Courtesy of The Art Institute of Chicago.)*

Great Hall, The Miller's House, Millbach, Pennsylvania, 1752

Among the Pennsylvania Dutch, the great hall was a combination kitchen and dining area, complete with large fireplace. This setting has a distinctive Rhineland flavor, particularly in the beautifully carved paneling, impressive staircase, and heavily beamed ceiling. The furniture, made of pine and oak, is based on Swiss and German designs. On the chest can be seen a painted "hex" symbol, an element of decoration found frequently in Pennsylvania Dutch furniture. Rugs were rare, the housewife wanting nothing to clutter her tidy sandstone floors. *(From the American Rooms in Miniature by Mrs. James Ward Thorne. Courtesy of The Art Institute of Chicago.)*

Dining Room, Wentworth Gardner House, Portsmouth, New Hampshire, 1760

This dignified setting represents an outstanding example of the interior of a mid-eighteenth-century Georgian home of the Portsmouth area. Scenic wallpapers were popular, this one patterned after a design of Parisian origin. Talented woodcarvers from the local shipyards were responsible for much of the ornamental woodwork. The furniture is Chippendale in character. Typical features include the ball-and-claw feet of the dining table and sideboard, and the straight fluted legs of the ornate ladder-back armchair and side chairs. *(From the American Rooms in Miniature by Mrs. James Ward Thorne. Courtesy of The Art Institute of Chicago.)*

Dining Room, Hammond-Harwood House, Annapolis, Maryland, 1770—1774

This generously dimensioned dining room reflects the expansive manner of life enjoyed by wealthy Southerners of this period, in contrast to the typically somewhat smaller interiors occupied by their affluent Northern counterparts. The elaborate headings of the doors and windows, as well as the coffer paneling of the shutters, are characteristic elements of the Southern approach to Georgian design. The pieces are fine examples of the Sheraton style made by American cabinet-makers. A particularly Southern contribution is the mixing table, standing between the two doors, which served as an adjunct to the sideboard. *(From the American Rooms in Miniature by Mrs. James Ward Thorne. Courtesy of The Art Institute of Chicago.)*

Living Room, Shaker Community House, c. 1800

The essence of simplicity, Shaker furniture was made as an act of religion by highly gifted craftsmen who regarded work as a form of prayer. The Shakers lived a communal life in a number of colonies across America. They built large, barnlike buildings and furnished them in the spartan style shown here. Shaker furniture is distinguished by its strong, clear sense of purpose and total absence of ornamentation. The pegboard, seen here holding hats and a hanging shelf, was a familiar sight in Shaker rooms. Frequently, chairs were hung on the pegs to provide more floor space in the rooms. The small black cast-iron stove with its long stovepipe was the Shaker's source of heat. *(From the American Rooms in Miniature by Mrs. James Ward Thorne. Courtesy of The Art Institute of Chicago.)*

Bedroom, Oak Hill, Peabody, Massachusetts, c. 1801

In this Federal setting we have a chance to view replicas of the artistry of Samuel McIntire, one of New England's most talented architects and furniture craftsmen. His work was rich in carved ornamentation, a talent for which he no doubt inherited from his father, a woodcarver and cabinetmaker. The bed and painted side chairs typify his skill. The superb bowfront commode and mirror are modeled on the work of the Boston cabinetmaker John Seymour. *(From the American Rooms in Miniature by Mrs. James Ward Thorne. Courtesy of The Art Institute of Chicago.)*

Parlor, Eagle House, Haverhill, Massachusetts, 1818

Prosperity is greatly in evidence in this fine example of the interior of a New England merchant's home of the Federal period. The furniture, with its clean, elegant lines, reflects the designs of Hepplewhite and Sheraton as interpreted by American cabinetmakers. The Hepplewhite influence can be seen in the classic shield-back side chair, while the high-backed armchair and sofa are clearly Sheraton-inspired. Girandoles (candle sconces with convex mirrors) were very popular, though rarely as handsome as the gilded ones shown here. The slender colonnettes of the woodwork flanking the fireplace, and the finely carved details of the mantel, were both characteristic of the time. *(From the American Rooms in Miniature by Mrs. James Ward Thorne. Courtesy of The Art Institute of Chicago.)*

Parlor, Waterman House, Warren, Rhode Island, c. 1820

The architecture here is distinctively local in style, as typified by the broken reverse-curve pediments and the delicate yet bold detail of the mantel and doorheads. The marvelous secretary dominating the setting, with its impressive stature and carved detailing, is an example of the style of the famous American cabinetmaker John Goddard, of Newport, Rhode Island. Although this piece appears here in a setting of circa 1820, it was produced some fifty years earlier. The chairs are outstanding examples of American Chippendale, their ornately carved legs terminating in ball-and-claw feet. *(From the American Rooms in Miniature by Mrs. James Ward Thorne. Courtesy of The Art Institute of Chicago.)*

Living Room, Cape Cod Cottage, 1750—1850

While no great furniture resides here, this snug little room is nonetheless noteworthy as it typifies the interior of a Cape Cod cottage during a span of more than a hundred years. The simplicity of the setting and its sense of tidy proportion convey a feeling not unlike that of a boat—in fact, the setting was the work of boatbuilders. Even the stairway is reminiscent of a boat's companionway. Simplicity also characterizes the furniture, a mixture of eighteenth- and nineteenth-century pieces. The butterfly table, Windsor chair, and modified Sheraton desk were familiar pieces, helping to convey the overall effect of neatness and snug comfort. *(From the American Rooms in Miniature by Mrs. James Ward Thorne. Courtesy of The Art Institute of Chicago.)*

Bedroom, New England, 1750—1850

Here we see a typical bedroom embodying features found in bedrooms throughout New England for more than a hundred years. The bare plaster walls have been decorated with a charming design applied with the use of a stencil, usually the work of itinerant journeymen. The furniture is made of maple and painted beech and includes such favorites as the Boston rocker, sewing table, highboy, and canopy bed. The familiar washstand with bowl and pitcher appears in the far left corner. The simple partition paneling and wide floorboards suggest the second half of the eighteenth century. (*From the American Rooms in Miniature by Mrs. James Ward Thorne. Courtesy of The Art Institute of Chicago.*)

Parlor, 28 East 20th Street, New York City, 1850—1875

Victorian in all its glory, this setting is reminiscent of the brownstone townhouse in which Theodore Roosevelt spent his childhood. The heavy ornateness of the period is well represented here in the popular furniture of John Henry Belter. These elaborately carved rosewood pieces, referred to as "rococo revival," were the successors to the more classic designs of Duncan Phyfe. The large and opulent chandelier, along with the imposing gilt mirror over the mantel, are good examples of the taste for generously sized furnishings that flourished in the Victorian period. (*From the American Rooms in Miniature by Mrs. James Ward Thorne. Courtesy of The Art Institute of Chicago.*)

A House in New Mexico, Contemporary

Southwestern architecture, with its heavily Spanish influence, is as much a part of the American heritage as the European-influenced architectural and furniture styles of the eastern states. The Spanish, Mexican, and Pueblo Indian influences persist to this day and find expression in this dining room of an adobe brick and plaster home. Notice the corner fireplace and characteristic ceiling consisting of saplings laid herring-bone fashion over heavy roof beams. The furniture has both a Spanish and Mexican flavor. Also of Mexican design are the candle sconces and old silver and pottery pieces. *(From the American Rooms in Miniature by Mrs. James Ward Thorne. Courtesy of The Art Institute of Chicago.)*

Living Room, George Washington Smith House, Santa Barbara, California, Contemporary

This southern California home represents a highly successful example of the adaptation of the Spanish Colonial style to contemporary requirements of comfort and convenience. The subtropical climate easily accommodates the Moorish and Latin influences of Old Spain—the open patio, heavy walls, and colorful tiles that give a cooling and spacious effect. In the furniture we see a blending of Spanish styles dating from the fifteenth through eighteenth centuries, all looking comfortably at home together. *(From the American Rooms in Miniature by Mrs. James Ward Thorne. Courtesy of The Art Institute of Chicago.)*

The Thorne Rooms can have an intimidating as well as inspiring effect on the collector. To those who find such perfection discouraging in comparison to what they can hope to accomplish with their own collection, we offer two consolatory thoughts. First, such absolute perfection is far from being an essential prerequisite for enjoying the hobby. And second, there are contemporary craftspeople making and selling miniatures whose work is clearly on a par with that of the Thorne Rooms. The work of these people is available to any collector who is able to pay the price.

A glance through the catalog of Chestnut Hill Studio should raise your spirits. Here is a wide selection of fine miniatures, representing a variety of periods, at extremely fair prices, considering their unusually high quality. Some of these pieces are shown on the next few pages to give you an idea of the high degree of period authenticity you can introduce into your own settings.

CHESTNUT HILL STUDIO

Ironically, Chestnut Hill Studio owes its existence to the Thorne Rooms, which inspired Reta Cowles Johnson to produce fine-quality miniatures that could be sold by mail. She began back in 1947, which makes Chestnut Hill Studio one of the earliest businesses of its kind. Mrs. Johnson made many of the original pieces herself and contracted the balance of the collection to various other craftspeople. Her husband, Arthur Le Roy Johnson (a direct descendant of Paul Revere), contributed many of the designs for the Colonial furniture they offer.

Since Mrs. Johnson's death, in 1962, the business has been managed by her son and daughter-in-law, Arthur and Mary-Dudley Cowles, both of whom have been deeply involved in antiques and the arts for many years. Most of the more than seven hundred items in the Chestnut Hill Studio collection were researched and designed by Mrs. Cowles. Mr. Cowles executes the first models and also handles much of the actual production. The rest are produced by talented relatives and friends.

(Photo by Arnold Beckerman.)

Ladder-back chair with arms, 17th century

Settle, mid-17th century

Cape Cod wing chair, early 18th centur

Moravian side chair, 16th to 17th century

Windsor chair, c. 1725

Queen Anne wing chair, 1700–1760

Corner chair, 18th century

American Shie Hepplewhite side cha late 18th century

Duncan Phyfe side chair, 1810–1820

Boston rocker, 19th century

Comb back rocker, early 19th century

Shaker chair, c. 1820

Shaker dining chair, early 18th century

Victorian Lincoln rocker, 1830–1860

Hitchcock chair, c. 1840

Hepplewhite drop-leaf table plus two half-round tables, and four matching shield-back Hepplewhite side chairs. The table is set with two Bohemian lustres, Canton plates, footed Bohemian wine goblets, and a Canton bowl holding a flower arrangement. A covered ginger jar stands on the Delaware Valley highboy. (Photo by Arnold Beckerman.)

The pieces in the Chestnut Hill Studio collection are based on originals found in museums, reference books, and private collections. Considerable effort is spent on making each piece an exact scale replica, so that in photographs they actually appear to be life size. This requires that the thickness of each piece of wood be carefully considered and specially dimensioned. Some of the more complicated designs require more than a hundred individual pieces of wood.

Grain is another matter of great importance where authenticity is concerned, and woods are selected for grain that will be in scale with the small dimensions of the furniture. For instance, to capture the mellow look of old pine—a look that can't be simulated with stains—Chestnut Studio uses actual aged pine, more than a hundred years old.

In addition to fine period furniture, Chestnut Hill Studio makes a large number of period accessories, from elaborate crystal chandeliers to unbelievably delicate-looking China Trade porcelains.

Chestnut Hill Studio miniatures are available only by mail order (see Chapter 18).

Victorian sofa in the style of John Henry Belter, hand-carved by Hermania Anslinger. (Photo by The Commercial Photographers, Spokane, Washington.)

CHAPTER 5

OUTSTANDING MINIATURE-MAKERS

Every field has its heroes, and miniature making is no exception. Some names, like Eric Pearson and E. J. Kupjack, both of Thorne Room fame, have already become legend. New legends are in the making; many of the craftspeople in this chapter are already well known among miniaturists. The others will gain recognition with exposure. These pages offer a sampling of the best work being done today by people at the top of their craft.

The common denominator of these craftspeople is a serious attitude about miniature making. To these men and women, the creating of fine miniatures is a dominant interest, life-giving and soul-satisfying, assuming a large and significant portion of their lives. They are in it for love as much as for money.

Like all outstanding artists, great miniaturists are in short supply, as is their work. There are only so many hours in each day, and the creation of one exquisitely detailed piece of period furniture could take a perfectionist the better part of a week. Many miniature-makers can accommodate only a limited number of orders, and some are booked up for as much as a year.

Publicity, for some of these people, can be a double-edged sword. We know of miniaturists who were driven to distraction by the volume of mail resulting from some well-intentioned article or book. No dedicated miniature-maker wants to spend half of every day answering mail, particularly with a heavy backlog of orders to fill. So if you plan to correspond with any of the people mentioned here, a self-addressed stamped envelope will go a long way toward showing your appreciation for their dilemma.

Addresses and catalog information will be found in Chapter 18.

"In high school I asked the professor if I could take manual training (now called shop) instead of sewing. He said, 'No. Girls don't do that sort of thing!'"

HERMANIA ANSLINGER

For more than thirty-five years, Hermania Anslinger, a modest craftswoman of enormous talent, has been creating custom miniatures for a select and very knowing clientele. Many of her customers are miniature-makers themselves—a tribute to Miss Anslinger's extraordinary skills.

As Mary Frances Cochran, herself an outstanding miniaturist, put it: "Hermania Anslinger will get *all* my money from now on, now that I finally have acquired my first piece from her."

Miss Anslinger's uniqueness lies in the fact that she excels in two distinctly separate, yet complementary, disciplines—woodcarving and furniture making. As a result, she can create miniature furniture with the most elaborately carved details—furniture that few miniature-makers would attempt.

The pieces shown here typify Miss Anslinger's talents. Ironically, Miss Anslinger had to develop this talent entirely on her own, having been denied access to shop instruction in high school. Nor was this to be the last time that Miss Anslinger was misguided. Back in the late 1930s, shortly after she had begun making miniatures, Miss Anslinger took an exhibit to the fair at Great Falls, Montana. When the woman in charge of the art display there advised her not to make her carvings so small because they wouldn't sell, Miss Anslinger turned to larger-size carvings. Fortunately, she began to advertise her talents for custom carving in *Hobbies Magazine,* and these ads attracted enough requests for miniatures that she was encouraged to resume her work in this area.

Today Miss Anslinger continues to create her extraordinary furniture and carvings on a custom-made basis.

Opposite page: *These pieces were made by Hermania Anslinger for a private collector. The basis for each piece is as follows, reading clockwise from top center: Fourposter bed, a combination of several Federal beds of this type. Secretary-bookcase from the Essex Institute Museum, Salem, Massachusetts, early 1800s. Round "Empire" table from the Philadelphia Museum of Art, c. 1815. This is an American version of the French "antique" type of circular-topped table on a triangular base. Chamber table from the collection of the City Art Museum of St. Louis, Missouri. Empire couch from Hamilton Hall, Salem, Massachusetts. Grandfather clock, a combination of two Simon Willard clocks. Chippendale mirror, from an original featured in* Antiques Magazine. (Photo by Arnold Beckerman.)

Mrs. Ash is an award-winning ceramist who has turned her talents to miniature making. She offers a considerable variety of beautiful miniature ceramics, all carefully researched and documented. Many of her designs are based on museum pieces.

Mrs. Ash's goal is to create "ceramic pieces that are not trite and ones that will add historic significance to your settings." In her catalog you'll find such diverse offerings as a Wedgwood "Colly Flower" tea-pot, English delft plates, and Chinese Export pieces of all descriptions.

"A few words about patterns and prices. I have spent more time trying to figure out a way to list these new patterns than I did drawing them! There seems no easy solution because I don't want to offer you just a few shapes in certain patterns, but give you a wide choice of ceramic shapes and designs, although my time and expense vary with each pattern . . . so . . . there is a separate price list for Tobacco Leaf, Chinese Ladies, and Japanese Bird Prints. The other patterns are listed as a group. Most of these new patterns are either Export pieces or European-made Oriental-type pieces.

"I realize that I have created a monster, offering so many patterns and shapes. If you think *you* are confused, think of *me* filling the orders! I guess I'm such an individualist that my idea of a dollhouse is one of individualism, too."

Mr. Atkins had to improvise most of his techniques, learning from trial and error like so many other self-taught miniature craftspeople. "I've had to learn to make tools for myself. Taking a course in jewelry making helped, too. I learned how to silver-solder, which was a good thing. I started off trying to weld everything with a full-size torch—one-eighth of a second too long and you burned the whole thing up. So I learned brazing with molten copper. Sometimes I go from a weld to a braze to a hard solder to a soft solder, and that way you can join things very close to one another without destroying the previous bond."

Among all the wonderful and unusual offerings in The Village Smithy catalog, one of the most interesting is a spiral staircase. "Some people build dollhouses and forget the stairs, or don't leave enough room for stairs, so that's where the spiral staircase comes in handy. I remember when I built a dollhouse for my little girl, after it was done it had no stairs, which didn't bother her a bit. To her the dolls fly up there. But it bothered the hell out of me. And that's when I started thinking about spiral staircases."

In addition to the wealth of items in his catalog, Mr. Atkins will also supply "bespoke" work. "You describe the item, specifying style such as 'Early American,' 'Renaissance,' 'Victorian,' etc. Include anything for clarification, rough sketch, pix from magazine, and I'll respond with a price estimate and (perhaps) a simple sketch. If the subject is a tricky one, send me $5.00 and I'll send you a sketch and price. You will send back the sketch with 'okay,' or send back sketch with corrections and I'll make a new one (no charge) and we'll keep going on this way until we are in accord or one of us drops dead. The $5.00 is merely to shake out collectors of free sketches."

If a sense of humor is a sign of intelligence, then Al Atkins is the smartest man in the business. His catalog is peppered with wit and brimming with wrought-iron creations, some of which look quite impossible to make.

Mr. Atkins was not always a miniature smithy. He became one by accident.

"I've been a commercial artist

"When something comes up in the course of making one of these little objects, something that I cannot prevent; such as a crookedness, a bump, a curve in what should be straight, a deviation from even measurements, a bit of good old early American rust; all of these things come under the umbrella phrase: 'part of its charm.' "

almost all my life. When I became interested in full-size iron work, I read every book I could find and eventually set up a forge. I learned some basics from a great blacksmith, enough to enable me to make chandeliers and other full-size pieces. Some of this work was displayed in a shop in Bronxville [New York]. They sold all right, but nothing spectacular.

"Then Kay MacLaren [publisher of *Nutshell News*], who lived in Bronxville at the time, called me up and asked me if I'd consider making miniatures. I didn't know what a miniature was. Kay invited me over to

see her collection and informed me that there wasn't much being done in metal miniatures. So I said I'd try it. I beat a few coat hangers into chandeliers. Kay liked them and wrote an article about it in *Nutshell News,* and from then on I was in a new business. And I liked it from the start."

How does a full-size smithy beat delicate miniatures into shape on full-size blacksmith equipment? He doesn't. "I don't use a forge at all because by the time you transfer a small thing from a forge to an anvil, you've lost your heat. I use an oxyacetylene torch."

ROBERT BERNHARD—DOLPHIN ORIGINALS

Before becoming a miniaturist, Bob Bernhard was an interior designer, and this orientation is reflected in his work. His pieces tend to be more unusual than most, such as his handsome turn-of-the-century wicker furniture in the Newport, Rhode Island, style. This sizable grouping includes a chaise lounge, two beds, a sofa, settee, four chairs, several tables, a lamp, and a fernery, complete with hanging birdcage.

Mr. Bernhard takes a decorator's approach to his upholstered furniture. Customers are sent swatches of fabric to allow them to choose the pattern and color they prefer. One of Mr. Bernhard's most popular fabrics is a handsome flame-stitch effect in rose and soft greens, which he offers on his "Philadelphia Museum Queen Anne wing chair."

Another highly unusual offering is a hand-painted kidney-shaped lady's book table with an adjustable book rest. As a considerate touch, Mr. Bernhard also includes a miniature blank diary.

Mr. Bernhard's interest in miniatures came as an outgrowth of building scale houses for model train layouts and working for a display studio that specialized in making scale models of different kinds. This background has served Mr. Bernhard well—he also makes beautiful custom dollhouses.

44

When we first saw Robert Carlisle's "oak rocker," our initial impulse was to see if we could find a flaw in it somewhere—it looked almost too perfect. After turning it over and examining it from all angles, we came away with a healthy respect for Mr. Carlisle's talents. Not only was the rocker perfectly built and the finish velvety-smooth, but it also inclined at just the right angle. Its precise balance produced an unexpectedly realistic rocking effect when set in motion.

We wondered what kind of a background enabled Mr. Carlisle to work with such precision.

"I suppose it was natural for me to get into miniatures. I always loved to build things. I was a cabinetmaker as well as a journeyman machinist. As a hobby I made miniature engines and machine tools that worked, and also collected antiques. Until someone gave me a miniature catalog, I wasn't even aware of the hobby.

"The idea of combining several of my hobbies and both trades appealed to me, so in March of 1974 I began to build miniature furniture with the idea of selling it in a flea market in Omaha. Sales far exceeded my expectations. Soon I was getting inquiries from dealers and they were followed by sizable wholesale orders. By July of the same year, things were so out of hand that I had to give up either my regular job or the miniatures. Tough decision. Took me all of fifteen seconds to make up my mind to quit my job and go full time on the miniatures. Have been building miniatures seven days a week ever since

and love it. Later that year I had to give up the flea market bit; mail orders were taking all of my time.

"Everything on my list and the things still on the drawing board are what would be found in an average turn-of-the-century American home, which could be anything from 'Golden Oak' furniture right out of the 1900 Sears Roebuck catalog to Grandma's old walnut bedroom suite."

Mr. Carlisle's price list gives additional insight into his working philosophy.

"These little pieces of furniture are made as nearly like their full-size counterparts as I can make them within practical limits. For example, all drawers are real and will open, but do not have dovetail joints. Scale is also followed within the same limits. The manufacturer's label on the back of cabinet-type pieces has print to scale, so small a magnifying glass is needed to read it. On the other hand, for the sake of strength, drawer sides are made 1/16" thick. True scale would be nearer 1/32". All pieces are signed and dated.

"Note: I feel oak is too coarse and open-grained for use in miniatures. It's like using burlap for curtains in a mini-house. Therefore, items described as 'oak' are actually made of birch, which is a finer but still slightly open-grained hardwood that looks like oak in miniature."

We found Mr. Carlisle's prices to be unusually low for furniture of such high quality. His work represents a real "find."

"I rather think we are on a Titanic, that the world of tomorrow will be likely to punish us for having partaken so delightedly of this pretend-world of miniatures."

In the Spring 1975 issue of *Nutshell News,* Mary Frances Cochran was the subject of an article entitled "Going Places—Maryland." As a result, Mrs. Cochran was first inundated with requests for her price list, then besieged by orders for her furniture. Most miniature-makers would be delighted with such a response, but Mrs. Cochran is a perfectionist who takes considerable time to make each piece. Even before the *Nutshell News* article, Mrs. Cochran was quoting six months for delivery of her furniture. "Probably other craftspeople are quicker than I am, but it takes me a minimum of one week to make the simplest piece, and a month or more to do a complicated one."

Mrs. Cochran offers a wide variety of classic furniture designs. "I get a lot of the measurements from Dover's *Masterpieces of Furniture* by Solomonsky, and the Lester Margon books, and some from our own collection of eighteenth- and early-nineteenth-century antiques. I am into carving and will be doing increasingly advanced work as my skill improves. I have the workbook of Chippendale, Sheraton, Hepplewhite, Thomas Hope's book and even Blackie (mid-Victorian cabinet-

maker). Everything is custom-made, which is slow, slow, slow."

In addition to being a craftswoman of considerable talent, Mrs. Cochran is a person of charm and ingenuity.

"My husband and I learned how to make things mostly by restoring antique pieces which, having lasted a century or two, seemed always to self-destruct about two weeks after coming into our possession.

"We also learned to work with wood by undertaking massive house remodeling. We simply bought power tools and how-to books, read the books and ruined hundreds of dollars' worth of materials until we finally grasped the idea of what the tool would do if we did our part correctly.

"I got into miniatures seriously in 1967 when I began refurnishing my own childhood dollhouse, which had suffered water damage during storage in a leaky garage. Deciding my male child might be subjected to ridicule if the other children knew of our joint restoration venture, I seized upon the idea of the Victorians, who presented shops to boys to complement the dollhouses the girls had.

"Seeking merchandise to stock

my son's miniature store, I found some of the well-known names in the business, from whom I began buying for his store and my dollhouse. As inflation took its toll, I realized I shouldn't support what was for me an expensive hobby. I started supplying my own insatiable demands for miniature period pieces to fill the rooms I made. I began sending pieces to antique shows. Then someone wrote Mrs. MacLaren about me, the *Nutshell News* article emerged, and I'm doing my best to fill the orders which have come from North, South, East, and West."

French bedroom, made by Mary Cochran, except for the plaster mantel from Molly Brody.

Pennsylvania kitchen (c. 1750), with simulated stone fireplace and an Edward Hicks painting in the overmantel. Room, furniture, and furnishings by Mary Cochran, including the painted tin trays and sconces. Chicken stewing in the open kettle, made by Peggy Barnes. Eighteenth-century Wedgwood "Colly Flower" pieces on table, made by Suzanne Ash.

MARIE FRIEDMAN

Marie Friedman is a virtuoso miniaturist. Completely self-taught, she makes miniatures of extraordinary variety. The remarkable thing about Mrs. Friedman's work is how thoroughly at home she is in so many different mediums.

Mrs. Friedman's leather saddle looks like the work of someone who has spent her life tooling leather. Her electrified hanging Victorian parlor lamp is undoubtedly the work of a highly skilled lamp-maker. Her china pieces are so perfectly scaled and incredibly thin that they could only be the work of a veteran ceram-

ist. Her spatterware is equally impressive. Her furniture shows a mastery of dovetail and mortise and tenon construction. And her log cabin, with its pegged floors and working fireplace, looks like the work of a full-time dollhouse builder. Everything Mrs. Friedman puts her hand to looks as though she had been doing it for years.

Mrs. Friedman, a former computer programmer, learned her miniature-making skills from trial and error. "I have no time or patience for classes. Techniques in miniature are usually a little different, anyway.

I've actually found it an advantage to be ignorant because then I'm not bound by conventional full-size methods.

"The motivation in each case has been the same. I wanted something that wasn't available at the time—flower pots, a clothespin bag with pins, china that was thin enough, etc.—and after making these things, I found that other people wanted them, too."

Mrs. Friedman's lighting fixtures are used by Noel Thomas in many of his dollhouses (see Chapter 8).

"I work in wood, leather, glass, fabric, metal, and ceramics."

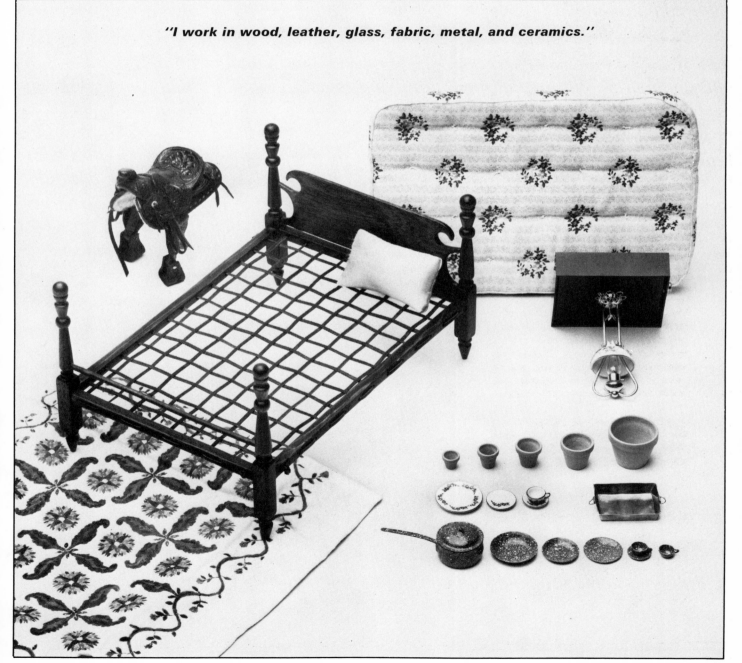

The furniture that you see here, with its clean lines and custom-made hardware, was created by a retired aircraft senior design engineer.

Philip Grande's first exposure to miniatures occurred in 1973. He had taken a job to pass the time, and during his lunch breaks he would browse at a miniature shop nearby. This gave him the idea of putting together a miniature kitchen to present to his wife for her birthday. He purchased all the pieces that he needed, but the idea of making miniatures himself began to germinate. A few months later he decided to take a try at building some miniature furniture for his own amusement. His first piece, a settle, turned out so well that his family urged him to build something else. The "something" was a chair table. It led to a set of ladder-back chairs, then to a country cabinet. A dry sink followed.

As Mr. Grande completed each new piece, he would take it to the miniature shop to get their opinion of it. The work was well liked and the shop sold quite a few pieces. At the shop's request, Mr. Grande built a pool table and an icebox, both of which are extremely handsome pieces.

Mr. Grande next ventured into the mail-order business. A custom request prompted him to build a set of miniature baby furniture, including a crib with working drop sides and casters. These pieces have become a permanent part of his collection.

Mr. Grande enjoys making miniatures and takes great pains to do a quality job. "My search for good hardware was fruitless. This led me into making my own hinges, casters, and icebox-door latches. I have made tools to aid me in the handling and making of small pieces, whether made of wood or metal. My ultimate aim is to custom-make those items that people desire and that are not ordinarily obtainable."

THE HOFFMAN COLLECTION

Shaker dining room includes trestle table with bench and four chairs. The two tall, slat-back chairs recline at a comfortable angle. The low dining chairs are made to tuck under the table. Armless rocker, footstool, and candlestand occupy the left front corner. On the right stand the familiar short stack, circulating heat stove and its woodbin, together with dustpan and brush. Two towels can be seen on the drying rack. Hanging on the peg strip are a wall cabinet, two low dining chairs, and a wall shelf containing a pair of oval boxes.

The dignity and simple beauty of Shaker furniture has been captured in miniature by the Hoffman family, who follows as closely as possible the original construction methods of the Shakers.

The Hoffman Collection is the work of George Hoffman, his wife, Sara, and their son, Mark. Together they have created a collection of pieces so authentic-looking that their work is sold at a number of Shaker museums, as well as at the Metropolitan Museum of Art in New York City.

The collection includes three varieties of Shaker rockers, a rope bed with working wooden casters, the ever-popular oval box, the distinctive black stove, and other endearing Shaker creations.

All the woods used by the Hoffmans are carefully selected with an eye to choosing the proper grains for miniaturization. All finished pieces are signed and dated by the family member who made it.

Most recently, the Hoffman family has been working in cooperation with the curatorial staff at Old Sturbridge Village in Massachusetts to create a series of miniatures based on the eighteenth-century antiques of that village.

Candlestand

Reclining ladder-back chair

Hanging wall shelf with oval boxes

JUDY JACOBS—MERRY MINIATURE BOOKS

Just as books lend personality and presence to a full-size room, so do miniature books help a miniature setting come alive.

Judy Jacobs has been creating miniature books since 1970. Her current price list contains more than one hundred different volumes, ranging in size from ⅛ inch to 2½ inches high. Most of the books are bound in real leather. Most have illustrations—many in full color. You'll find such old favorites here as *Winnie-The-Pooh* and *Peter Rabbit,* as well as art books, animal books, poetry books, and lots more.

What prompted Ms. Jacobs to become involved in this unusual specialty?

"My Merry Miniature Books began as a hobby. I had always loved tiny objects. Then, one day, I was given a ticket to an antiquarian book fair, where I acquired my first two tiny volumes. The prices and scarcity of small 'real' books soon led me to create my own. A visiting friend told me there was money to be had in mini-creations, and gave me a copy of *Hobbies Magazine,* with their spe-

cial 'Miniatura' section and ads. Not really believing much would result, I printed up a list of my available books and sent them out to several of the miniature advertisers. Joen Ellen Kanze, one of the first to get a copy, not only placed an order but sent me a complimentary copy of the first *Nutshell News.* By the second issue, Editor Catherine MacLaren had given my books a lovely mention—by the third, I was an advertiser with a large catalog of books, and really 'in business.' "

JACK JARQUE—MARITIME MINIATURES

Jack Jarque has translated an interest in maritime history into an unusual miniature specialty. He makes models of models—one-inch scale replicas of ship models which were themselves scale replicas of real ships. Mr. Jarque's miniature ships are based on famous sailing vessels from America's maritime past, and include such historic ships as Columbus's *Santa Maria,* Francis Drake's *Golden Hind, The Mayflower,* John Paul Jones's *Bon Homme Richard,* and full-rigged clipper ships.

Each ship is available in waterline or pedestal models. The ships are made of wood, beautifully de-

tailed and painted, with sails of cloth. They measure roughly two inches in length and the same in height, and look perfect on a miniature fireplace mantel.

Mr. Jarque also offers handsome miniature framed paintings of ships. And in case you have nautical requirements of your own, Mr. Jarque will build a ship model to your order, be it a Mississippi River Paddle Wheeler, private yacht, or family pleasure craft.

One of Mr. Jarque's ships, in any form, will lend a warm "salty" touch to a miniature collection.

JEAN KIRKWOOD AND BETSY ZORN—THE GINGER JAR

Sheraton-style bookcase has tapered legs with casters. Chippendale library table. Chippendale chair with crewel upholstery. Cellarette with hinged top and pull-out tray.

The handsome eighteenth-century furniture you see here is the work of two craftswomen who have combined forces under the name of The Ginger Jar.

Jean Kirkwood and Betsy Zorn are transplanted New Yorkers who are both mothers and retired nurses. Each has a workshop in her basement, "and a very understanding husband." They specialize in reproducing eighteenth-century antiques. The pieces are thoroughly researched in order that the miniature be as faithful as possible to the original. Their list carefully documents each piece and gives the exact dimensions. The furniture itself is dated on a paper label with the cabinetmaker's mark, as was done in the eighteenth century.

The Ginger Jar furniture is beautifully made with a wonderfully mellow finish. Woods are mostly cherry and maple. The graceful cabriole legs of the Queen Anne chairs and the intricate openwork backs of the Chippendale chairs give evidence of the considerable talents of these craftswomen.

The Ginger Jar is now in its fifth year of business, with customers from coast to coast as well as from overseas.

Chippendale chair with intricately pierced splat, straight legs with stretchers, and silk upholstery. Embroidered stand (c. 1800), with hand-turned legs and stretchers, has petit point work in progress. Williamsburg bracket shelf. Queen Anne mirror. All pieces are cherry wood.

Cherrywood day bed (c. 1725), with hand-caned seat, six cabriole legs with turned stretchers, and adjustable back.

E. J. Kupjack.

Eugene Kupjack is the closest thing to a living legend that the miniature world has produced. His miniature rooms, which he signs, bear the unmistakable stamp of the man who worked with Mrs. James Ward Thorne for three and a half years on the American Rooms.

Mr. Kupjack's work can be seen at the Art Institute of Chicago and at the Illinois State Museum. Several hundred of his rooms are in private collections, and two exhibits of his work are touring the country under the sponsorship of national manufacturers of home furnishings.

The essence of realism, Mr. Kupjack's work often borrows from the art of illusion. Mr. Kupjack explains:

"A miniature setting is an art form whose success depends on its realism. But realism in 1/12 scale is not easy to bring about.

"Using the actual materials of the original in building the miniature does not always produce the proper effect. For example, marble is the wrong scale with regard to figure, and in thin slices it loses its marble

Detail of Pennsylvania Dutch Tavern. (Photo courtesy of Chicago Historical Society.)

*Benjamin Franklin press
From the collection of Marc Rosen.*

Pennsylvania Dutch Tavern and Inn, c. 1760. (Photo courtesy of Chicago Historical Society.)

Room from the Potts House in Valley Forge, used by George Washington as his headquarters. In the private collection of E.J. Kupjack.

"When planning a miniature room, keep in mind that such a setting is like a hundred pictures—a new composition appears at every angle."

Fireplace area of Pennsylvania Dutch Tavern and Inn. (Photo courtesy of Chicago Historical Society).

effect and takes on a translucent quality. Brick, when cut to scale, is too coarse in texture. Full-scale carpeting is impossible to use in a room. Most wool fabrics are too thick for miniatures. The list is long in the 'don't' department.

"The problem of materials is part of the challenge of making miniatures. Train your eye to see one material as another. And be on the lookout for common objects such as small pictures and labels that can be made into usable miniatures.

"When planning a miniature room, keep in mind that such a setting is like a hundred pictures—a new composition appears at every angle. So try to make the composition appealing from as many angles as possible.

"The single most important factor in a miniature setting is scale. Composition, lighting, color, and theme are compromised if the scale is mixed or off. I find that one inch to a foot is a good workable scale; it affords a finished model of comfortable size and is small enough to not require absolute detail.

"The art of miniaturizing is to know what detail to leave out, still keeping the character of whatever is being miniaturized. Select items that have a good profile and strong design and they will carry the proper effect.

E. J. KUPJACK

Remember, most miniatures will be viewed with the naked eye, so detail which cannot be seen unaided is useless to the total effect. Knowing what you left out, what material you substituted, and all the other tricks you used will color your appreciation of the finished miniature. Viewers will see only the finished model and the total effect. What they don't know won't hurt them. It's all part of the art of miniaturization."

Mr. Kupjack works on commission under the firm name of E. J. Kupjack & Associates. He also offers a collection of sterling silver miniatures, based on pieces in museums and private collections. His catalog documents each piece in detail.

Wayside Inn

Example in Garvan Collection Yale University Art Gallery, New Haven, Conn.

Covers do not open

Tankard Circa 1762

Tea Pot Circa 1770

Circa 1710

4 arms

2 ½"

2 ½"

1 ⅞"

Central Chandelier, Four Arm

Rare — Example in private collection Maker's Mark   Daniel Garnier

Each piece sterling silver

Circa 1689-1700

Short Candlestick William and Mary English Silversmith Unknown Example in private collection

Circa 1761

Round Footed Tray Original by Paul Revere Early American Silversmith

Example in Metropolitan Museum of Fine Art, New York, N. Y.

Pheasant

18th Century Table Ornament English and American

Table Silver Spoon, Fork, & Knife
English Silversmith Unknown
Example in private collection

Circa 1820

Coffee Pot Circa 1712

Original by John Burt, Boston Ma Early American Silversmith Example in Metropolitan Museum of Fine Art, New York, N. Y.

Cover does not open

English Sheffield Plate English Silversmith Unknown Example at Carlyle House Alexandria, Virginia

Double Arm Candelabra Circa 1762

Circa 1715

Monteith Bowl
Early American Silversmith, John Coney Franklin D. Roosevelt Library, Hyde Park, New York Each piece sterling silver

Ladle   Circa 1780
Designed by Daniel van Voorhis Example in Garvan Collection Yale University Art Gallery, New Haven, Conn.

John Adams's law office

HARRY LITTWIN—COPPER CORNER

When you're ready to outfit your kitchen, Harry Littwin can supply most of your needs. Mr. Littwin, a retired jewelry manufacturer, has re-directed his skills toward producing a varied collection of handmade copperware, with an emphasis on pots, stoves, and cooking utensils. The excellent quality of his work has earned it a place in the gift shop of the Museum of the City of New York.

Mr. Littwin's copper pots and pans are most realistic. Covers fit perfectly. Handles are just the right size. The total effect is one of an expensive piece of copper cookware shrunk to 1/12 its original size. Photos of Mr. Littwin's pieces have appeared in *Gourmet* magazine, *House and Garden,* and the National Geographic Society's book entitled *The Craftsman in America.*

Mr. Littwin is yet another example of an excellent craftsman who became a miniaturist by chance. He happened to enter a store one day where several dollhouses were being outfitted for Christmas. The proprietress had all the furniture she needed, but no kitchen pieces. Mr.

Littwin volunteered to make some. He produced thirty-two pieces for her selection, and she bought them all.

Today Mr. Littwin sells through several museums, in miniature shows, and by direct mail via his catalog.

NORMAN NELSON—CLARE-BELL BRASS WORKS

Once while we were photographing a dollhouse, we saw, in one of the bedrooms, an extraordinary brass bed. We wondered how any craftsman could have worked brass with such precision. After digging further, we found out.

The bed was designed and made by Norman Nelson, a brass manufacturer of twenty-five years who specialized in making precision parts for industry. Mr. Nelson's company even supplied some of the brass hardware for the U.S. astronauts' backpacks.

It also happens that Mr. Nelson operates a flea market on weekends. It was here that one of the dealers asked him if he would make a miniature mortar and pestle. From that moment on, Mr. Nelson found himself in the miniature business. His products now include spitoons, candlesticks, decanters, goblets, and a wonderfully realistic-looking doorknob that screws together on both sides of the door, just like a real one.

But back to the brass bed. This is Mr. Nelson's real *tour de force.* It

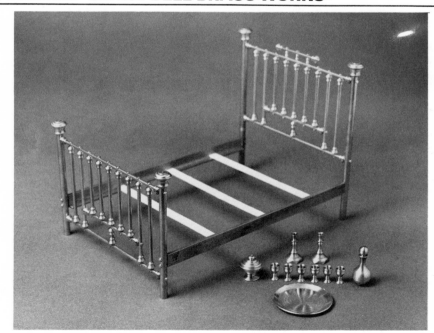

took three months of planning and tooling. The headboard alone consists of 156 individual pieces, the footboard another 150. It's doubtful that anyone without Mr. Nelson's brass

expertise and resources could have achieved anything like it. Here is an unusual case of space-age technology applied to the making of fine miniatures.

The collector of Victorian miniatures is most fortunate to have a resource such as Franklyn Morley. His Victorian miniatures are superb reproductions of outstanding pieces from private collections, reference books, and museums.

Mr. Morley's sleigh cradle, copied from a piece in the Shelbourne Museum, serves as a good example of his work. This delicately shaped bed has a bentwood bottom and rolled ends. Few miniaturists have been successful in bending wood to the extent that Mr. Morley has done here. The finish is a rich walnut.

All of Mr. Morley's pieces are very accurately scaled reproductions. In order to achieve realistic detailing, some of the wood pieces that are used measure less than 1/32 inch in thickness. There is a meticulous quality about everything connected with Morley Miniatures, from the furniture itself to their fine catalog, and even to their letterhead.

"I have been a commercial and industrial artist for forty years and the nature of the work that I have done all of my life has trained me well for the detailing and accurate scaling of our miniatures.

"I started making miniatures four years ago when we were unable to find authentic, finely detailed furnishings for our own collection. The Victorian era, although considered by many antique collectors to be a bizarre and vulgar period for design, interested me most. In miniatures, it was a period that almost didn't exist.

"The few pieces that I made as an experiment were seen by many of our friends who were also interested in this period, and I was enticed to create for them, too. Before I realized my plight, I was in business. Most of the pieces that I started with were cabinetwork, especially for the kitchen. Although we have branched out into pieces for other room settings, cabinetwork is still my preference. I only make things that I consider to be a real challenge because of their complexity, and things that are not made by other miniaturists. I have also made many custom pieces."

The Morley Miniatures catalog is a handsome and informative booklet that the Victorian enthusiast will delight in owning.

Early-Victorian full-length dressing mirror with cabriole legs.

Turn-of-the-century tilt-bin table with hutch top.

FRANKLYN J. MORLEY—MORLEY MINIATURES

*"I only make things that I consider to be
a real challenge because of their complexity, and things
that are not made by other miniaturists."*

*Early-Victorian armoire
with double-mirrored doors.*

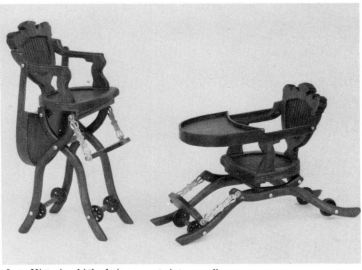

Late-Victorian high chair converts into a walker.

Early-Victorian sleigh cradle with bentwood bottom and rolled ends.

*Early-Victorian pie safe.
Double doors and side panels are pierced tin.*

MARY PAYNE–POSY PATCH ORIGINALS

Caladium

Snapdragon

For that finishing touch in your miniature setting, why not put a sansevieria on that side table? Or a spathiphyllum on the desk? Or perhaps an aphelandra or two on the mantel? If these suggestions strike your fancy, the person to turn to is Mary Payne, a talented craftswoman who makes these and other delightful plants and flowers.

In the five years since she first began making miniature flora, Mary Payne's work has become progressively smaller and more realistic-looking. Today she can make an entire basket of ivy smaller than a single petal on her first flower.

Mrs. Payne makes her tiny creations out of bread dough. Her catalog contains a sequence of photographs showing the creation of a rose that will give you an idea of the complexity of this art form. The catalog is a plant fancier's delight. It offers calla lillies, snapdragons, African violets, ferns, caladiums, rubber plants, and much more.

In creating a new plant, Mrs. Payne purchases a live specimen to use as a model so she can reproduce accurately both color and proportion.

Among Mrs. Payne's more elaborate creations are a bride's bouquet and a Williamsburg Colonial flower arrangement—both seemingly impossible works of mini-horticulture.

Posy Patch Originals is a mail-order business, with customers in all fifty states as well as abroad.

Ribbon plant *Williamsburg Colonial arrangement* *Fiddleleaf fig*

It seems only natural that with a background in architecture and a mother who creates extraordinary miniature plants and flowers, Braxton Payne should create a miniature greenhouse. As a matter of fact, Mr. Payne has designed several different models of greenhouses, plus gardening equipment to go with them—benches, hand tools, flower pots, wheelbarrows, hoses, and other hard-to-find items.

Mr. Payne built his first greenhouse as a present for his mother to house the growing collection of plants and flowers of Posy Patch Originals. As an architect of institutional buildings, he found the idea of creating a greenhouse both challenging and exciting. In order to make his greenhouse architecturally and structurally accurate, Mr. Payne studied plans of actual greenhouses and visited several that were in his vicinity.

His research resulted in models with a high degree of realism. The largest of his greenhouses rests on a simulated-stone foundation. The canopy lifts off the base for easy access, and the door swings open on tiny hinges. Interior detailing includes trusses, which make perfect supports for hanging baskets. The workmanship is meticulous throughout.

With his greenhouses and gardening accessories, Mr. Payne has added an extra dimension to miniature collecting.

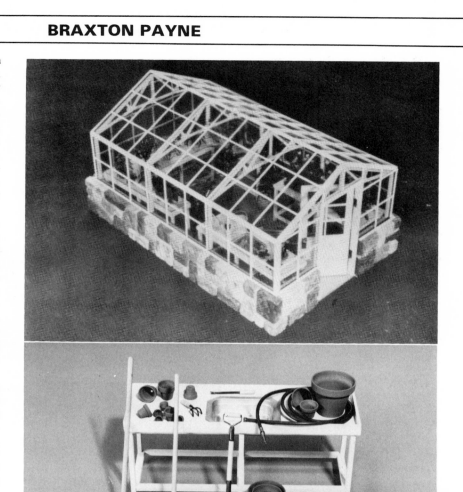

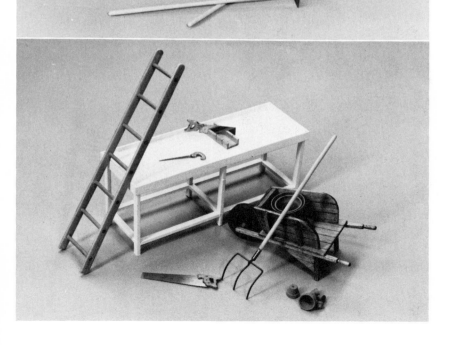

MELL PRESCOTT

Among the more than thirty items on Mell Prescott's list is an 1803 piano. The cover opens to reveal mother-of-pearl keys and hand-painted mother-of-pearl trim. An upholstered piano stool completes the offering. This unusual and beautifully made piece is a current specialty of Mrs. Prescott's.

A well-known craftswoman for many years, Mrs. Prescott started collecting and making miniatures when a friend refused to lend her a small cradle. "I needed one to use in a flower-arranging lecture I was giving. That day I went into Springfield and bought myself saws, drills, squares and came home to produce an adorable cradle. Then I decided it would be fun to reproduce many of the Queen Anne pieces in my home. This led to lowboys, highboys, game tables, and especially good upholstered chairs and sofas.

"I measure a large chair and reduce it to one inch to the foot in every detail. The materials must also be in scale and the thinness of it cut down to look correct."

1803 piano, made in a limited edition of twelve signed pieces.

In addition to the handsome Queen Anne, Victorian, and other furniture offered on her list, Mrs. Prescott will also copy any piece within reason from a photo or picture.

As with many other senior craftspeople, miniature making has become a source of great pleasure to Mrs. Prescott. "The building of these small pieces has proved to be a real joy, and makes my older years so worth living."

Room setting and all furniture made by Mell Prescott, except desk and Windsor chair.

BETTY ROCKOFF

The most appetizing miniatures we've ever seen are Betty Rockoff's dinners. Mrs. Rockoff prepares a miniature meal with such realism that you can almost smell the food. Menu choices include a turkey, ham, or New England dinner, complete with a variety of appetizing vegetables.

Mrs. Rockoff also makes a three-tiered wedding cake and a rose-topped party cake, with improvised techniques and materials.

"A lifelong fascination with small things was responsible for my venture into food making. At the time I began collecting miniature furniture and dolls, there was no food available that I felt was suitable for my settings. I began experimenting with various materials and found that certain foods lend themselves to certain mediums."

As with so many other miniaturists, what started out as an excursion into miniature making to satisfy her needs as a hobbyist became, for Mrs. Rockoff, a full-fledged business.

CONSTANCE SIMONE–SOMETHING DIFFERENT MINIATURES

The finest miniature tinware we have seen is made by a remarkable woman who is completely self-taught. Connie Simone can make a solder joint that's virtually invisible to the naked eye. Somehow she has managed to teach herself the secret of forming tin into the most minute and graceful shapes.

Her tiny painted coffee pot, with its tapered spout and perfectly contoured handle, causes you to wonder how she could possibly have made it. Many of her tiny creations leave you with the same sense of awe.

All of Ms. Simone's pieces are carefully researched from books and museums, and reproduced as authentically as possible, including the painted designs and the colors them-

selves. The designs are based on regional country tinware from Maine, Pennsylvania, Connecticut, New York, and Vermont, all dating back to the early 1800s.

Ms. Simone, like many other craftspeople, started out as a collector. Unable to find good quality miniature perfume bottles, she decided to try to make them herself. Her efforts were surprisingly successful, encouraging her to sell them by mail order. When someone suggested advertising in *Early American Life* magazine, Ms. Simone set about making the kind of pieces she thought would appeal to that magazine's audience—and her tinware collection was born.

While Ms. Simone had no previous miniature-making experience,

she possessed the rare combination of a mechanical as well as an artistic background. This enabled her to improvise the tools and techniques needed to fabricate and decorate her delicate works of tin.

Ms. Simone still makes her original perfume bottles, as well as beautiful mirrors of Federal and folk art design. She sells her work at shows and by mail order.

Left row, top to bottom: *painted document box; coffin lid trays from Pennsylvania.* Center row: *Federal gilt mirror with reverse glass painting of ship in top panel; perfume bottles; bread tray from Maine; small coffin lid tray from New York; candlestick; wall sconce.* Right row: *book box; coffin lid trays from Maine, Vermont, and New York.* (Photo by Arnold Beckerman.)

Harry Smith holding cherry bonnet-top highboy with brass pulls and complete dovetail construction. (Photo by John Hammer for the *Courier-Gazette*, Rockland, Maine.)

A man who can definitely do anything in miniature is Harry Smith of Camden, Maine. This well-known and highly respected craftsman ranks as one of the world's outstanding miniaturists. His work is sought after by museums as well as advanced collectors.

Mr. Smith spares no effort to make each of his pieces the finest of its kind. His bonnet-top highboy, a work of unbelievable delicacy, requires three full weeks to make. All the details of the original are there: a full steam-bent bonnet top, sculptured molding, turned vases, curved-top drawers, cabriole legs, and full dovetailed construction. The brass escutcheons and drawer pulls were all made by Mr. Smith. Viewed from any angle, there is nothing that betrays the fact that this remarkable piece of furniture is a 1/12-scale miniature.

Such extraordinary perfection is commonplace in all of Mr. Smith's miniatures. His working spinning wheel incorporates thirty-two separate turnings pegged together. His delft fireplace contains fifteen hand-painted tiles, each with a different scene. His model of the *Constitution* stands only 1¾ inches high, yet is fully rigged with standing rigging and ratlines of specially thin wire. And Mr. Smith's versatility extends to tinware, stoneware, and wrought iron as well.

Mr. Smith is a firm believer in detailing. "I dovetail drawers, mortise-and-tenon or rabbet most joints, hand paint all designs, hand make all hardware, hand rub and wax the finish. I use antique wood, mostly about a century old and properly seasoned. The grain has to be really fine so it will be in keeping with the scale."

Mr. Smith's tools are as unique as his skills. He works mostly with small knives and surgical scissors. For his microscopic hardware requirements he has adapted a miniature metal lathe.

While not all collectors can afford work of Mr. Smith's caliber, it's nonetheless exhilarating to see what's being done at the pinnacle of the craft.

Cherry delft tile fireplace with 2 1/2-inch model of U.S.S. Constitution, *including all spars and 250 lines. Flanked by a walnut side chair with velvet-covered seat and a walnut center table holding a "Gone with the Wind" Victorian lamp.*

Queen Anne lowboy with carved fan and brass pulls.

Spinning wheel for flax

Pierced-tin pie safe

Hand-painted sea chest with rope pulls.

Black and gold deacon's bench with hand-painted designs.

Ash carver chair with rush seat.

CHAPTER 6

POPULAR MINIATURE FURNITURE AND ACCESSORIES

The work of individual, recognized crafts-people constitutes only a small portion of the miniature marketplace. The great majority of miniatures comes from a legion of less well known craftspeople and a handful of companies that do a volume business, either through mail order or by wholesaling their products to retail stores.

Chrysnbon, in Western Springs, Illinois, is one such company. Their remarkably well made accessories can be found in many stores, tempting the collector with a great variety of unique offerings in neatly organized display cases. We counted more than a dozen different types of lamps alone. Our favorite Chrysnbon item is a standing gumball machine, of extraordinary quality for the price.

A sizable collection of lead-free pewter pieces is offered by Colonial Craftsmen Pewter Workshop, Inc., of Cape May, New Jersey. Back in 1971, when they first began making miniature pewterware, Colonial Craftsmen had two employees. Today they employ thirty people to service 1,400 retail customers. Need a twelve-arm chandelier? A candle mold? A Victorian paper holder complete with a roll of wrapping paper? Any Colonial Craftsmen dealer can supply these and dozens of other equally unusual and well-made pewter items.

Sonia Messer Imports of Los Angeles, California, offers a large number of high-quality furniture pieces, many in walnut, in a wide variety of styles, including eighteenth-century French, Queen Anne, Colonial and Victorian. The work is done in South America, and the workmanship is remarkable in the number of different pieces offered in each style.

What follows is a sampling of the miniatures produced by the larger suppliers described above.

French Limoges miniatures, from Block House.

CHRYSNBON

Duxbury chair, from a Chrysnbon furniture kit.

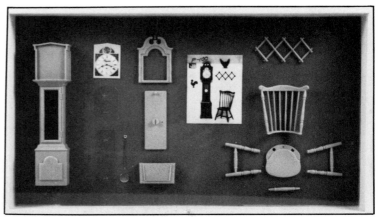

Chrysnbon furniture kits showing the component parts of a grandfather clock and Duxbury chair. The basic material is wood-grained polystyrene, to which a special fruitwood finish paint is applied to simulate wood.

Chrysnbon miniatures. Back row: jars of preserves; carpet beater; candy jars; lamps. *Front row:* relish trays and two serving trays; place mat; flower bowl, Cracker Jack boxes.

Lundby, a Swedish firm, is one of the largest companies in the business. They make furniture and accessories for every room, mostly in plastic, which suits their contemporary design. Unfortunately, their pieces are made to ¾-inch scale, but even so, some of them manage to look correct in a 1-inch-scale setting, particularly their floor lamps. The Lundby line includes such unusual items as a sauna, a stall shower, a ping-pong table and a garden glider. Lundby also makes a simplified 4-volt electrical system for miniature rooms and dollhouses.

The Chrysnbon, Sonia Messer, and Lundby lines are distributed by the well-known New York firm of Block House, which also carries a line of French Limoges china.

One of the largest firms producing dollhouse accessories, quaintly named Grandmother Stover's, Inc., is also one of the oldest, having been founded in 1940. Their familiar little packages can be found hanging on racks in miniature shops, stationery stores, and toy stores throughout the country. Among Grandmother Stover's notable achievements over the years has been the miniaturizing of *The New York Times, Amy Vanderbilt's Complete Book of Etiquette* and *Webster's Dictionary.* Grandmother Stover's can supply you with a vacuum cleaner, mixer, coffee maker, iron, bathroom scale, and more than four hundred other household items. Many national brand products are represented in their collection, including miniature packages of Kellogg's Corn Flakes, Kleenex, Ivory Soap, and Duz.

In addition to these large popular sources, a vast number of anonymous craftspeople produce their miniature specialties for local shops on a limited basis. Many of these people make their miniatures as a sideline. Among the numerous craftspeople who supply the Mini Mundus shop in New York is a convict who makes miniature furniture.

(From the Colonial Craftsmen catalog.)

18-58-5B   18-58-5C   18-58-5D   18-58-5E   18-58-5G   18-58-5K

18-58-4F   18-58-4M   18-58-4N   18-58-4Q   18-58-4R

18-34I   18-35E   18-34F   18-34H   18-34H-I

18-33   18-33A   18-35   18-35A   18-35B   18-35C   18-35D

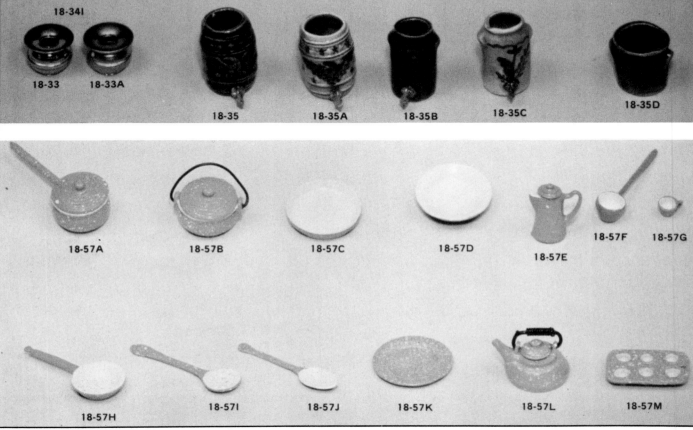

18-57A   18-57B   18-57C   18-57D   18-57E   18-57F   18-57G

18-57H   18-57I   18-57J   18-57K   18-57L   18-57M

-1 -2 -3 -4 -5 -6 -7 -8 -9 -10 -11 -12

-13 -14 -15 -16 -17 -18

18-68A 18-68A-1 18-68B 18-68B-1 18-68C 18-68C-1

18-48 18-48A 18-50F-10 18-51A 18-51B 18-51C 18-51D

18-8 18-8B 18-8C 18-8D 18-9 18-9A 18-9B

18-9D 18-9C 18-9E 18-10 18-10A 18-10B 18-12

18-12A 18-13 18-14 18-15 18-17 18-17A 18-17B

(From the Grandmother Stover's catalog.)

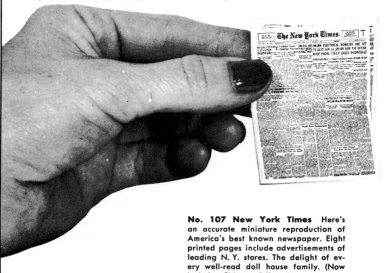

No. 107 New York Times Here's an accurate miniature reproduction of America's best known newspaper. Eight printed pages include advertisements of leading N. Y. stores. The delight of every well-read doll house family. (Now includes Chicago Tribune)

No. 144 Scales Blue composition scales with black tread and hand painted dial. Also a diet book and box of Kleenex.

*No. 181 Pair Candlesticks Very elegant metal candlesticks with silver finish. Will take regular birthday candles.

No. 111 Checker Board Red and black. 24 plastic checkers ⅛″ in diameter. You can really play on it if you have fingernails and plenty of patience.

No. 250 Cat on Rug A gay little crocheted wool rug is the favorite resting place for this tan and white doll house cat. Put it in front of the fireplace or stove.

No. 247 Fish Plaque Mounted minnow-size speckled trout is colorfully hand-decorated. Great gift for a serious fisherman.

No. 265 Steeple Clock Since time stands still in the doll house, this is a very appropriate clock. The clock is metal, painted brown, and the door frame is a separate metal casting painted gold.

No. 103 Magazines Printed four colors on heavy cardboar_ these tiny replicas are startling_ real. Scatter them around the livi_ room for realism. Five for

No. 208 Nest of Bowls Three wood bowls finished in bright red, yellow and blue enamel. Very useful.

No. 271 Vacuum Cleaner Every detail is faithfully reproduced in metal . . . except for the room-length cord. Realistically hand-decorated.

No. 148 Bean Pot Decorated in two tones of brown and white and filled with very realistic baked beans.

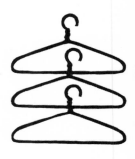

No. 170 Coat Hangers Here a_ three heavy wire hangers exac_ like those in your closet. These, _ course, are just the right size f_ doll house doll clothes.

No. 246 Round Mirror This is a very popular mirror for any room. Gilt frame and real mirror.

GRANDMOTHER STOVER'S

No. 203 Carving Set Steel color cast metal knife, fork and butcher steel. Handles carefully decorated to look like bone.

No. 225 Ham Has a golden glaze and is very carefully hand decorated in pink and black cloves. Bright blue platter with parsley and sweet potatoes.

No. 101 Playing Cards Fifty-two miniature cards and the joker. Each tiny detail is accurately reproduced so the cards can be used. They're ⅜" long and printed in red and black with back design printed in blue.

No. 252 Bag of Oranges A real mesh bag (handmade) filled with tiny oranges. Unlike Florida and California oranges, these from Ohio are never out of season.

No. 151 Radio Table model radio with real cord and printed dial. Appropriate for any room in the house. Available in ivory or bright red. Black knobs.

No. 226 Ship Print Here in a narrow gilt frame and mat is an authentic print of the Clipper Ship, Flying Cloud. Hand-tinted.

No. 263 Coffee Maker First appeared in our 1950 catalog. The original supplier is again making the seven precision parts of lucite and steel which we assemble and decorate by hand. In thirty years only the cost has changed.

No. 185 Cookie Jar Red painted wood filled with pretend cookies. Pennsylvania Dutch decoration in white, green and pink.

No. 149 Electric Iron This tiny metal iron is very realistic with its cord and its shiny black handle. Won't scorch.

No. 275 School Set The ABC book contains all the alphabet and the tablet pages are ruled. The wood framed blackboard is black, the eraser erases. But, alas, the chalk won't chalk.

No. 262 Mixer & Bowl. Cast metal with baked white enamel finish. Hand decorated aluminum blades, black handle and red button.

No. 211 Teakettle This, too, is a solid metal casting. Chrome finish, has red stopper and black handle.

No. 245 Salad Set A natural wood bowl of lettuce, tomato and hard-boiled egg salad with four matching individual bowls. Colorful and healthful. Serves four.

CHAPTER 7

AN INTRODUCTION
TO DOLLHOUSES

The first thing to consider in contemplating the purchase of a dollhouse is whether you really want a dollhouse at all. Some people, for example, collect miniatures as art objects and display them the way they would any small, precious object, housing their collections very happily on bookshelves or in display cabinets of one kind or another. Most collectors, however, prefer to assemble their miniatures into settings. These can range from simple vignettes containing just a handful of objects to complete dollhouses, furnished from top to bottom. In between these extremes are miniature rooms (shadow boxes), one of the most popular types of housing. Even here there is a range of choices, from simple, unpainted plywood boxes to beautifully constructed rooms made by cabinetmakers, with handsome veneers and hinged-glass doors.

In this chapter you'll see a number of different ways of housing your collection of miniatures. If you feel ambitious and want to build your own housing, Chapter 13 will guide you.

The miniature room or shadow box provides an easy way to enter the hobby. By keeping the cost of housing to a minimum, it allows the new collector to concentrate on the miniatures themselves. It also provides the novice with a fairly inexpensive way of trying the hobby on for size before making a more substantial commitment and investment. In addition, a miniature room setting takes considerably less time to decorate and furnish than does a dollhouse, and this is likely to give the eager beginner a more immediate feeling of accomplishment.

VARIOUS APPROACHES TO HOUSING YOUR MINIATURES

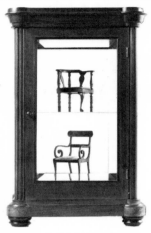

VITRINE, OR DISPLAY CASE

Chairs from Chestnut Hill Studio.

VIGNETTE

From the cover of the Block House catalog.

MINIATURE SHOP

From The Enchanted Dollhouse.

ANTIQUE DOLLHOUSE

From the collection of Iris Brown.

DOLLHOUSE BUILT FROM PATTERNS

From The Ark.

FANTASY DOLLHOUSE

From The Enchanted Dollhouse.

BOOKSHELF ARRANGEMENT

Wing chair and rug from Chestnut Hill Studio. Victorian lyre console table and tufted side chair from the collection of Robert Milne.

SHADOW BOX, OR MINIATURE ROOM

From Mini Mundus.

READY-MADE DOLLHOUSE

From The Enchanted Dollhouse.

DOLLHOUSE BUILT FROM PLANS

FINISH-IT-YOURSELF DOLLHOUSE

By Joen Ellen Kanze.

CUSTOM-MADE DOLLHOUSE

By Robert Dankanics.

Wing chair and rug from Chestnut Hill Studio. Victorian lyre console table and side chair from the collection of Robert Milne. Candlestick from the collection of Valerie Rosner.

Advanced collectors use the miniature room to re-create period room settings. In the hands of an expert, the single room can emerge as a work of art in itself, with intricate paneling and moldings, inlaid floors, bay windows, stately doors, perfectly scaled hardware and ingenious lighting effects. The miniature room is also a popular form among collectors with special interests, such as general stores and old-fashioned schoolrooms.

Because of its size, the miniature room can fit on a shelf or stand on a small table, and it can be moved around with ease and transported to shows with a minimum of trouble. It also serves as an excellent housing for a collection of antique miniatures, where high cost and rarity prohibit assembling an entire houseful of objects.

A still simpler form than the miniature room or shadow box is the vignette—a shallow box, no more than a few inches deep, which is usually framed and hung on the wall. While the structure is simple, the art of creating vignettes is not, for this is the art of illusion. Working with only a handful of objects, the vignettist tries to create the feeling of an entire room or reveal something of the personality of the room's "occupant." A skillful vignette conveys more than the sum of its parts. If you think you'd like to explore this challenging art form, do yourself a favor and obtain a copy of Susan Brown's excellent book, *Miniature Vignettes*.

Handsome housings for a collection of miniature silver or china are the unusual display cases made by Micro-Creations of Dayton, Ohio. These museum-quality cases, in a soft cherry finish, resemble store fronts and have interior display units. They can be obtained as self-standing or wall-hanging cases.

The same pieces as before now assembled in a room setting, with the addition of a Delaware Valley highboy, Hepplewhite half-round table, corner chair, ginger jar, and Canton bowl, all from Chestnut Hill Studio. Tufted armchair from the collection of Robert Milne. Painting by Jack Jarque. Shadowbox room from Mini Mundus.

The same pieces from the room setting on the previous page, now installed in a dollhouse made by the author. The painting has been replaced by a Federal round mirror from the collection of Valerie Rosner.

A dollhouse represents a true commitment to the hobby. There, in front of you, stands an empty house, waiting for you to move in. It's even emptier than a real house, since you usually have to provide your own fireplace, kitchen appliances, bathroom fixtures, and other amenities that usually come with a life-sized dwelling.

On the other hand, here is where one of the great pleasures of the hobby lies—in confronting those empty rooms and turning them into a home based on your own taste and ideas. The possibilities are unlimited, since virtually anything you can think of you can do. If there's something you can't buy, you can make it yourself, or have it custom-made. A dollhouse gives you the most room for expression. It allows you to create an entire home.

The job of finding the right dollhouse is a little like looking for a real house. The main considerations are ordinarily price, style, and quality. Price, of course, has a bearing on the other two factors. In a low-priced house, don't expect too much authenticity of architectural style or excellence of workmanship. If, on the other hand, you want a dollhouse of pleasing design and meticulous detail, be prepared to pay for it. One thing you can be fairly sure of: Whatever you pay for a *well-made* dollhouse, you'll be getting your money's worth. A hand-made dollhouse is a labor of time; the more detailed the house, the more hours it has taken to build it. An exquisitely made dollhouse, in which every shingle has been applied individually and every strip of interior molding is exactly to scale, might be cheap at a thousand dollars, while a poorly made house, with oversized hinges, rough edges all around and acetate windows, might be overpriced at fifty dollars. Many children's dollhouses (but not all) fall into this latter category.

Unless you already have a distinct preference in architectural style, an enjoyable warm-up exercise before seriously shopping for a dollhouse is to go for a drive in the country armed with a camera. Stop and take pictures of any houses that appeal to you. At home, lay out the pictures side by side, and by process of elimination, zero in on the style you'd most like to own in a dollhouse. The job then becomes one of trying to approximate that style in a ready-made dollhouse of acceptable quality, or to consider having it custom-built. A good illustrated book on houses will give you additional possibilities.

The photographs on the following pages represent some of the classic categories of house design. They're intended to stimulate your appetite for "house-hunting."

Photographed at The Dollhouse Factory, Lebanon, New Jersey.

CHAPTER 8

SHOPPING
FOR A DOLLHOUSE

This chapter will attempt to answer the question "What do I have to spend for a good dollhouse?"

To a certain extent the question is subjective, for it depends in part on your own taste and requirements. Inflation is also a factor, of course, forcing us to use those all-too-familiar words "Prices subject to change."

It's safe to say that you'll have difficulty finding a satisfactory dollhouse for less than $100 unless you "think small." While the larger houses in this price range are fine for children, they lack the quality of materials and attention to detail that an adult collector would want. It's a question of economics. In a large house, the cost of materials is higher and is accordingly offset by the use of lesser quality materials (wood substitutes and plastics) and short-cut construction methods, which keeps it within the lower price range. In a smaller house of the same price, you can expect to find better quality materials and better workmanship.

When the price of a full-size dollhouse gets up between $100 and $200, you'll begin to find more architectural detailing, although it will probably be more fanciful than accurate. Houses in this price range are made of wood, have at least six rooms and an attic (usually accessible by way of a hinged roof), are electrified, have one or more staircases, and sometimes come wallpapered.

In their overall dimensions, such houses will run between 2 and 4 feet in length, 1 and 1½ feet in depth, and about 2 feet in height. Any child would be thrilled to get his or her hands on one of them, and so would many adult collectors.

The houses that you'll see on the next few pages represent a good cross section of ready-made dollhouses. All of them were provided for us by a single source—The Enchanted Dollhouse, in Manchester Center, Vermont. Here, under one roof in a marvelous sprawling Colonial, Mrs. Jean Schramm, a woman of great charm and energy, has assembled nine rooms of dolls, dollhouses, miniatures, toys, games, books, and other delights. Mrs. Schramm's remarkably thorough collection of dollhouses and miniatures in all price ranges is intended to appeal to all levels of collectors, and to young and old alike. If you're ever in the neighborhood, make it a point to stop in. You'll find the visit most rewarding.

One-room cottage, brick effect on sides
and simulated shingles.

Modular dollhouse made up of separate rooms that
are stackable. One room with roof.

Outhouse, 9″ high, made of simulated barn wood.

Townhouse in box, hinged front doors and painted details.

Simple two-story townhouse.

Basic two-and-a-half-story house,
assembled or in kit form.

One-and-a-half-story log cabin dollhouse, with removable roof, separate porch, and ladder to loft.

Three-story townhouse, with dormer.

Four-story townhouse, with scalloped roof.

Three-story "Betsy Ross" townhouse, with three rooms.

Three-story, three-room "Independence Row" townhouse.

One-room schoolhouse, complete with bell.

Small log house or general store, with detachable porch.

Three-story townhouse, with six rooms and two staircases. Comes unassembled.

Two-story dollhouse, with four rooms plus attic.

Four-room Southern Colonial mansion, with columns.

Basic two-story house, with four rooms plus attic.

Farmhouse, with four large rooms plus attic with lift-up roof. Front porch comes with ceiling swing and hanging plant.

Large Colonial, with six rooms and an attic, features wallpaper in all rooms, carpeted staircase, and fireplace.

Two-story Colonial house, with six rooms plus staircase. Wired with lights.

Five-room house, with staircase and attic. Wallpapered and with curtains. Extensions can be added on either side.

Pepperbox, garrison-type house of log construction, made in three sections and containing movable ladder-type staircase.

Miniature room, fully wallpapered, complete with chair rail and corner fireplace.

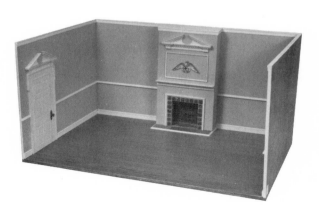

Miniature room, wallpapered, and ready to be decorated.

Above $200, a whole new world of possibilities opens up, becoming wider and more elaborate as the prices get higher and higher. From here on, the sky's the limit. You can have anything you want, provided you're willing and able to pay the price.

At first you may have to swallow hard at the thought of spending more than $200 for a dollhouse, but just consider what's happened to the prices of full-size houses in the last few years. The cost of materials and labor has increased in the mini world just as it has in the full-size world. But unfortunately, a dollhouse-maker can't live on one-twelfth the income of the rest of us.

One dollhouse-maker estimates that a dollhouse which she sells for $500 takes her three hundred hours to make. While the $500 price tag may seem like a lot of money at first, when you consider the time it takes and deduct the cost of materials, it turns out that the builder is selling her considerable talents for a mere $2 an hour.

With these economic factors in mind, come with us now on a tour through the rarefied upper reaches of the dollhouse world. The houses we'll encounter in this chapter are ready-made; in the next chapter we'll look at custom-made houses. The prices start at $250, and styles range from fanciful Victorian to architecturally perfect Georgian based on measured drawings. Along the way you'll meet the builders of these miniature wonders. You'll also gain an insight into what it's like to have a dollhouse built for you.

For the addresses of these dollhouse builders, refer to Chapter 18.

PAULA MacLEAN

For about $250 (plus shipping charges of about $30), you can own one of Paula MacLean's charming four-story "Hearts-and-Flowers" Victorian-style dollhouses. The cost of crating is included in the price; and when you consider that the house stands 40 inches tall and 34 inches wide, you can appreciate that the crating is a job in itself.

The house is constructed entirely of wood and contains six rooms, three hallways—each with a staircase—and a full attic. The house derives its charm, architecturally, from its wrap-around porch, bay windows, and second-floor balcony. Other distinctive features include twenty "stained-glass" windows, French doors, and window boxes with flowers. The customer can choose his or her own exterior colors at no extra cost.

Considering the work that goes into one of Paula MacLean's houses, and the price, we consider it a rare bargain.

"I received my first dollhouse at age six, and I've never gotten over the magic of miniatures. The dollhouse was a metal one, lithographed, with plastic furniture. It gave me years of happiness, but I always dreamed of a dollhouse made of wood, with wood furniture and real

rugs and paintings, not just painted on. When I turned twelve, I decided regretfully that I was too old for the dollhouse and put it away in the attic. It stayed up there only two weeks. I missed it too much and got it down again to play with.

"At fourteen, I drew up a floor plan for my dream dollhouse. It had a kidney-shaped swimming pool, a four-car garage, and, among the usual things, a total of thirteen bathrooms! It was a little ambitious for me at that age, and it never got off the drawing board. I tried again at age twenty-two, but I didn't have the skill or woodworking equipment needed, and I put it off to do 'some day.'

"When I was twenty-five, married and very busy being a wife, and working full time, I happened across a magazine article about getting the most out of life. The article said to list the things you'd always meant to do when you had the time. Then it said to pick the things you would do if you only had 6 months to live. And finally, it said that if you wanted to get more out of life, you should do those things now and not put them off. I set about building my dream dollhouse.

"It was a duplicate of my childhood dollhouse, except that it was made of wood, with real rugs and electric lights and much more. I enjoyed building and furnishing it so much that I wanted to build another one. I took a woodworking class to improve my skills, and then designed and built a Victorian dollhouse. That started me in business. I still don't have a Victorian dollhouse for myself —rather ironic, like the cobbler's kids who have no shoes. But perhaps when I get caught up on orders, I can build myself one."

(Photos courtesy of Paula MacLean.)

If you have $395 to spend on a dollhouse, you qualify for the extraordinary Victorian mansion produced by My Uncle of Fryeburg, Maine.

Anyone who has ever built a dollhouse and knows how much work and costly materials go into it will be baffled at how My Uncle can sell a house of this quality for the price.

Consider the dimensions of the house: 46½″ wide (that's almost 4′), 29″ deep, and 44½″ high. Few dollhouses are this big. The construction is entirely of wood; no Masonite, particle board, or wood substitutes are used. The house has two full floors; an attic; dormers; a total of 39 windows, including a bay window; a full porch with hand-turned columns, and individually cut clapboard siding. Among the many interior features are two railed staircases, and fireplaces on the first and second floors.

The house is completely enclosed on all sides. Access to the inside has been ingeniously and tastefully provided by four hinged sections that swing outward. Magnetic latches keep these sections securely closed.

The house comes completely assembled and painted white, inside and out. Door-to-door delivery is free if you live in New England; otherwise, there is a shipping charge. The total weight is 250 pounds.

This marvelous house, like most better dollhouses, is made in limited numbers. My Uncle advises customers to allow eight weeks for delivery.

(Photos courtesy of My Uncle.)

These are two-room structures, averaging 30 inches tall, 14 inches wide, and 12 inches deep. The ground-floor room makes a perfect shop, with the upstairs room functioning as living quarters. Access to these houses is through the front, which opens, and the roof, which can be raised. Details have been carefully and inventively handled, right down to the random-plank oak-veneer floors, which have been given the patina of a business establishment.

Amity Petites also makes larger houses and beautiful miniature furniture—all the collective output of a very talented family consisting of Dorothy Rawlings and Linda and Larry McKibbon, her daughter and son-in-law. Occasionally Dorothy's son William and Larry's brother Ron add their talents in the creating of miniature furniture and accessories. Friends help out, too, and the result is a marvelous pool of talent devoted to miniature making.

If you've been wishing you could find a beautifully made dollhouse of smaller-than-average size yet still 1-inch-to-1-foot in scale, and you happen to find yourself at either the spring or fall miniature show sponsored by N.A.M.E., you'll get your wish. For there (and only there) you will find the exquisite little houses made by Amity Petites.

(Photo courtesy of Amity Petites.)

(Photos courtesy of Jim Marcus.)

Jim Marcus specializes in San Francisco Victorian townhouses and builds them to perfection. His prices range from about $750 for the kind of house shown here to $1,100 for a model of the Russian consulate building—a San Francisco structure dripping with ornamentation.

Mr. Marcus is a master of detail. A former woodcarver, he is capable of reproducing anything the original builder could build. His houses are modeled after the type of Victorian townhouse in which virtually all of the detail was concentrated on the front, and he tries to capture these details accurately enough for his houses to serve as historic models as well as dollhouses.

Mr. Marcus's approach to making dollhouses is unique. Each year he selects a particular design which he considers to be an outstanding example of the Victorian townhouse style and makes a limited edition of about ten houses. Working on these houses full time, he takes an entire year to complete an edition. After that, he begins work on another design "edition," never duplicating, treating each in the same way that a printmaker treats a limited edition of prints. By changing the edition each year, Mr. Marcus keeps his interest high and is able to produce work of which he can be proud. Each new design is chosen so that the house can be placed alongside the houses from former editions to eventually simulate an entire San Francisco block.

"My most recent Victorian is closely modeled after an elegant house on McAllister Street in San

Francisco. This dollhouse offers excellent visibility of the interior through the large bay windows; thus, the front of the house does not have to be opened in order to view the collection inside.

"A special feature of this dollhouse is the full basement, which is seen through the window beneath the bay. 'Ground level' has been established by surrounding the bottom four inches of the house with a finely jointed wood base, which has been richly finished in the old style with six coats of orange shellac. This helps to create the impression that one is looking down into the basement from street level.

"The front doors and the interior of the house have a finish similar to that of the base; the stairs are graced by carefully turned newel posts and scale handrails. Thirty-nine hand-carved brackets of five different designs and seventeen other intricately carved areas adorn each house. Lighting is of the reflected type, with the wiring completely concealed, and an outside on-off switch for convenience.

"This dollhouse will be produced in a limited edition of ten; each house will be signed and numbered. The houses are completely finished on the outside, and the backs and interior stairs may be removed for ease in applying your choice of wallpaper. These houses are one room deep, but the width of the rooms on the top and bottom floors may be determined by one's placement of the movable inner walls."

GOTFRED O. HOFFMANN– MINIATURE MANSIONS OF CHESHIRE

A dollhouse can tell you a great deal about the person who constructed it. After studying one of Gotfred Hoffmann's houses, you'd probably conclude that its builder had either an engineering or architectural background, a sound knowledge of woodworking and materials, and a high degree of intelligence. You'd be right on all counts.

Mr. Hoffmann designs and builds several different models of dollhouses, and also does custom building. One of his designs in partic- ular is worth singling out because it is so uniquely the product of its creator. This is the Colonial dollhouse that the Hoffmanns refer to as Model 411.

Unlike most dollhouses, which tend to be one room deep, this house is two rooms deep, giving it the overall proportions of a real house. The beautifully handled exterior detailing furthers this illusion of reality. A hinged front panel swings open to provide access to the front rooms, while the back has been left open for access to the rear rooms.

There's a precision to the house that makes it look like an architect's model, but the thing that strikes us most is its ingenious design, which enables it to accommodate a host of "options."

The basic house is priced at around $425. It has seven rooms, a fireplace in the living room, a staircase with a hidden closet beneath it, and an attic under the hinged roof. However, you can modify the house to your own taste (and pocketbook) with a tantalizing variety of optional features. You can elect to have either a hip roof with dormers or a peaked roof with dormers. You can have clapboard siding as well as shingles on the roof. The house can be electrified for you. A lighted fireplace can be added. Two different porches are available. You can have a doorbell and chimes on the front door, and carpeting on the staircase. By going the whole route, you can boost the price of the finished house to around $800, but it's worth it. Many customers who start out intending to buy the basic model can't resist coming away with the deluxe version.

Whatever options you choose, your house will have a little brass plate on the back with your name, the date, and Mr. Hoffmann's name as architect/builder. Under the brass plate is a hollow space to hold a mini deed.

Another appealing feature of this house is that it comes apart without difficulty. The entire house can be packed away in about twenty minutes. Also, because dismantling is so easy, you can get to the walls to wallpaper or paint them.

The wiring has been cleverly designed with plugs and sockets that allow for easy disconnecting when the house is being disassembled. Consequently, no soldering or unsoldering is required. And because the basic house is made of rock maple—a wood so hard it takes carbide-tipped drills to work on it—it should last for generations.

The mind that figured all this out belongs to a former electrical engineer, the son of a building contractor, whose lifelong hobby of woodworking has become a full-time occupation. Mr. Hoffmann began building dollhouses about three years ago, when he realized there were very few good ones on the market. At his daughter's insistence, he exhibited his first house at an art show, and the reaction encouraged him to turn it into a business. Mr. Hoffmann, ably assisted by his wife, sells his houses at miniature shows and by mail order.

(Photos courtesy of Noel Thomas.)

Elaborate detailing includes hand-cut siding and shingles, dentil molding, and roof ornamentation.

If you can afford the best and would like to acquire a dollhouse that surely ranks as a work of art, get in touch with Noel Thomas of Open House.

Mr. Thomas's houses are so beautifully made that even the most casual passer-by is compelled to stop in his or her tracks and marvel at the talent that produced such an artifact.

We had the pleasure of seeing one of Mr. Thomas's houses work its fascination in the front window of F. A. O. Schwarz in New York several Christmases ago. Children had trouble making their way to the window through the dense crowd of admiring adults.

Mr. Thomas has both a taste for complex architectural styles and the ability to reproduce them faithfully in miniature. And through it all, the hand of the artist is clearly visible. His is not the perfection of a machine but the perfection of the craftsman.

In his detailing, too, Mr. Thomas has an approach that is as distinctive as his signature. His flooring, shingles, siding, window panes, staircases, and interior molding all have a special character, for Mr. Thomas makes all of these components himself—he uses no ready-made elements. It's this total authorship of even the smallest detail that gives Mr. Thomas's houses their originality, unity, and integrity.

NOEL THOMAS—OPEN HOUSE

It's easy to see why these houses sell as fast as Mr. Thomas can build them. But no one can get rich working this way. The price tags of $1,000 and $1,500 can hardly compensate Mr. Thomas for the work involved.

Because of their considerable beauty and limited numbers, Mr. Thomas's houses, we feel, will become much-sought-after collectors' items in the years to come.

Mrs. Thomas gives us some interesting background about her husband's approach to dollhouse building:

"I think the key to Noel's work is that he doesn't build toys, he builds real houses in miniature. And he builds them for himself, not according to some elusive standard of what the buyer might pay for. He loves the work, likes to make inaccessible places in each house that you can only see through a window. And each house is different from and more intricate than the last.

"We don't have price categories for our houses. Noel works on one until it's done and then decides upon a price. So far we've had no difficulty selling them this way. He does work within a basic price on a pre-ordered house; otherwise, he works completely on his own. His favorite period of architecture is the Pacific Northwest Victorian, and again, everyone seems happy with it.

"As for houses, Noel has always noticed details. He has lived in New York and Connecticut as well as on the West Coast. I guess he learned from all his exposure to older homes how to really see a house and remember the details.

"It's difficult to calculate how many hours Noel puts into a house. He puts only the basic design down on paper before he begins to build. The final shape or contents of a house are never determined until a house is completed. I guess that's the real joy of working in a small scale. You could never decide you wanted another gable or upstairs porch halfway through a full-size house. I guess

an estimate of from 200 to 300 hours per house would be roughly accurate. Each one becomes more complex, though, and he'll do things like spend days on a front porch or a butler's pantry. He loves the detail work.

"There are sources for almost everything you would need in dollhouse construction, already pre-cut, but Noel has found he'd rather make them himself. There's something reminiscent of mobile homes about pre-cut siding and shingles. Nothing is more real than the real thing, so everything (with minor exceptions like electrical channeling) is individually made and cut, from shingles to oak flooring to stairs, handrails, etc. We think it's this sort of thing that makes Noel's houses special. They're real, and don't merely give the suggestion of reality. His fireplaces, part of each finished house, are burned with real soot, hand-rubbed in. The difference between that and a spray-painted or quick-aging method is very noticeable."

To further heighten the illusion of reality, here Mr. Thomas has papered his attic with miniature newspapers.

Detail of staircase showing handmade interior woodwork.

CHAPTER 9

THE CUSTOM-MADE DOLLHOUSE

If you have something special in mind—a dream dollhouse that you would like to see become a reality—you need the services of a custom dollhouse-builder. Several excellent builders are presented in this chapter, along with examples of their work. If none of these people are located near enough to you for a visit, you can always deal with them by mail. Or you could contact your local miniature shop for the name of a builder nearby.

A good dollhouse-builder is a combination architect, carpenter, decorator, and psychologist. He or she has to sort out someone's dream clearly enough to be able to turn it into something tangible. It helps if the client can furnish a photograph or sketch, but frequently a verbal description of the house is all the builder will have to work from.

Most important for a successful custom dollhouse is a meeting of minds between client and builder. Misunderstandings are both difficult and costly to rectify. For that reason, the builder first submits a set of drawings to the client, just as an architect does. It's a lot easier to make adjustments at this stage of the project than it is once work has started.

A dollhouse-builder is usually prepared to carry the job all the way through to the finished house, doing the painting, wiring, construction of built-in fireplaces, and anything else the client would like. Many clients, however, prefer to do the interior decorating jobs, such as painting and wallpapering, themselves.

The next few pages will give you some idea of what it's like to have a custom dollhouse built for you.

ROBERT DANKANICS—THE DOLLHOUSE FACTORY

Robert Dankanics is a custom dollhouse builder of enormous versatility. He seems to be able to build anything with which his clients challenge him. His houses are meticulously detailed and incorporate such specialized architectural touches as complicated lathe turnings and stained-glass windows.

As a former practicing psychotherapist, Mr. Dankanics is patient and understanding. He realizes that dollhouses are very important to his clients, and works hard to meet their expectations.

Mr. Dankanics is willing to lavish a considerable amount of attention on his houses, thinking nothing of finishing off a roof with thousands of individual shingles applied one at a time, or bricking an entire façade with miniature clay bricks of his own manufacture.

(Photos courtesy of Robert Dankanics.)

Victorian villa, 6 rooms, wallpapered throughout, fully electrified. Tower has secret room and attic has a trapdoor and ladder.

Country house with gazebo porch, 5 rooms, full attic, 4 dormers, electrified.

Georgian brick townhouse made with 2,600 hand-laid mini-bricks.

As much as he enjoys building dollhouses, Mr. Dankanics is just as happy to have you try your own hand at dollhouse building. His shop, in Lebanon, New Jersey, is well stocked with building supplies in addition to miniature furnishings. He and his wife, Judy, will help you in every way they can. A photo album in their shop attests to their success in this area—it's filled with photos of houses that their customers have built for themselves. But beyond that, if you're thinking of having a dollhouse built for you, Mr. Dankanics is a good person to bring your dreams to.

"In the dollhouse business I can get the kicks in one month that it takes an architect, a builder, and a contractor a year and a half to get.

"It takes a while to develop a feeling for how much to charge. By now, in most cases, I can judge beforehand the amount of work involved. I can't break it down into hours or material costs, but I know what I have to make to be willing to produce the house. In that way I can give a pretty firm price at the outset. Frequently I lose out because halfway through I fall in love with it and spend more hours on it than I had anticipated.

"My beach house, for instance, takes me more than a month to build. It has over 3,000 hand-split shakes. That means that first I have to saw the wood, then I have to split them again the other way. The preparation alone takes two weeks before I even start to build anything.

"If you wanted me to build you a custom house, the first thing I'd ask is whether I have to work from fantasy or whether you have a picture of the kind of house you want. Working from fantasy is much more difficult because a client may have had pieces of ideas in mind for twenty years or more. If you can't sketch your ideas, then I have to try to sketch them for you. It's a little like doing a police 'work-up.'

"Most people aren't used to coming into a place where you can have just what you want, where you can tell me what's on your mind and I go back and build it. To most people it's a very novel experience, unlike ready-made dollhouses where you just walk over to a shelf and say, 'That's the one I like.'"

Southern Colonial, 8 rooms, full attic, electrified, with clapboard siding and cedar-shake roof.

English baby house, 3 stories, 8 rooms, fully electrified.

Victorian Dollmansion, 3 floors, 8 large rooms, with an electric elevator and lights in all rooms. A stained glass solarium extends over a patio made with 1,050 mini-bricks. The front tower contains a spiral staircase.

To custom dollhouse builder Joen Ellen Kanze, no house is too big or too small to construct. Mrs. Kanze recently completed a carefully researched replica of a thirty-room mansion for a client who lived in the house as a child. Although she reduced the number of rooms for the sake of practicality, Mrs. Kanze kept such original features as a working elevator and three built-in fireplaces.

Mrs. Kanze has also built simple one- and two-room dollhouses. Her specialty, however, is reproducing the house one lived in as a child, or any other fondly remembered structure, such as a schoolhouse or general store—you name it. She constructs the house up to the finishing stage, and then the client takes over and does the finishing—the work that Mrs. Kanze refers to as "the fun part."

"We can take on only one order at a time, and we won't accept down payment on a new house until the current one is finished. This makes for poor economics, but who ever got rich having so much fun? The house which is now on the drawing board measures 3 inches too wide to fit through the cellar door, so we will have to do some hassling with the client to shrink it a bit. A sticky wicket, as the people do have very definite ideas about exactly what they want.

"Sometimes a client will send a sketch that is good enough to send a firm quote on, but sometimes the sketches are unrealistic, dollhouse-wise. Mostly, a client will send a picture, and I work up a dollhouse version on graph paper and quote a price according to how elaborate the structure is. There is no way to give a 'basic' price. There are too many variables. The range is generally about $75 for a one- or two-room cottage or store, unfinished (sanded smooth) and ready to decorate. The big elaborate houses run around $500, ready to finish."

"All houses include a 7-watt fixture in each room, bulb, cord and plug, and switches for different levels of the house. All work on regular house current. We've tried transformers and batteries, but the direct current is the best; and, as my husband is a trained electrician, the houses are wired completely safe. Windows are real glass.

"We've never really clocked the number of hours that go into putting a house together, but I would estimate that our big 'tower houses' take at least 200 hours."

(Photos courtesy of Joen Ellen Kanze.)

The dollhouse pictured here is a fastidiously accurate replica of a historic 1760 Dutch Colonial house in Upper Saddle River, New Jersey. It was built on commission and reflects the Conleys' meticulous and original approach to dollhouse building.

Before going into dollhouses full time, Mr. Conley was a theatrical set designer, and many of his unusual and highly effective construction techniques reflect this discipline.

In making the exterior of the Saddle River house, for example, Mr. Conley used a technique that included both hand-carved detail and no less than eleven layers of paint to simulate the original sandstone blocks. The outer walls of the house were constructed 2 inches thick, permitting the realistic-looking setback of the doors and allowing for window seats in each of the downstairs rooms.

The house has been electrified with two separate wiring systems, one for overall illumination and the other to power the tiny chandeliers.

Old pine was used to make the pegged, random-plank floors. The chimneys terminate in two built-in illuminated fireplaces and a walk-in kitchen hearth, complete with beehive oven.

In addition to building museum-quality custom dollhouses, the Conleys also offer several models of ready-made dollhouses.

(Photo courtesy of Doormouse Dollhouses.)

CHAPTER 10

ANTIQUE MINIATURES

Another interesting option open to the miniature enthusiast is the collecting of antique miniatures. This is generally an expensive area of collecting and requires a great amount of diligent shopping, for antique pieces are hard to find and much sought after.

Antique collectors relish the endless searching and the thrill of discovery. They also know that the scarcity of a piece will cause it to increase in value, so in a sense they can justify their hobby as a form of investing.

Antique collecting frequently starts with the purchase of an antique dollhouse. The job then is to find sufficient furnishings of suitable kind and antiquity. This is the challenge of antique collecting, and a considerable challenge it is.

Before you seriously consider collecting antique miniatures, you should make an effort to learn everything you can about them. There are several excellent books on the subject, in particular the two highly authoritative books by Flora Gill Jacobs (see Bibliography). Read, visit dealers, go to shows and museums. Only by having a sound awareness of the field will you be able to appreciate good examples of antique miniatures when you come across them, and be able to collect them wisely.

German castle in ½-inch scale, c. 1875, with detachable turret and elaborate fret-saw work throughout. The right half of the front section swings open for access to the interior. From the collection of Robert Milne.

The difference between a toy and a true
miniature is dramatically illustrated by
these two groupings. The German
Biedermeier parlor set, c. 1850–1860,
shown here, while elaborately detailed,
is still toylike in its heavy design and
construction. The pieces are more
impressionistic than realistic.

Shown here are true miniatures—a Victorian-style cameo sofa, gentleman's chair, and lady's chair, refined in every detail and so realistically proportioned that in a photograph they could easily be mistaken for full-size furniture. Note the exquisitely carved frames and the delicacy of the tufting. Made by Frank Matter in the late 1940s. From the collection of Robert Milne. (Photo by Arnold Beckerman.)

The word *antique* is a very broad term in miniature circles and has nothing to do with the legal definition. Legally, an antique is any work of art or handicraft over one hundred years old. This is the current definition of the term. Until very recently, *antique* took its definition from the U. S. Tariff Act of 1930. According to the *Encyclopaedia Britannica:*

"The act exempted from duty 'artistic antiquities, collections in illustration of the progress of the arts, objects of art of educational value or ornamental character . . . which shall have been produced prior to the year 1830' . . . a year widely accepted as proper because it marks approximately the end of traditional handicrafts and the beginning of industrialization. Industrial products at first were poor in design and in quality; attempting to recover earlier standards, people became more and more interested in the products of ages past."

Encyclopedia International suggests a less exacting definition.

"In the broadest sense of the word, an antique is an object not in current production. . . . In actual practice a shorter passage of time [than 100 years] is enough to turn an artifact into an antique. Two generations, about 60 years, are usually sufficient; our fathers' possessions are out-of-date, our grandfathers' are antiques."

Robert Milne, a highly respected dealer in antique miniatures, goes further yet, and his definition comes closest to practice. Mr. Milne applies the term *antique* to those things that are no longer being made and that are in demand by collectors. He draws the line at World War II. A visit to any miniature show or toy show will reveal that Mr. Milne's definition is the prevailing one. At one show recently, I saw a child pick up a toy ray-gun from the 1930s. The dealer quickly snatched it away, exclaiming: "Don't touch that. It's an antique!"

For many collectors of antique miniatures, the word *antique* means "Victorian," referring to a period when dollhouses flourished. Most of today's antique miniatures are from this period. Although most of the better examples are tucked away in museums and private collections, from time to time some good pieces do appear on the market.

Recent vintage "antique" miniatures from the collection of Robert Milne. Clockwise from top: Swan bed, 1947; grandfather clock, c. 1940s; Hepplewhite sideboard, c. 1930s; Louis XV armchair, c. late 1940s; Chinese step tables, c. late 1940s; Chippendale settee, c. late 1940s; Queen Anne highboy, c. 1940s. (Photo by Arnold Beckerman.)

Small German dollhouse, c. 1900, with embossed paper railing on second floor and painted front door. From Iris Brown Antiques.

English dollhouse, late nineteenth century. Contains four rooms, a staircase, two fireplaces, and the original wallpaper. From Iris Brown Antiques.

From a dealer's point of view, antique miniatures carry little risk. "If you sell it, great, you've made a profit," says Ms. Brown, "and if you don't sell it so fast, it goes on appreciating anyway. There are very few things in life that you can have both ways like that."

Most antique pieces are sold either at shows or at the shops of the handful of antique miniature dealers around the country. It's easier to make a mistake buying a piece at a show than in a shop because a show puts you at an emotional disadvantage, much as an auction does. A shop provides a much more leisurely environment in which to make a carefully considered purchase.

"In a show you feel compelled to buy the piece right away," explains Robert Milne, "or somebody else will buy it first, whereas in a shop you can think about it. There's a risk there too, but in a show you have hundreds of people plus dealers all competing in one day. A shop may have only five or so customers in a given day."

A show does have one advantage—it provides you with an opportunity to see the offerings of many dealers at a single time. Working against you, however, is the fact that the dealers at the show buy from one another before the show even opens. It's not uncommon for a piece to change hands—and price—several times before the doors are opened to the public.

From time to time, antique miniatures also turn up at auctions. This is likely to happen with increasing frequency in view of the rapidly growing interest in the hobby. Even the prestigious auction house of Sotheby Parke Bernet in New York has had miniatures up for auction recently, an indication of the seriousness with which miniatures are regarded in art circles.

In the collecting of antique miniatures, unity of scale assumes little importance; in fact, the lack of a consistent scale contributes a certain naïveté that has a great deal of charm. The objective here is not to create a historically accurate room setting, but rather to re-create (or preserve intact) the contents of an old dollhouse. As we discussed earlier, many of the early dollhouse-builders paid little attention to exact scale. Their sole concern was to represent a house and its contents in miniature for use as a child's plaything, not as a scale model. Interestingly enough, many antique miniatures, while considerably cruder than their exact-scale counterparts made today, seem to capture better the feeling of the life-sized original piece.

French chateau-style dollhouse, late 1800s. Contains windows on three sides and a special side entrance with a working door. From Iris Brown Antiques.

Dollhouse, c. 1929, with fireplaces in all rooms, simulated carved shingles, and a stucco-effect exterior. From The Enchanted Dollhouse.

Left to right:

German Biedermeier parlor chair, c. 1850–1860, upholstered in cut velvet.

German walnut pier mirror, in the style of the Victorian Renaissance Revival of the 1870s. Representative of a line of middle- to late-Victorian furniture that was widely exported to the United States.

Marble-top table with base of embossed filigree pewter. A German toy of the late-Victorian era.

German natural oak desk, of the Eastlake (Medieval Revival) style, c. 1880. Stamped embossing was used to simulate carving.

Marble vanity, of the German Renaissance Revival style of the late-Victorian era. Representative of a large line of similar "golden oak" pieces that were marketed in the United States.

French Victorian brass bed, c. 1880–1890. Representative of a line of stamped, embossed brass pieces of late-Victorian design. Although many of these pieces were sold in the United States, most French pieces of this period were not exported to this country.

German painted lady's desk, part of a collection produced between 1900 and World War I, contemporary with our "Mission" pieces. Made of wood (and sometimes pressed paper), with a painted finish.

Stained mahogany bookcase of the Empire Revival style, made during World War I and into the 1920s.

Mahogany secretary, made in Germany just prior to World War I.

"Roper" iron stove, one of a large line of cast-iron kitchen and bathroom pieces manufactured by the Arcade Company of Freeport, Illinois, in the 1920s and 1930s, and patterned after typical, full-size pieces of their time.

From the collection of Robert Milne. (Photo by Arnold Beckerman.)

Left to right:

Tinie Toy grand piano, 1 1/4-inch scale, with music-box mechanism, made in the 1930s. Tinie Toy produced dollhouse furniture in Providence, Rhode Island, from the early 1920s until World War II.

Art Deco kitchen sink, made by Strombecker of Moline, Illinois. Whole households of dollhouse furniture were produced by Strombecker from the early 1930s through the late 1950s, with styles conforming to the contemporary, full-size furniture of the time.

Console cabinet, a representative piece of the famous Linfield furniture, made in Linfield, Massachusetts, between 1930 and 1958. These pieces were exceptionally well made for children's dollhouse furniture.

Grandfather clock made by Wilfred T. Victoreen, a retired cabinetmaker from Pittsfield, Massachusetts, who made Early American miniatures of exquisite detail during the 1940s and early 1950s.

Victorian tufted lady's chair, made by Frank Matter around 1948.

Victorian lyre console table, made by Carl Forslund in the late 1940s. Mr. Forslund had a furniture factory in Minnesota, where he produced a line of full-size reproductions of Victorian furniture. He also made a line of miniatures that were exact copies of his own full-size replicas.

Mahogany Hepplewhite sideboard, made by Eric Pearson, a famous cabinetmaker who made exquisite miniatures during the 1930s and 1940s.

Chinese step tables of inlaid teakwood, made in the late 1940s.

Swan bed, custom-made by Frank Matter in 1947.

Queen Anne highboy, made by William Kauter of New York City, a cabinetmaker who produced a limited number of miniature replicas of his own full-size pieces during the 1940s and 1950s.

Louis XV armchair, made by Eric Pearson in the late 1940s. Although of 1-inch scale, the extraordinary delicacy of this piece makes it appear smaller.

Petite Princess refrigerator, a representative piece of a wide line of plastic dollhouse furniture made by Ideal during the years 1964–1966. The Petite Princess line was made for all the rooms of the household and included many accessories. The bathroom and kitchen pieces were made only during one year and are relatively rare. The entire line was discontinued in 1966. Although little more than ten years old, Petite Princess furniture has become sought after by collectors. From the collection of Robert Milne. (Photo by Arnold Beckerman.)

116

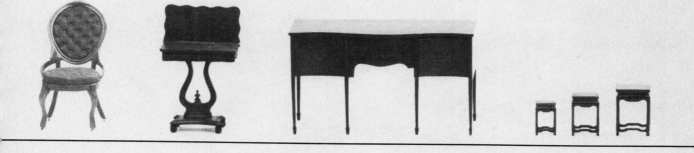

Antique miniatures come in many sizes, and scarcity in the marketplace forces the antique collector toward a greater flexibility of attitude. "In these times," points out Iris Brown, a New York dealer, "when antique miniatures are so difficult to find, who's going to turn down a great Victorian piece because it's a little larger than what you had in mind?" A collector as well as a dealer, Ms. Brown is adamantly pro-antique. She has no interest in miniatures of current manufacture, no matter how beautifully made, and is frankly shocked at some of the prices that new pieces are selling for. "Today, when the arts are holding their value more than money—more than stocks and bonds—more than anything, antiques are where the value is. Many of my customers are buying antiques as a hedge against inflation. I can't see why anyone would pay a huge price for a new piece when they could pay less and buy a great antique piece that's going to keep appreciating."

French filigree metal bed; French metal telephone, with removable receiver and ivory mouthpiece; French commode, pre-1900, with high-relief carvings and turnings.

Set of German Biedermeier furniture in 1/2-inch scale, upholstered in purple velvet, with gold-embossed paper edging; dressing mirror.

German tin stove, c. 1860–1870, with attached pot and removable cover, hanging tin cup, and simulated brick design. Alongside are various small, metal miniatures.

Metal tray with flowers; French metal gambling wheel that spins; silver lavabo, with gold wash and dolphin motif.

French metal sled and dollhouse toys.

German filigree pewter cradle, dated May 9, 1893; filigree basket; small goblet. From Iris Brown Antiques.

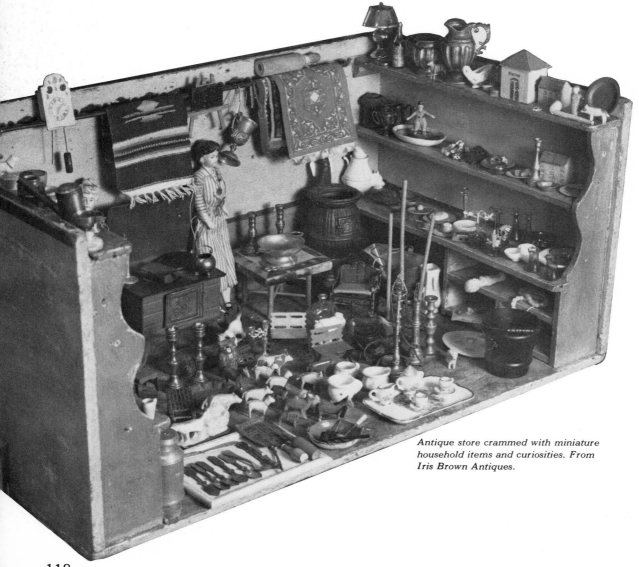

Antique store crammed with miniature household items and curiosities. From Iris Brown Antiques.

CHAPTER 11

TOOLS AND SUPPLIES FOR MAKING MINIATURES AND DOLLHOUSES

One of the great pleasures of the hobby comes from making things yourself. It takes very little effort to turn a small slice of a dowel into a hatbox, but the thrill of accomplishment is considerable.

Sooner or later most miniature collectors try their hand at making something, whether it be kitchen curtains or an entire dollhouse. And most are surprised to learn that they can do far more than they had imagined.

It doesn't take very long to go from a "not-me-I-could-never-make-anything-like-that" frame of mind to the "I-can-make-nearly-anything" level of self-assurance. It's a simple matter of building confidence. You try something and you succeed at it. Then you try something a little more difficult, and you find you can do that, too—maybe not perfectly at first, but better than you had thought.

The things you'll be willing to tackle at this point may still be fairly simple. But you're learning—learning how to use tools, learning how to use new materials. If you continue to do this long enough, a time will come when you'll think automatically of making something for yourself rather than purchasing it.

One of the nice things about making miniatures is that it's a tabletop operation that doesn't demand a lot of working space or cumbersome equipment. The necessary tools are few and simple to use. Chances are that you already own some of the basic tools.

If you decide to become deeply involved in the craft, particularly making furniture, you'll want to acquire one or two power tools designed especially for the model-maker. These are not only easy to use, but they allow you to do things that would be difficult to do with hand tools.

Building a dollhouse is a more complicated undertaking than making miniatures, requiring considerably more energy, work space, and tools.

The type and number of tools you should own will depend entirely upon what you intend to build and how serious you become about building. It doesn't pay to make an investment in tools unless you plan to use them.

On the pages that follow, we've provided a comprehensive view of most of the tools and supplies that are useful to miniature making and dollhouse building. The list is divided into basic categories, starting with drafting supplies because it's always a good idea to commit a project to paper before attempting any actual construction.

Hutch cabinet, made by Herb Kolb.
Magnifying glass from Brookstone Tools.
Hardware from The Dollhouse Factory.
(Photo by Arnold Beckerman.)

DRAFTING SUPPLIES

The first tools you'll use aren't for building your project but for planning it.

A working drawing can be anything from a freehand scribble on a napkin to a plan neatly drawn on graph paper. The only requirements are that it show you what the finished piece will look like, indicate the placement of each component part, and reveal the object in three dimensions: length, width, and height.

The more complex the piece, the more carefully made the drawing will have to be; nothing should be left to guesswork. To make careful drawings, you'll want to tape the paper to your work surface with masking tape so it won't shift while you're drawing. A T-square is very helpful for achieving perfectly aligned horizontals. The 90° triangle, moved back and forth along the T-square, will provide perfectly aligned verticals. These items plus a ruler, pencil, and eraser are the basic drafting supplies that every miniaturist should have.

It's also a good idea to acquire a protractor, compass, and dividers—those familiar articles from high-school geometry.

In addition to this basic equipment for drawing straight lines, you might want to acquire a few simple devices for drawing curves and special shapes. Plastic templates of many kinds are available at art supply stores. They allow you to achieve ovals and other shapes that would otherwise be difficult to draw accurately. A set of French curves (not shown) will also prove helpful in this area, as will a flexible rule—a device that can be bent into any number of smooth curves.

Other useful drafting supplies that are not shown here include a sketch pad, tracing-paper pad, 45° triangle, Scotch tape, scissors, and a scale ruler. This last item is most helpful in converting full-size dimensions to 1/12 scale with a minimum of effort. It can be purchased at many miniature shops.

All supplies courtesy of The Bee-ko Company, New York City. (Photo by Arnold Beckerman.)

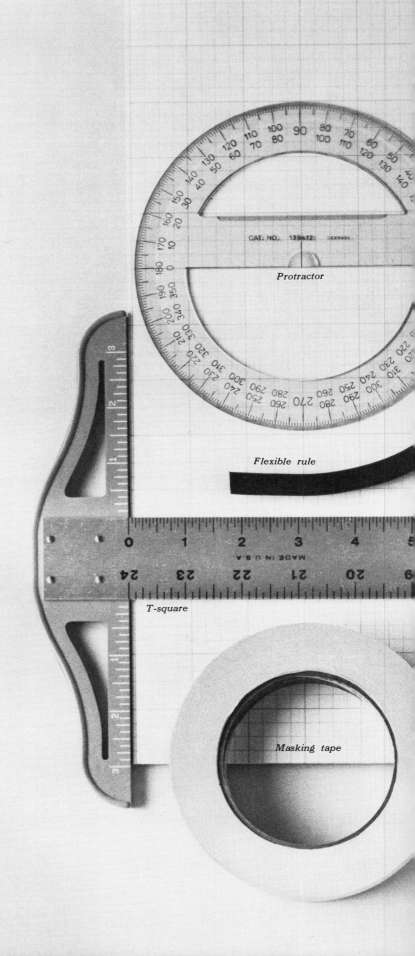

Protractor

Flexible rule

T-square

Masking tape

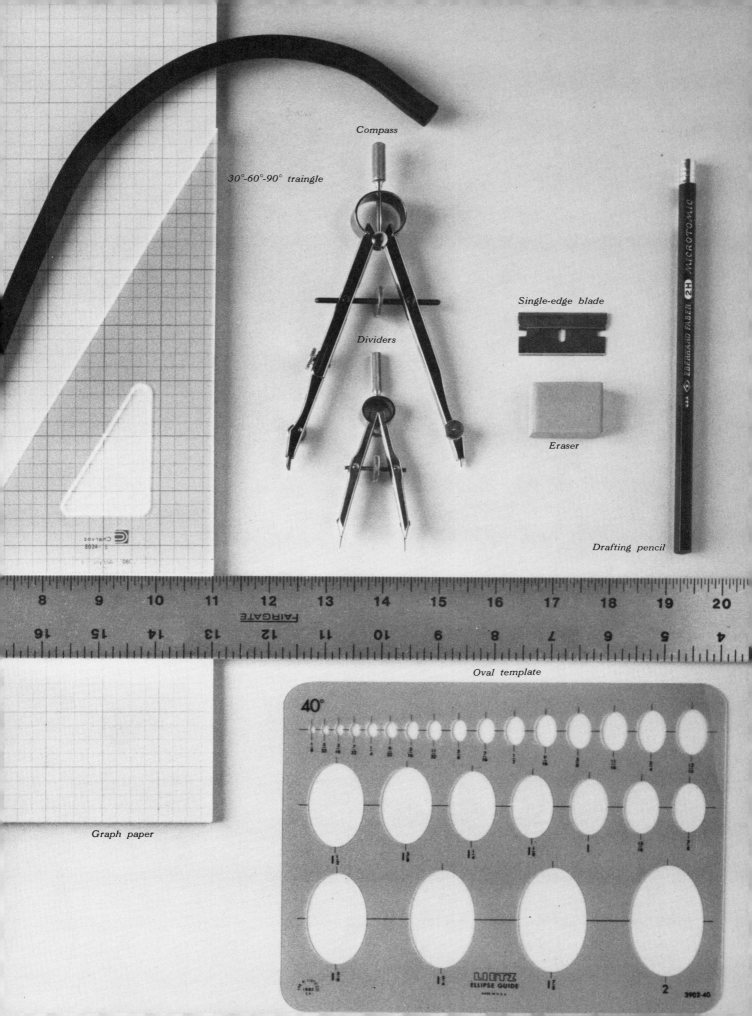

Compass

30°-60°-90° traingle

Dividers

Single-edge blade

Eraser

Drafting pencil

Graph paper

Oval template

40°

HAND TOOLS

Most of the tools found in the typical toolbox will be of little use to the miniaturist because of their size. Fortunately, proper tools of the right size do exist, and at relatively low prices.

All the tools on this page are made by X-acto, a company that has been creating tools for model-makers and hobbyists for more than forty years.

The X-acto story is an interesting one. Originally, X-acto was a small company making surgical blades. When World War II began, the U. S. Navy decided to develop a program that would train civilians to spot and identify planes. The "Spotter" program centered around the building of scale-model planes, and thirty million balsa-wood spotter kits were produced. The Navy contracted with X-acto to supply the knife blades for these kits, and the name X-acto became synonymous with model-making. Today, the company makes more than five hundred products for the hobbyist, which can be found in hobby and hardware stores, toy stores, and miniature shops.

Since cutting and joining are two of the fundamentals of woodworking, you'll need several different kinds of cutting tools, starting with a good knife, like the ones shown here, and a supply of extra blades. You'll also need a saw—maybe several saws. The coping saw is probably familiar to you; the razor saw is probably not. The latter, a very thin back saw that makes clean, perfect cuts, can be used by itself or in combination with the X-acto miter box.

Holding devices, such as a small vise and a variety of small clamps, are essential. The vise shown here has a vacuum-grip base that allows it to be attached firmly to any smooth surface simply by moving a lever. The vise is just as easily removed and leaves no mark.

Holes are readily made with a small pin drill. You will need a variety of drill bits, however, to make holes of different sizes.

For shaving, shaping, and smoothing, we recommend a sandpaper block, spoke shave, block planer, and small files.

As you get deeper into miniature making, you may find yourself improvising tools of your own to help you handle special problems.

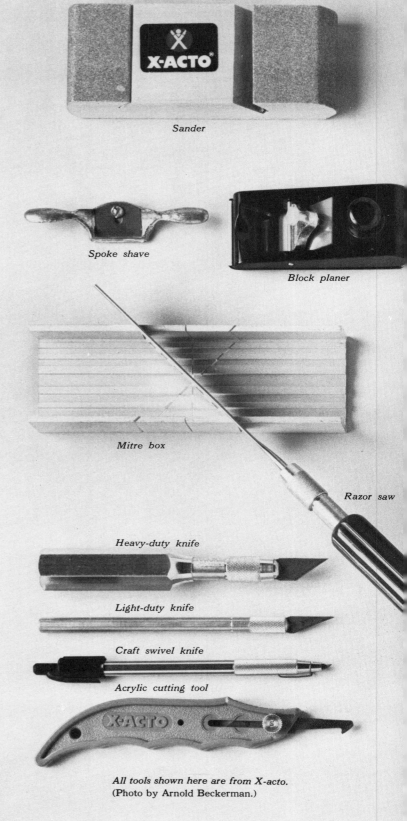

Sander

Spoke shave

Block planer

Mitre box

Razor saw

Heavy-duty knife

Light-duty knife

Craft swivel knife

Acrylic cutting tool

All tools shown here are from X-acto.
(Photo by Arnold Beckerman.)

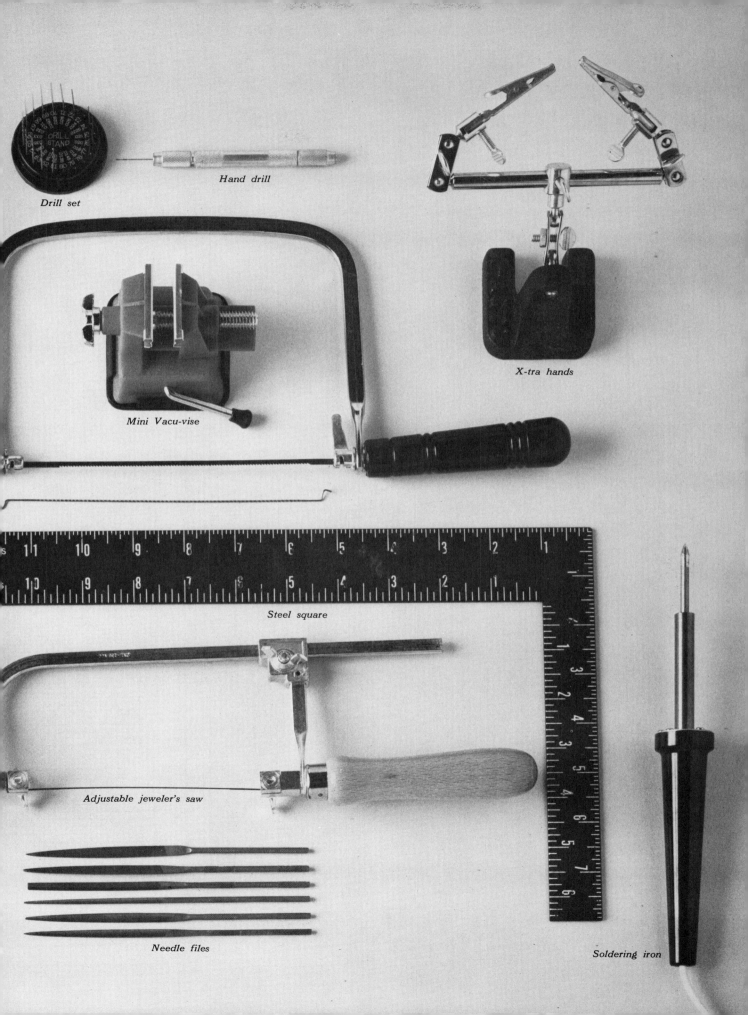

Drill set

Hand drill

X-tra hands

Mini Vacu-vise

Steel square

Adjustable jeweler's saw

Needle files

Soldering iron

HAND TOOLS

Brookstone, another well-known tool company, offers a great many useful tools for miniature making, including all of those shown here.

Brookstone tools are available by mail. Their catalog emphasizes that "most of our customers' orders are filled and mailed the same day we get them," and you can believe it. We've never experienced a prompter response from any mail-order company. Send for the Brookstone catalog (see Chapter 18); it's an excellent resource for interesting and unusual tools.

Of all the items pictured here, perhaps the least familiar is the caliper, an extremely useful tool that gives very accurate inside and outside measurements. Use it to determine the thickness of a piece of wood, the diameter of a dowel, the size of a piece of electrical wire, the width of an interior opening.

The keyhole saw is particularly useful for sawing openings *within* a piece of wood rather than sawing from the edges inward. You first drill a hole to allow the saw to enter the area to be cut out.

There are many magnifying devices that help reduce eyestrain, which can result from doing close work. The headband magnifier shown here has a movable lens holder that can be swung up out of the way when not needed.

For building dollhouses, you'll need some of the conventional tools commonly found in the toolbox, such as a rip saw, crosscut saw, hammer, screwdriver, pliers, and perhaps a wire cutter.

All tools shown here are from Brookstone Tools. (Photo by Arnold Beckerman.)

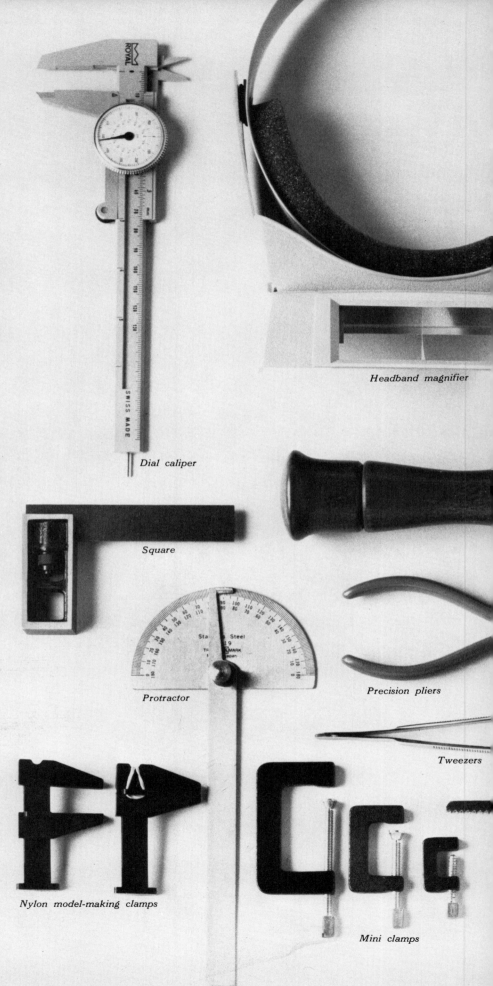

Headband magnifier

Dial caliper

Square

Protractor

Precision pliers

Tweezers

Nylon model-making clamps

Mini clamps

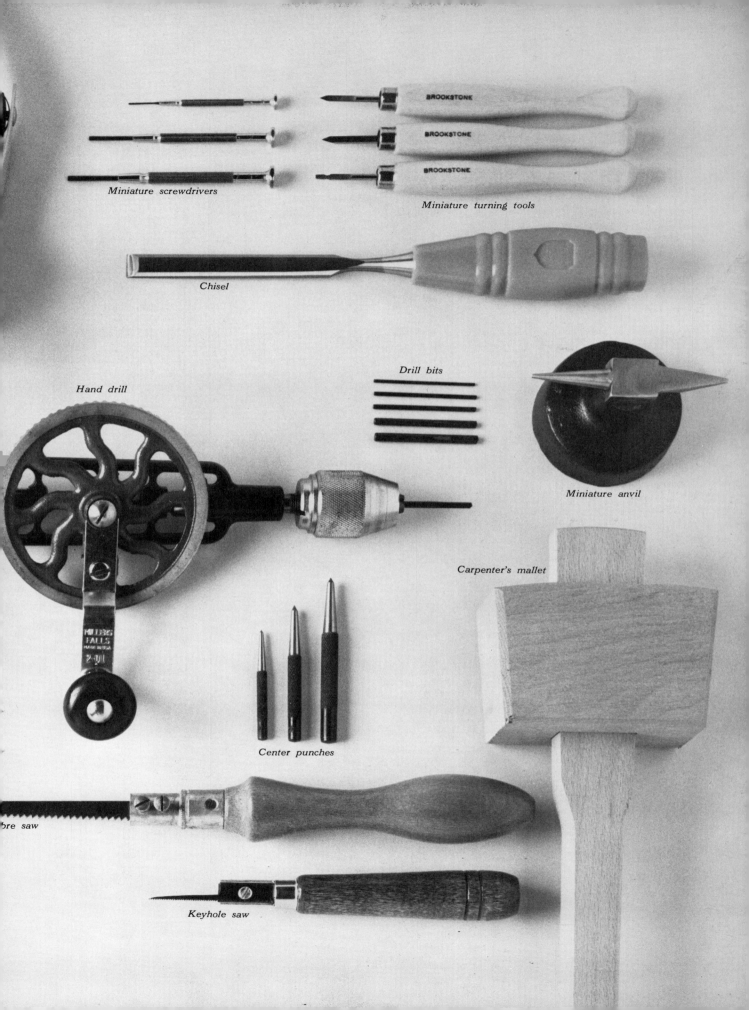

Miniature screwdrivers

Miniature turning tools

Chisel

Hand drill

Drill bits

Miniature anvil

Carpenter's mallet

Center punches

bre saw

Keyhole saw

POWER TOOLS

Power tools take most of the physical labor out of woodworking. It's a lot easier and more accurate, particularly when working on a large project such as a dollhouse, to guide a power-saw blade along a line than to do the cutting manually.

If you've never used power tools before, you may feel a little wary of them; but after using one, you'll wonder how you ever did without it. It's a lot like using a vacuum cleaner instead of a carpet sweeper, a sewing machine instead of a needle and thread, a cake mixer instead of an egg beater. When strenuous or time-consuming work is involved, only the most ardent purist would forgo the aid of a power tool in favor of a hand tool.

Power tools can be divided roughly into two groups: those intended for full-size work and those made specifically for model making. Among the former group, a sabre saw and ¼-inch power drill are the two most useful tools for our purposes, particularly for dollhouse building.

A sabre saw makes short work of most cutting jobs and requires no effort other than that of guiding it along. It can cut circles and curves in addition to making straight cuts. However, when you use a sabre saw, there are a number of safety precautions you should observe, and they shouldn't be taken lightly. Keep your fingers away from the moving blade. Cut away from rather than toward your body. Use a grounded outlet which accepts the three-pronged plug that comes with the saw (an air-conditioning outlet will usually do). Make sure that your work is securely clamped down and that nothing will get in the way of the moving blade. Finally, try a few practice cuts to get the feel of the sabre saw and what it can do.

A ¼-inch power drill will give you nice straight holes in a flash, with no effort. Be sure to have a variety of drill bits of different sizes to go with it.

Even more useful than the sabre saw and ¼-inch drill are the power tools made specifically for the hobbyist. These tools are designed to handle the exacting requirements of small-scale model making. The Dremel Company produces a number of extremely useful tools, and American Edelstaal makes an extraordinary multi-purpose tool called the Unimat, which any serious hobbyist will want to know about. All of these are described in detail below.

DREMEL MOTO-SHOP

The Moto-Shop, long a favorite tool of advanced miniature-makers and dollhouse-builders, is a complete power workshop in one compact, tabletop unit. A rugged jigsaw handles all sawing requirements, from doing intricate scrollwork to cutting long boards. This saw can handle wood up to 1¾ inches in thickness as well as light-gauge metals, plastics, felt, and other similar materials.

A power takeoff on the side of the saw drives a number of useful attachments, among them sanding discs; buffing wheels; and a versatile, flexible shaft attachment for drilling, grinding, and routing.

MOTO-TOOL

The versatility of this tool is demonstrated by the fact that Dremel offers more than one hundred fifty accessories to be used with it. These include high-speed steel cutters for cutting, shaping, and hollowing most metals, plastics, and woods; grinding, polishing, and sanding accessories; and brushes, engraving cutters, drill bits, and router bits.

Moto-Tools come in several models and prices. We recommend the variable-speed model, which allows you to dial any speed from 5,000 rpm to 25,000 rpm and can be used with a great variety of materials. The slower speeds permit you to work on fragile model parts and soft materials such as plastics, and to do intricate wood carvings. The faster speeds are for routing, grinding, cutting, and engraving.

DRILL-PRESS STAND

This accessory converts your Moto-Tool into a drill press for work where extreme accuracy is demanded. It allows you to exactly line up your work with the Moto-Tool in order to drill straight holes, thereby eliminating imprecisions that could occur when handholding the drill.

MOTO-LATHE

The ability to turn wood opens up a world of possibilities to the miniaturist and dollhouse-builder. Imagine being able to make your own professional-looking turned legs for furniture or your own balustrades and porch rails for a dollhouse. The Moto-Lathe is a low-priced, easy-to-operate miniature lathe that strips away the mystery of wood-turning and makes it available to any hobbyist. In addition to wood, the Moto-Lathe can be used for turning soft metals and plastics, handling materials up to 1½ inches in diameter and 6 inches in length.

ROUTER ATTACHMENT

A very useful accessory for dollhouse work is an attachment that converts your Dremel Moto-Tool into a router. With it you can make perfect slots, grooves, and other cuts that would be difficult or impossible to do by hand. For example, in dollhouse construction, a router is invaluable for making clean, accurate slots in floors and ceilings to hold walls in place. There are various router bits for the different types of cuts. Protective goggles are recommended when working with a router. (Routing is discussed more fully in Chapter 14.)

MOTO-SAW

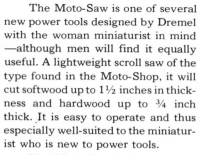

The Moto-Saw is one of several new power tools designed by Dremel with the woman miniaturist in mind —although men will find it equally useful. A lightweight scroll saw of the type found in the Moto-Shop, it will cut softwood up to 1½ inches in thickness and hardwood up to ¾ inch thick. It is easy to operate and thus especially well-suited to the miniaturist who is new to power tools.

The Moto-Saw is also inexpensive, as it was Dremel's intention to put a power saw within the reach of every miniaturist. And because it weighs only nine pounds, the Moto-Saw is simple to set up and store away.

COMPONENT PARTS

For the miniaturist who wants to build his or her own shadowbox room or dollhouse but doesn't care to make the more difficult elements such as doors and windows, component parts are available from several sources. We call your attention in particular to these excellent all-wood kits from X-acto.

The window kit comes pre-assembled except for mullions, which are also supplied, so it's virtually ready for use when you buy it. All you need is an opening in the wall that measures 2 15/16″ × 5″. The windows are the popular six-over-six variety and slide up and down with precision. The detailing is extremely fine.

The raised-panel door faithfully duplicates the construction method used in making high-quality, full-scale doors. The kit contains fifteen perfectly machined, ready-to-assemble wooden pieces, as well as hinges, screws, and two brass doorknobs. The pieces fit together flawlessly, and the result is a very professional-looking door measuring 2¾″ × 6⅝″, which is ready to be finished (see the end of this chapter for finishing supplies).

ADHESIVES

Modern technology has produced a bewildering variety of adhesives for bonding just about anything to anything. For our purposes here, we've narrowed the field down to a handful of products that we consider the most useful for serving the specialized needs of the miniaturist.

In our opinion, the best all-purpose glues continue to be the white resin glues such as Elmer's Glue-All and Sobo. Both are safe and easy to use, and produce an extremely strong bond—more than adequate for most dollhouse and miniature work. Use them for gluing wood, fabric, paper, leather, Styrofoam, pottery, and most other porous materials.

For joining nonporous materials such as glass and metal, try Duco Cement, a well-established product that forms a clear, flexible, waterproof bond.

Epoxy is a superadhesive that will take over the jobs that other glues can't handle as readily, such as joining different materials together and bonding porous surfaces to nonporous surfaces.

For applying wallpaper, we recommend that reliable old favorite, rubber cement, which allows the paper to be peeled off if need be.

A magical adhesive that was indispensible to us is contact cement—extremely useful for applying shingles and siding. This cement bonds instantly on contact, which makes it ideal for joining pieces that are awkward in shape or too delicate to be clamped. We used contact cement to join the balusters to the handrail of our staircase—a very difficult job to glue otherwise.

For mini-electrical work, we found silicone adhesive to have a double advantage. It acts as an insulating material as well as an adhesive, and it bonds readily with wood, glass, metal, masonry, rubber, canvas, and ceramics.

"Mini-mortar" is a fast-drying, pre-mixed, cement-type product sold in one form or another by miniature shops that carry dollhouse-building supplies. The mini-mortar we have used—with great success—came from The Dollhouse Factory, in Lebanon, New Jersey. We used it for making the stone fireplace project described in detail in Chapter 12. The consistency is just right for application onto a wooden surface, into which stones can then be embedded. The mortar hardens in about fifteen minutes.

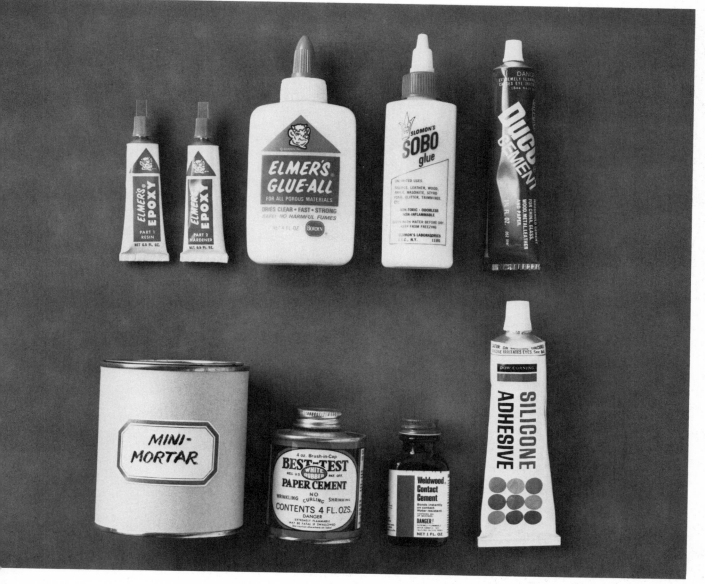

BUILDING SUPPLIES

The rapid development of this hobby has produced a bonanza for the miniaturist in terms of supplies. Not too long ago, if you wanted cedar shingles for your dollhouse roof, you had to take a block of cedar wood and split it into shingles yourself. Today, you can buy cedar shingles by the bagful, ready to use. Similarly, you can buy miniature bricks, turned balusters, moldings of every description, and a wealth of other ready-made materials that formerly you would have had to make yourself.

The company that has done the most to supply building materials that meet the specialized needs of the miniaturist is Northeastern Scale Models, of Methuen, Massachusetts.

For twenty-five years, Northeastern has been supplying wooden building materials for hobbyists and model-makers. Through Northeastern—or the many miniature shops that carry their products—you can obtain miniature "lumber" for any furniture-making or dollhouse-building project. The lumber is made from bass-wood, a wood similar to pine in its softness but, unlike pine, with a barely noticeable grain, more in keeping with 1/12 scale.

In addition to providing lumber, Northeastern makes dozens of different moldings, all in perfect scale. Such moldings are indispensible in building a feeling of reality into miniature settings. As an example of the unbelievable scope of their line, Northeastern offers all the various moldings needed to build an exact-scale working double-hung window system—a total of fourteen different moldings.

The dollhouse-builder will be helped further by Northeastern's various floorings, sidings, stair stringer and handrails, shingles, and structural shapes of many kinds.

Hardware has come a long way, too. Where once it would have taken a detective to find a source for door-knobs, hinges, and escutcheons, today such hardware items are readily available at miniature shops.

This recent availability of supplies and materials has opened up the hobby to many new participants. After all, few of us are prepared to bake our own miniature bricks, but a good many of us are willing to build something, given the bricks.

Wood-veneer tape

Cedar shingles

Wood turnings

Bricks

Hardware

Miniature bulbs

Supplies courtesy of The Dollhouse Factory. (Photo by Arnold Beckerman.)

BUILDING SUPPLIES

Molding, siding, flooring, and shingles.
From Northeastern Scale Models.
Wood strips and sheets of various sizes,
available in basswood and basswood mahogany.
(Photo by Arnold Beckerman.)

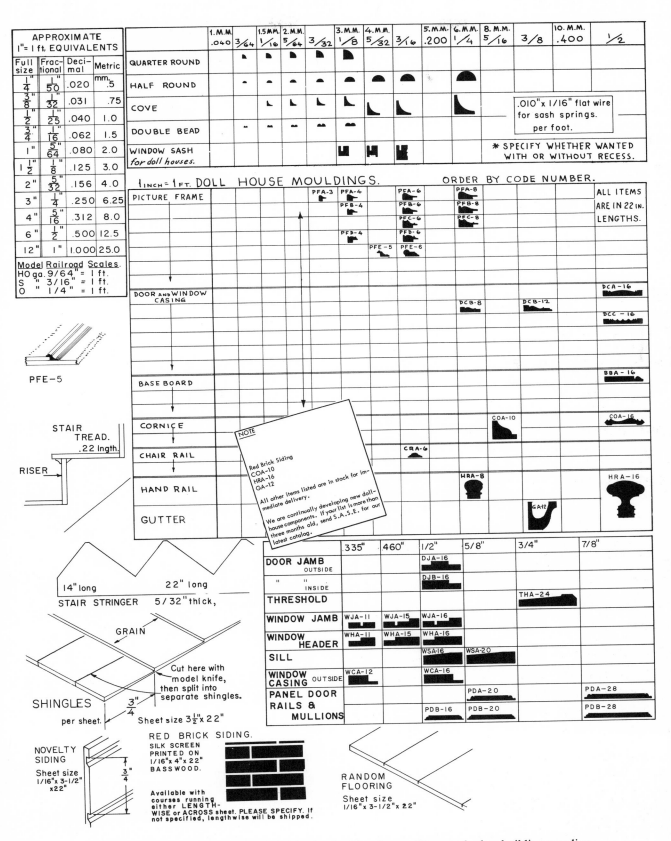

Page from Northeastern Scale Models' price list showing moldings and other building supplies.

ELECTRICAL SUPPLIES

Nowhere in the miniature world is the "revolution of availability" more dramatic than in miniature lighting. To appreciate the advances that have been made in this area, one has only to contrast the tiny grain-of-wheat bulbs, and the considerable illumination they provide, with the oversized and underlit bulbs of the recent past.

For dollhouse lighting at its simplest, the Swedish toy firm of Lundby makes a neat little 4-volt system that is easily installed and safe to use. Lundby also offers a wide variety of floor, table, and ceiling lamps that plug into their electrical system.

For most dollhouse lighting, we recommend a 12-volt electrical system. The undisputed authority in this area is Illinois Hobbycraft, masterminded by an electrical wizard named Ed Leonard. Illinois Hobbycraft "wrote the book" on miniature lighting, and supplies everything the hobbyist could possibly need for wiring a dollhouse or miniature-room setting.

Illinois Hobbycraft offers several step-down transformers to convert 115-volt house current to a safe and effective 12 volts. The power of the transformer determines the number of bulbs it can light.

The two common types of miniature bulbs are the screw-base bulb and the tinier grain-of-wheat bulb. As the "Illinois Hobbycraft Technical Bulletin 5B10" points out: "Grain-of-wheat bulbs do not screw into sockets but, instead, are equipped with two tails of wire called 'leads,' which are connected directly to the transformer or circuit wires. The elimination of bulky sockets allows the fixtures to be more compact and therefore more realistic but inhibits easy replacement of the bulb." This same bulletin discusses the various sizes of wires and when each should be used.

To give you an idea of the scope of miniature lighting supplies that are available, we have reprinted several pages from the Illinois Hobbycraft catalog.

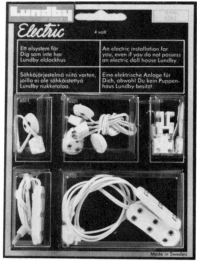

Components of the 4-volt dollhouse lighting system, made by Lundby of Sweden.

Lighted shop, The Enchanted Dollhouse.

ELECTRICAL SUPPLIES

POWER SOURCES - TRANSFORMERS, BATTERIES, ACCESSORIES

Fig. P-1

Fig. P-2

TRANSFORMER, 12 VOLT, 1,200 MILLIAMPERE - Fig. P-1

Industrial quality transformer. Enough power to supply electricity for a large dollhouse. Has wires extending from primary and secondary windings for connecting to line cord and feed or circuit wires. Not self-protecting. Recommend use of fuse #640-017-2 to protect against overload. Body of transformer measures 2" high X 2-3/8" wide X 2-1/4" overall depth. Width over mounting feet, 3-1/2". Order line cord separately.

12 volt, 1,200 ma. transformer, Order number 620-003-1

TRANSFORMER, 12 VOLT, 500 MILLIAMPERE - Fig. P-2

Residential grade transformer. Enough power to supply electricity for a medium size dollhouse or large miniature room. Has wires extending from primary winding for connecting line cord. Screw terminals for connecting feed or circuit wires. Has built-in thermal protection against overload. 2" high X 2-1/4" wide X 2-1/4" overall depth. Order line cord separately.

12 volt, 500 ma. transformer. Order number 620-001-1

TRANSFORMER, 12 VOLT, 150 MILLIAMPERE - Fig. P-1

Industrial quality transformer. Enough power to supply electricity for average miniature room, an Illinois Hobbycraft Christmas tree string or other small display. Has wires extending from primary and secondary windings for connecting to line cord and to feed wires or terminal strip. Not self-protecting. Recommend use of fuse #640-017-1 to protect against overload. Body of transformer measures 1-1/4" high X 1-1/2" wide X 1-3/8" deep. Width over mounting feet, 2-1/8". Order line cord separately.

12 volt, 150 ma. transformer, Order number 620-002-1

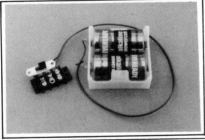

Fig. P-5

PRE-WIRED BATTERY PACK, 3 VOLTS, LARGE. Fig. P-5

Will supply 75 milliamperes of electricity for 50 to 70 hours, continuous duty. Lasts much longer if used intermittently. Batteries may be replaced when exhausted. Complete with on-off switch and terminal strip. Ready to install. No splicing or soldering required. Suitable for use with miniature room or small display. Includes two "D" size alkaline cells, battery holder, terminal strip, on-off switch, instructions for use. 18 inch wires between battery holder and terminal strip. Battery holder meas. 2-3/4" X 2-1/2" X 1-1/4"

Pre-wired battery pack, 3 volts, large. Order no. 621-001-1

PRE-WIRED BATTERY PACK, 3 VOLTS, MEDIUM. Fig. P-5

Will supply 75 milliamperes of electricity for 35 to 45 hours, continuous duty. Description same as #621-001-1, above except: includes two "C" size alkaline cells, battery holder measures 2-1/8" X 2-3/8" X 7/8".

Pre-wired battery pack, 3 volts, med. Order no. 621-002-1

PRE-WIRED BATTERY PACK, 3 VOLTS, SMALL. Similar to Fig. P-5

Will supply 75 milliamperes of electricity for 8 to 12 hours, continuous duty. Description same as #621-001-1, above, except: includes two "AA" size alkaline cells, battery holder measures 1-1/8" X 2-3/8" X 5/8".

Pre-wired battery pack, 3 volts, small. Order no. 621-003-1

Fig. P-3

Fig. P-4

PLUG-IN TRANSFORMER, 12 VOLT, 400 MILLIAMPERE - Fig. P-3

Hobby grade transformer. Suitable for miniature rooms which have two or three bulbs, single lighted Christmas tree or other small display. Plugs directly into wall. Eliminates need for transformer inside miniature room. Not self-protecting. Recommend fuse be installed at miniature room to protect against overload. Use fuse #640-017-3. 2-1/2" wide X 2-1/4" high. Extends 2-1/8" from wall.

Plug-in transformer, 12 volt, 400 ma. Order no. 620-005-1

PLUG-IN TRANSFORMER, 12 VOLTS, 1,000 MILLIAMPERE - Fig. P-4

Industrial grade transformer. Recommended for large miniature room or dollhouse. Plugs directly into wall. Eliminates need for transformer inside dollhouse or miniature room. Has screw for anchoring to wall outlet plate. Screw terminals for connecting 12 volt feed wires for miniature lighting system. Not self-protecting. Recommend fuse be installed at dollhouse or miniature room. Use fuse #640-017-2. Measures approx. 2-1/2" wide X 3-1/2" high. Extends about 2-1/4" from wall.

Plug-in transformer, 12 volt, 1,000 ma. Order no. 620-004-1

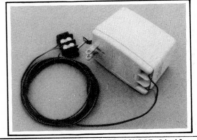

Fig. P-6

PRE-WIRED 12 VOLT, 1,000 MA. POWER SOURCE Similar to Fig. P-6

Recommended for large miniature rooms and small or medium dollhouses. Ideal for place where transformer space was not planned or transformer can not be fitted inside. Includes transformer #620-004-1, eight foot low-voltage cord, terminal strip, fuse for protection against overload, instructions for use. No on-off switch provided. Recommend transformer be unplugged from wall when not in use.

Pre-wired 12 volt, 1,000 ma. pwr. source. Order no. 620-104-1

PRE-WIRED 12 VOLT, 400 MA. POWER SOURCE. Similar to Fig. P-6

Recommended for miniature rooms having 2 or 3 bulbs. Ideal for case where transformer can not be installed inside room. Includes transformer #620-005-1, eight foot low-voltage cord, terminal strip, fuse to protect against overload, instructions for use. No on-off switch provided. Recommend transformer be unplugged when not in use.

Pre-wired 12 volt, 400 ma. power source. Order no. 620-105-1

(From the Illinois Hobbycraft catalog.)

ELECTRICAL SUPPLIES

<u>BULBS AND SOCKETS</u> - CHRISTMAS TREE LIGHT STRINGS

DESCRIPTION	Order No.
16 VOLT GRAIN OF WHEAT BULB. About 1/8" dia. X 1/4" long, with 6" wire leads. Consumes 65 milli-amperes. Use with 12 volt transformer for long life. Clear only.	610-010-1
12 VOLT LONG-LIFE GRAIN OF WHEAT BULB. About 1/8" dia. X 1/4" long, with 6" wire leads. Consumes 60 milliamperes. Warranted 10,000 hour life when used with Illinois Hobbycraft transformer. Clear only.	610-001-1
12 VOLT CANDLE FLAME BULB. About 3/32" dia. X 1/4" long, with 6" wire leads. Consumes 45 milli-amperes. Warranted 10,000 hour life when used with Illinois Hobbycraft transformer. Pointed shape makes this bulb ideal for applications where appearance of a candle flame is desired. Clear only.	610-005-1
SMALL 12 VOLT GRAIN OF WHEAT BULB. About 3/32" dia. X 1/4" long, with 6" wire leads. Consumes 50 milliamperes. Smaller size than regular grain of wheat bulb useful for wiring very small lamps, etc. Clear only	610-007-1
6 VOLT GRAIN OF WHEAT BULB. About 1/8" dia. X 1/4" long, with 6" wire leads. Consumes 75 milli-amperes. Clear only.	610-006-1
3 VOLT GRAIN OF WHEAT BULB. About 1/8" dia. X 1/4" long, with 6" wire leads. Consumes 75 milli-amperes. For use with 3 volt battery packs. Clear only.	610-002-1
1-1/2 VOLT GRAIN OF WHEAT BULB. About 1/8" dia. X 1/4" long, with 6" wire tails. Consumes 100 milliamperes. Clear only.	610-003-1

GRAIN-OF-WHEAT BULBS

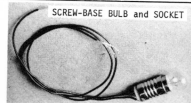
SCREW-BASE BULB and SOCKET

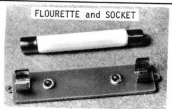
FLOURETTE and SOCKET

DESCRIPTION	Order No.
16 VOLT FLOURETTE BULB. Flourescent-like bulb with frosted glass, about 1/4" dia. X 1-1/2" long. Ideal for back-lighting miniature rooms or for general lighting in dollhouse. Medium brightness. For long life, recommend connecting to 12 volt transformer. Consumes 80 milliamperes. Use socket listed elsewhere in this catalogue.	610-008-1
16 VOLT MINIATURE SCREW-BASE BULB. Replaceable bulb which screws into tiny socket (listed else-where in this catalogue). Overall length- 9/16", diameter of glass- 1/4". Consumes 60 milliamperes. For long life, connect to 12 volt transformer.	610-009-1
SOCKET, FLOURETTE. For use with #610-008-1 flourette bulb. Has solder terminals for connecting wires which run to transformer.	640-015-1
PRE-WIRED FLOURETTE SOCKET. Same as above but with 24 inch, two-conductor wire soldered to terminals. Ready to install and connect to transformer or terminal strip. Wire can be painted.	640-015-2
MINIATURE SCREW-BASE SOCKET. For use with bulb #610-009-1. Outside diameter of socket about 7/32". Length about 3/8". Has 6" wire leads attached.	640-016-1
CHRISTMAS TREE LIGHT STRING KIT, 12 VOLT. Includes 12 grain of wheat bulbs and illustrated instructions for assembly. For use with 12 volt transformer. Consumes 90 milliamperes. Bulbs are clear. Use paints, listed elsewhere in this catalogue to color bulbs.	610-203-1
ASSEMBLED CHRISTMAS TREE LIGHT STRING, 12 volt. String of twelve bulbs, completely assembled and tested, ready to install on your tree. For use with 12 volt transformer. Consumes 90 milliamperes.	610-203-2

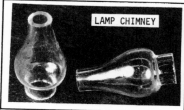
LAMP CHIMNEY

LAMP BASE
Top   Underside

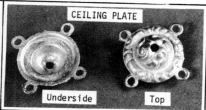
CEILING PLATE
Underside   Top

<u>WIRING ACCESSORIES</u>

DESCRIPTION	Order No.
LAMP CHIMNEY, fire-tempered pyrex, 21/32" high, 7/32" dia. at base, 11/32" dia. at widest part. Glass approx. 1/32" thick. Accepts any grain of wheat bulb in this catalogue. Crystal clear. Optically true. Without a doubt, the finest miniature chimney available.	680-005-1
LAMP BASE, round, cast metal. 9/16" dia. X 1/4" high. As an add-on, this piece gives weight and stability to commercial plastic dollhouse table lamps. Use it to hide the splice to the wall plug "cord" on a table lamp you've wired yourself. Drilled through the center to take wire.	680-001-1
CEILING PLATE, Cast metal, about 1/2" dia. For suspending hanging lamps and fixtures from ceiling. Hollow back provides place to hide splices between fixture wires and circuit wires. Fasten in place with cement or small brads. Can be painted.	680-002-1

(From the Illinois Hobbycraft catalog.)

FINISHING SUPPLIES

You'll find most of the finishing supplies you'll need at a hardware store. Most woodworking projects will require several grades of sandpaper, particularly the extra fine grades. Superfine steel wool (No. 0000) helps achieve a velvety-smooth finish. If you're working with plywood and find yourself confronted with holes on the edges, you can patch them easily by using plastic wood.

There are several excellent products for obtaining a rich wood finish. Minwax Wood Finish, easy to apply and available in fifteen colors, penetrates the wood and seals it with a hard, protective finish. The Minwax Company offers a helpful booklet entitled "Tips on Wood Finishing" (see Chapter 18).

The Floquil-Polly S Color Corporation, a long-time supplier of quality paints and finishes for modelmakers, has several fine wood stains which can be used on both polystyrene and wood. These stains go under the names Polly S and Flo-Stains.

X-acto offers a miniature-furniture-finishing kit that includes two base stains, glaze stain, sealer, two top coats, and tinted glue. Detailed instructions tell how to obtain a professional quality finish.

Several of the companies mentioned above also make excellent paint products.

Testors, a familiar name to model-makers, offers finishing enamels in a spectrum of colors for use on virtually any surface—wood, metal, glass, paper, Styrofoam, plaster, polystyrene plastic, leather, and even concrete.

For dollhouses where larger areas are involved, commercial house paints can be used. We were very pleased with the results we obtained with Martin Senour's Williamsburg colors, which reproduce the wonderfully rich and subtle tones of Colonial Williamsburg.

Today's miniaturist is also fortunate in the variety of fabrics and wallpapers available. It's no longer a case of trying to make the best of a full-size pattern; today there are many patterns available in perfect 1/12 scale. One of the most innovative contributions has been made by X-acto in creating a handsome collection of coordinated wallpapers and fabrics, as well as panoramic outdoor scenes for use in shadowbox rooms. Check your local miniature supplier for other interesting wallpapers and fabrics.

CHAPTER 12

MAKING MINIATURE FURNITURE YOURSELF

There are several different ways to get started in miniature making. Perhaps the quickest and easiest route to satisfaction lies with kits, which provide all the necessary materials and instructions. Frequently, the pieces are pre-cut and require only sanding, gluing, and finishing. Many excellent furniture-making kits, including kits for making upholstered furniture, are available today.

To make furniture entirely from scratch, you will need patterns (actual-size drawings of the various pieces to be cut) or plans (drawings that show the various pieces and indicate their relationships and measurements). Examples of both are given in this chapter, which includes complete instructions for three exciting projects.

You can also make your own plans by measuring actual furniture, then reducing the dimensions to 1/12 scale. Or you can find plans in furniture-making books and reduce their dimensions in the same way.

After you've built a few of your own miniatures, you'll begin to get into the habit of thinking like a miniaturist. Very likely, you'll find yourself sizing up things in the real world in terms of converting them into miniatures.

Custom dollhouse builder Joen Ellen Kanze provides an insight into how this thinking process works:

"When you first start to furnish your house, almost anything in the way of furnishings will do; but as you progress, your buying will become more selective and your imagination stimulated . . . you will look at a counter full of dainty handkerchiefs and see curtains . . . glass beads turn magically into cut-glass jars for a dressing table . . . bottle caps are mentally sprayed copper or silver and end up in the kitchen as pie plates . . . tapestry samples turn into room-size rugs. You will literally 'see double' at almost every turn.

COLVIN ORIGINALS

Making upholstered furniture is easy with Colvin kits. "Even a ten-year-old child can do it," says Mrs. Audrey Colvin, who has tested the kits on many of her friends. Each kit contains all the elements necessary to make each piece—patterns, pre-cut bases, Styrofoam, padding, fabric, fringed skirting, and clearly written instructions. All you need is white glue.

There are Colvin kits for making a tufted club chair, a wing chair, a tufted couch with throw pillows, and a tufted canopy bed with velvet headboard and pillows.

The finished pieces are virtually indestructible. Even if stepped on by accident, they can be bent back into shape.

(See Chapter 18 for information on where to obtain Colvin kits and all other items referred to in this chapter.)

LILLIE PUTT

Lillie Putt Furniture, of Chatham, New Jersey, offers a well-thought-out kit that enables the do-it-yourselfer to create a three-piece set of upholstered living room furniture—couch, chair, and footstool. The kit contains everything you need, including a cheerful calico print in various colors and a stuffing of 100 percent polyester.

Mrs. Velma McCann originated the construction method, having been inspired to create her own miniature furniture by the dollhouse in the Children's Room of the old Summit, New Jersey, library.

Introduced in April of 1975, the living room kit met with such a good reception that Mrs. McCann has begun the development of a bedroom kit.

REALIFE MINIATURES

Scientific Models, of Berkeley Heights, New Jersey, offers a collection of furniture-making kits by the roomful.

The bedroom kit, for example, includes a canopy bed (complete with bedspread, canopy top, trim, and mattress), a dresser, and two night tables. The living room kit contains an upholstered wing chair, a love seat, a secretary, a coffee table, and an end table. There are seven pieces of furniture in the dining room kit—four upholstered chairs, a pedestal dining table, a hutch, and a dry sink. Other kits allow you to assemble a complete nursery and a contemporary kitchen.

All of the furniture in the Realife Miniatures kits are made from pre-cut, basswood parts. The kits contain all the materials needed to complete the project: fabrics, upholstery stuffing, brass hardware, wood stain and gloss coat, glue—even decals for the nursery pieces. The instructions are clear and easy to follow.

Realife Miniatures kits are widely distributed. Check your local miniatures shop.

(Photos courtesy of Scientific Models.)

Heritage Series Nursery, Kit 192

Heritage Series Dining Room, Kit 190

Heritage Series Bedroom, Kit 188

Heritage Series Kitchen, Kit 191

Heritage Series Living Room, Kit 189

"I have been guilty of raiding my son's fishing-tackle box and finding what he calls 'treble hooks' but what I call 'chandeliers'—one glass bead on the end of each hook makes a marvelous, small light fixture. He has also been instructed to bring home all the empty .22-caliber rifle shells from his target-shooting expeditions—the brass shells are beautiful mugs or small vases when polished.

"If you have infinite patience and a pair of sharp cuticle scissors, cut a ping-pong ball in half and, with different colored Flair pens, make a dome-shaped 'Tiffany' lampshade. Use a wide-headed roofing nail for the base and attach it to the shade with florist's clay. Hardware stores are paradise when you are thinking small. . . . L-shaped cup hooks become brass faucets in the bathroom or kitchen; or, screwed into a wall, they are gaslight fixtures—a bead of suitable size will be the 'shade.' One-inch roofing nails, suitably painted, become candlesticks . . . two-inch roofing nails become lamp bases . . . 1/2″ brads painted yellow turn into pencils for the desk . . . bits of lace edging glued onto tube caps of various sizes become lovely lampshades—stuff the cap with Styrofoam and impale it in a roofing nail and *voilà!*—anything from a boudoir lamp up to a parlor lamp, according to the size of the cap.

"Scrounge for old, soft leather wallets and pocketbooks. Cut the leather to fit a piece of heavy cardboard, approximately 7/8″ × 3/4″, and glue on and you can make row after row of books for the really literate dollhouse. Those aren't buttons you see at the notions counter, they are cake plates, right? The holes are covered by the cake (made of Play-Doh and iced with acrylic paint). That broken wristwatch can turn into a mantel clock, with the proper mounting. That is not a cap from a shampoo bottle—with a little painting, you turn it upside down and it's a wastebasket. Those are not swab sticks in your doctor's office—they are hardwood curtain rods . . . glue a small, wooden bead at each end and hang the rods on fancy upholstery tacks driven into the window frames. A fistful of tongue depressors from the same doctor will yield lumber for bookshelves—just saw off the rounded edges and cut to size.

"Soon, if you are like me, you will have no shame in scrounging stuff. I no longer tell people, 'I'm buying this for my niece's dollhouse.' I come right out and tell 'em!"

The X-acto people have put their considerable hobby expertise to work in developing an outstanding collection of miniature-furniture kits. Called "The House of Miniatures Collectors Series," the offering currently includes more than twenty different furniture kits, and X-acto plans to expand the line as time goes on.

In addition to the furniture designs shown here, X-acto kits for making several different Chippendale chests, a Chippendale desk and dry sink, a hutch cabinet, side chairs, a tall case clock, a Hepplewhite round table, and other classic pieces as well are now on the market.

While developing their furniture designs, X-acto conducted extensive research in order to find the best examples of full-size furniture of the colonial period. Great care has been taken to reproduce these designs as accurately as possible in precise 1/12 scale, right down to the hardware. All drawer pulls and pendulum pulls are made of solid brass. The furniture is made entirely of wood, beautifully machined to metal tolerances. The detailing is exceptional for miniature furniture of its price.

X-acto furniture kits are an excellent way to obtain quality miniatures at very modest prices, along with the added pleasure of watching a piece of furniture come to life by your own hands.

Chippendale canopy bed, c. 1750–1790

Chippendale wing chair, c. 1750–1790

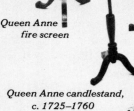

Queen Anne fire screen

Queen Anne tilt-top table

Queen Anne candlestand, c. 1725–1760

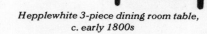

Hepplewhite 3-piece dining room table, c. early 1800s

Chippendale sofa, c. 1750–1790

Hepplewhite side table, c. early 1800s

(Photo by Arnold Beckerman.)

If you want to make your own miniatures from scratch but don't quite know where to begin, you might consider working from an actual-size pattern such as those provided by Green Door Studio, of St. Paul, Minnesota. Mrs. Beverly Nielson, the originator of Green Door Studio, has developed nearly a hundred items for which patterns are available, at very modest cost. There are simple projects like a kitchen table, a child's sled, and a country bench, as well as slightly more difficult projects such as a rolltop desk, a grandfather's clock, and an upright piano.

To develop a pattern, Mrs. Nielson first creates the actual piece; then her husband, Thor, a commercial artist, translates it into drawings of actual size.

Each pattern, of course, can be used over and over—there's no limit to the number of pieces you can make from it.

Working from a pattern is a good warm-up exercise before attempting to make miniatures entirely on your own.

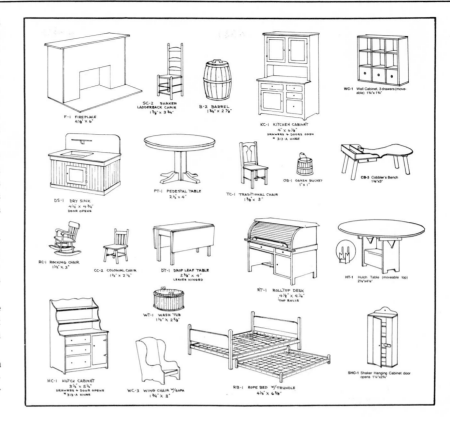

Shaker ladder-back chair

Open cradle

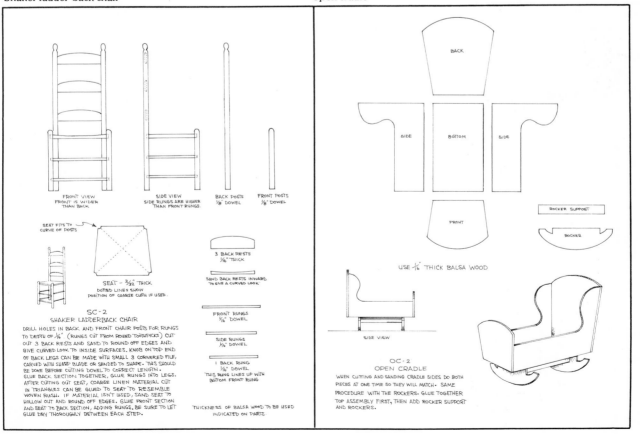

TRESTLE TABLE

This trestle table, a variation of the classic colonial design, is the first of three projects you can build right from this book. It's a little more difficult than the average project for beginners—and deliberately so. It is intended to familiarize you with the use of the jeweler's saw or jigsaw to cut curves and, at the same time, to develop your confidence in working with angles other than right angles. All too many furniture-making projects designed for beginners are based entirely on right angles, which contribute to the toylike appearance of many such pieces. By comparison, the canted legs of this trestle table help convey a greater feeling of realism.

TOOLS AND MATERIALS NEEDED

- 3/32″ basswood, 2 1/2″ × 9″ (for the top and sides)
- 1/8″ basswood, 5/8″ × 4 1/8″ (for the beam)
- 1/16″ basswood, 1″ × 1″ (for the wedges)
- Knife plus extra blades
- Jeweler's saw or jigsaw
- Sandpaper (fine and finishing grades)
- Small, round file
- Stain and paintbrush
- White glue
- C-clamps (one or two)

Start by cutting the table top from your 3/32″ basswood to the dimensions shown in Figs. 1 and 2. Clamp your wood firmly to the work surface, making certain to pad the clamps so that they don't mar the wood. After sawing, sand the edges and both surfaces.

To make the sides, cut two identical pieces of 3/32″ basswood, each 2 1/2″ × 2″. On one of these pieces, trace the shape shown in Fig. 3 (drawn to actual size). Then clamp the two pieces of wood together and cut both pieces simultaneously, using your jeweler's saw or jigsaw. Lightly sand all surfaces. If necessary, use your file to smooth the curves.

Next, bevel the sides slightly on top and bottom to conform to the angle shown in Fig. 1. To do this, place your sandpaper on the table and rub the piece back and forth over it, creating the appropriate angle.

Now cut the center beam from your 1/8″ basswood to the shape and dimensions shown in Fig. 4. Sand lightly.

The wedge effect has been simulated by cutting each of the wedges into two separate pieces, then gluing them to the top and bottom of the beam. This gives the appearance of a single wedge going right through the beam. Using your knife, cut four pieces for the wedges from the 1/16″ basswood, following the dimensions shown in Fig. 1. Sand lightly.

Finally, we want to cut a slot in each of the sides to hold the ends of the beam. Rule a 1/8″ slot on each side, centered top to bottom and right to left. Make the slot slightly longer than the 1/2″ height of the beam to allow for the angling of the sides (slot dimensions: 1/8″ × 17/32″). Use your knife to cut the slots. Sand or file the slots smooth.

Once you've made all your component parts, stain them whatever shade you've chosen. When they are dry, wipe off any excess stain.

To assemble the table, first glue the sides to the beam. When fairly dry, glue this assembly to the table top, working with the pieces upside down. Weight the beam to facilitate drying.

Lastly, glue the wedges into place.

You now have a finished trestle table. The next project is a bench that is designed to go with the table.

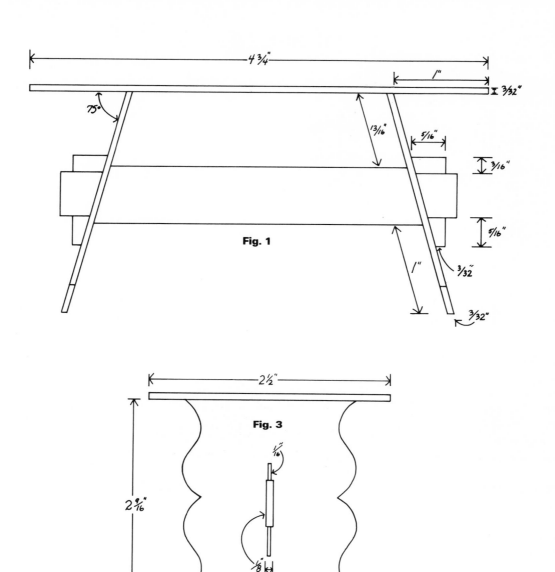

Fig. 1

Fig. 3

Fig. 2

Trim to fit leg slot

Beam

Fig. 4

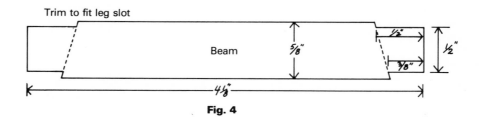

Trestle table designed and built by Herb Kolb.

BENCH

Start by cutting the back, seat, and support strip from 1/8″ basswood, using your jeweler's saw or jigsaw and following the dimensions shown in Figs. 1 and 2. When the pieces are cut, use sandpaper to round the upper edge of the back and the front edge of the seat. This gives the bench a nice, finished look. Sand all of the remaining surfaces smooth.

The sides are cut in the same way that we cut the sides for the trestle table. Start by cutting two identical pieces of 3/32″ basswood, each 2″ × 3 1/2″. On one of these pieces, trace the shape of the side, as shown in Fig. 2. Clamp the two pieces of wood together, padding the clamps so that they don't mar the wood, and cut the shape with your jeweler's saw or jigsaw. Sand the pieces lightly. Use your file to clean the curves.

Stain all the pieces. When they are dry, wipe off any excess stain.

Glue all the parts together in the positions shown in Figs. 1 and 2. Use rubber bands to hold the bench together while drying.

With the bench and trestle-table projects under your belt, you'll have no trouble building the fireplace that follows.

The bench about to be described is very similar in construction to the trestle table. It incorporates shaped sides and a gently sloping seat and back, which give it a realistic look.

TOOLS AND MATERIALS NEEDED

- 1/8″ basswood, 1 1/2″ × 8″ (for the back, seat, and support strip)
- 3/32″ basswood, 2″ × 7″ (for the sides)
- Knife plus extra blades
- Jeweler's saw or jigsaw
- Sandpaper (fine and finishing grades)
- Small, round file
- Stain and paintbrush
- White glue
- C-clamps
- Rubber bands

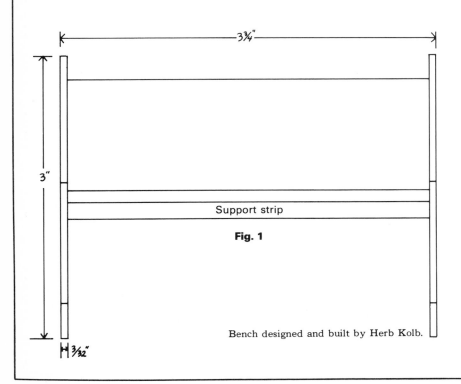

Support strip

Fig. 1

Bench designed and built by Herb Kolb.

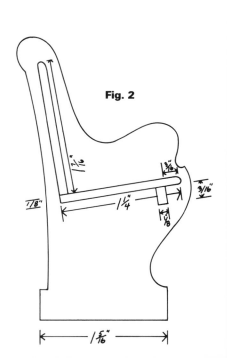

Fig. 2

STONE FIREPLACE

One of the more satisfying miniature pieces to make is a stone fireplace such as the one shown here (the same fireplace as the one on the front cover). It would be hard to find a project that yields such exciting results for the amount of time and effort involved. We made this fireplace in a single afternoon, using mostly scrap materials.

The overall dimensions are 6 3/8″ wide × 4 7/8″ high × 1 5/8″ deep (2 1/2″ deep at the hearth). The fireplace opening measures 3 1/2″ wide × 2 7/8″ high × 3/4″ deep and will realistically accommodate andirons, logs, and any other accessories. These measurements can be modified, of course, to suit your particular requirements.

We built our fireplace using small, colorful stones we picked up on the beach. They were fairly well rounded and polished from the action of the surf, and well suited to our purpose. But any stones will do. Rough, angular stones have a character all their own. Larger stones will give a feeling of boulders. For an entirely different effect, slate can be cut or broken into small pieces and used in place of the stones. Miniature bricks can also be used successfully.

The first step is to assemble the necessary materials and tools listed here.

TOOLS AND MATERIALS NEEDED

- 1/2″ plywood, 6″ × 4 3/8″ (for the back)
- 3/4″ pine or plywood, 6″ × 4 3/8″ (for the main fireplace)
- 3/32″ basswood, 6 3/8″ × 2 1/2″ (for the hearth)
- 3/8″ balsa wood, 6 3/8″ × 1 5/8″ (for the mantel)
- Mini-mortar
- Small stones
- White glue

- Matte black paint (such as Testors Military Flat Colors: "Flat Midnite Black")
- Wood stain in desired shade (for mantel)
- Saw (coping or sabre saw)
- Drill (hand or power variety)
- Drill bits, 1/4″ or 5/16″
- Screwdriver
- Sandpaper (fine grades)
- Knife
- Paintbrush for paint
- Paintbrush for stain
- Brush cleaner
- C-clamps
- Rubber bands

Fig. 1 will give you an overall idea of how the fireplace is assembled. After that, it's only a question of masonry and finishing.

Let's begin. Cut the various wood pieces to the dimensions given in the list above. The 1/2″ plywood piece will become the back of the fireplace (Fig. 2). Cut this piece first, then sand the edges and the front surface.

The 3/4″ pine will create the main shape of the fireplace (Fig. 3). To cut the opening, see Fig. 4. The trick here is to first drill a hole in the approximate location shown, using your 1/4″ or 5/16″ drill bit. This hole will allow you to get your saw blade positioned properly for cutting the arc. After drilling the hole, make straight cuts A and B. Then insert your sabre- or coping-saw blade through the hole and carefully cut part of the arc C. Now remove your saw and place it back through the wood at point X, facing the opposite direction, and carefully cut along the arc. When you reach point Y, the entire opening will fall out cleanly. Sand all edges.

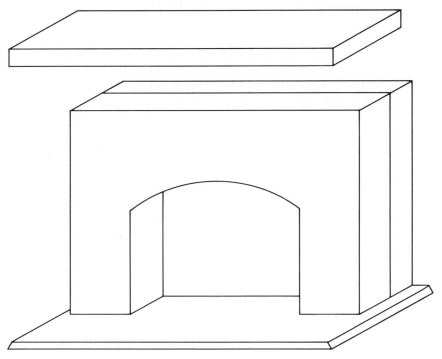

Fig. 1

Place the plywood backing piece and the pine main piece together, and with a pencil, trace the shape of the fireplace opening onto the backing piece. This will give you guidelines for gluing. Spread an ample coating of glue on the two surfaces to be joined, wait three minutes, then join, using C-clamps or rubber bands to hold the two pieces together until the glue sets (about 30 minutes). Clean off any excess glue that may have seeped into the fireplace opening.

While the glue is drying, cut the basswood hearth to size (Fig. 5). Then, with your knife, cut a beveled edge along the front and the two sides as shown. You might first want to practice cutting a bevel on a piece of scrap wood. Lightly sand the surface of the hearth and the beveled edges.

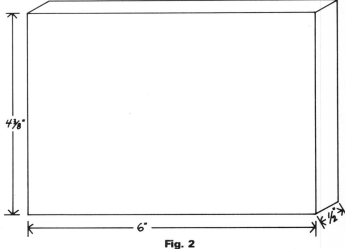

Fig. 2

Paint the entire surface of the hearth with your matte black paint and put it aside to dry.

Now cut the balsa mantel to size (Fig. 6). Use your knife to round the edges crudely on the front and sides to create a look that simulates a large plank of rough-hewn wood (leave the back edge flat). We even marred the surface in a few places to create an antique effect; this is easily accomplished as balsa wood is very soft and responsive. It's not necessary to sand the mantel, since we want to preserve the rough appearance. When you're satisfied that you've achieved the appropriate look, brush or wipe on the stain, then wipe off the excess. Some of the balsa wood grain will show through as fine white lines, which will heighten the illusion of antiquity.

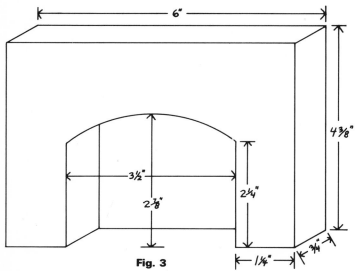

Fig. 3

By this time the glued pieces should be dry. Remove the clamps or rubber bands. You're now ready to become a mini–stone mason.

Start at any of the outer surfaces and apply a liberal amount of mini-mortar, using the blade of your screwdriver as an applicator. Do a small section at a time (see Fig. 7). When you've applied the necessary mortar to a section, tightly close the can so that the mortar doesn't dry up. Now press the stones into the mortar, embedding them deeply enough to be firmly gripped by the mortar. Space the stones in any way that pleases you. After embedding the first few stones, you'll begin to develop a feeling for the consistency of the mortar and how to handle it. The mortar sets fairly quickly, so don't interrupt your work by answering the phone

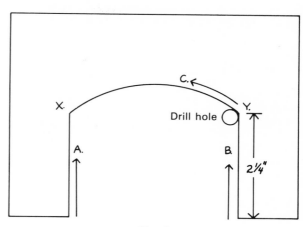

Fig. 4

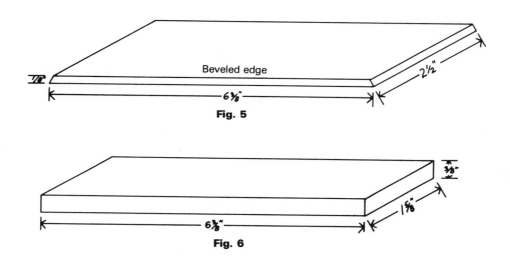

Fig. 5

Fig. 6

or taking a break until you finish the particular section you're working on. Then apply mortar to another section and embed your stones. Et cetera. We'd be very surprised if by now you aren't becoming a little excited with the results.

When you've finished your masonry work, let it dry for about thirty minutes. You'll have your finished fireplace soon after that.

All that remains is to glue on the mantel and the hearth —making sure the straight edges of each are aligned with the back of the fireplace—and to paint the inside of the fireplace with the matte black paint.

Your stone fireplace is now ready to warm your doll-house

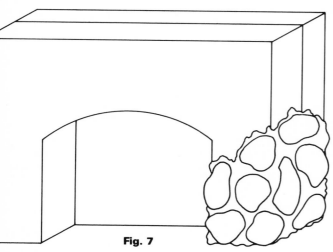

Fig. 7

...replace designed and built by author.

CHAPTER 13

BUILDING YOUR OWN DOLLHOUSE – SEVERAL APPROACHES

As we saw in Chapter 7, there are many different approaches to owning a dollhouse. In building a dollhouse, too, there are several options open to you. You can work from a kit, which is comparable to building a prefabricated house, where all the pieces are provided and you do the assembling and finishing. Or you can work from patterns, which is similar to the way a dressmaker works. Or, lastly, you can work from plans, which are analogous to the blueprints of an architect.

Of the three methods, the kit approach is by far the quickest and surest route to a successful dollhouse. It can satisfy the needs of the hobbyist who wants to have a hand in building his or her own dollhouse but has neither the time, the tools, nor the inclination to do it from scratch.

Patterns and plans are basically sets of instructions. How well your house comes out depends upon how well you follow the instructions. Both methods give you the satisfaction of building the house entirely yourself. Plans, however, allow for greater complexity of design.

Examples of all three approaches—kits, patterns, and plans—are given in this and the following chapter.

Mini-workman in Victorian dollhouse made by Gotfred O. Hoffmann.

DOLLHOUSE KITS

AFTON CLASSICS

An inexpensive but well-produced dollhouse kit is the Williamsburg model made by Afton Classics. Mike Lombardo, the owner and designer, has built in many quality features that make this a highly satisfying house to construct and own.

The six-room dollhouse measures 32″ long × 17 1/2″ wide × 28″ high. The components, all wood, are pre-cut, pre-drilled, and ready to be assembled. The kit also includes plexiglass windows, a center hall stairway, flower boxes, hardware, sandpaper, and nails.

A variation of this house, called "The Mount Vernon," is also available in kit form. It features the addition of a portico with round pillars, plus two large flower boxes.

MY UNCLE

Two excellent and modestly priced dollhouse kits are offered by My Uncle, of Fryeburg, Maine. One is a Nantucket Cape that measures 25″ wide × 17″ deep × 22″ high—a compact house well suited to the beginning collector or to a small miniature collection. The hinged front opens to reveal a living room, complete with oversized fireplace, plus a kitchen. The roof, also hinged, swings up to give access to a commodious upstairs bedroom.

The second house is described as a "Beacon Hill Townhouse," consisting of three floors and six rooms. The overall dimensions are 24″ wide × 13 1/2″ deep × 42 1/2″ high—a good-sized dollhouse. Its features include two stairways, two movable fireplaces, five flower boxes, plexiglass windows, and a characteristic townhouse roof, with a pair of double chimneys and a double balustrade.

Both houses are entirely of wood, with pre-cut parts ready to sand and assemble. All the necessary hardware, sandpaper, glue, and nails are included. These kits offer the collector the satisfaction of being involved in the construction of his or her dollhouse with a minimal expenditure of time and effort.

DOLLHOUSE PATTERNS AND PLANS

THE ARK

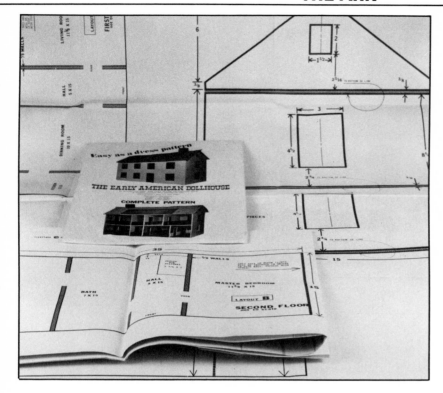

The easiest way to build a dollhouse from scratch is to work from a set of patterns, such as these designed by Gloria Pack of The Ark Miniatures. Choose the style of house you prefer—The Ark currently offers an Early American and a Colonial design, with more to follow. Then lay out the patterns, trace them onto plywood, and cut out the pieces —just as you'd handle a dress pattern. All instructions are given on the pattern sheets, including how to make wainscoting, attach shingles, and apply wallpaper.

The resulting dollhouses are of ample size, the Colonial model measuring 29″ in length, 24 1/2″ in depth, and 32″ in height, with a total of twelve rooms.

Mrs. Pack estimates the cost of the finished house at roughly $45, which covers all materials, plus the cost of the patterns. If you have to buy tools, your costs naturally will run higher, but the tools will serve you over and over again.

JOAN EASTMAN

Among the various dollhouses for which plans are available, the "Bradford House," a replica of a 200-year-old homestead located near Bradford, New Hampshire, ranks high in architectural integrity. The plans are the work of Joan Eastman, who researched and constructed the house with the help of her husband. The finished dollhouse attracted so much interest that the Eastmans decided to publish the plans and offer them for sale through mail-order advertising.

The Bradford House measures 36″ wide × 27″ high × 15″ deep. It has four rooms and a large attic in the main structure, plus a kitchen in the "addition" on the side of the house. A center staircase leads to the second floor, and a trap door and ladder provide access to the attic.

The plans consist of over thirty drawings and photographs, together with clear and detailed instructions covering every step of the project. The Bradford House has been especially designed to permit construction by the home craftsperson using simple hand tools and readily available materials.

Plans for additional houses are on the drawing board.

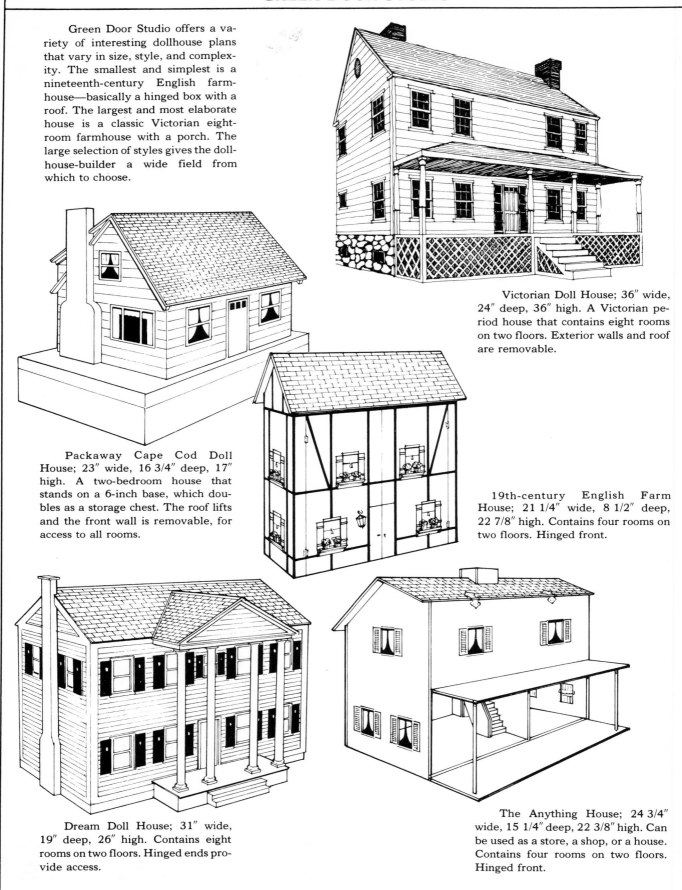

Green Door Studio offers a variety of interesting dollhouse plans that vary in size, style, and complexity. The smallest and simplest is a nineteenth-century English farmhouse—basically a hinged box with a roof. The largest and most elaborate house is a classic Victorian eight-room farmhouse with a porch. The large selection of styles gives the dollhouse-builder a wide field from which to choose.

Victorian Doll House; 36″ wide, 24″ deep, 36″ high. A Victorian period house that contains eight rooms on two floors. Exterior walls and roof are removable.

Packaway Cape Cod Doll House; 23″ wide, 16 3/4″ deep, 17″ high. A two-bedroom house that stands on a 6-inch base, which doubles as a storage chest. The roof lifts and the front wall is removable, for access to all rooms.

19th-century English Farm House; 21 1/4″ wide, 8 1/2″ deep, 22 7/8″ high. Contains four rooms on two floors. Hinged front.

Dream Doll House; 31″ wide, 19″ deep, 26″ high. Contains eight rooms on two floors. Hinged ends provide access.

The Anything House; 24 3/4″ wide, 15 1/4″ deep, 22 3/8″ high. Can be used as a store, a shop, or a house. Contains four rooms on two floors. Hinged front.

MINIATURE PATTERNS BY ELSPETH

If you'd prefer to make a room setting rather than build an entire dollhouse, try one of the Miniature Patterns by Elspeth. Each of these patterns, carefully thought out and marvelously detailed, allows you to create an entire room setting, furniture and all. The country store, for example, gives patterns and instructions for making not only the room itself but a coffee grinder, platform scale, broom, potbelly stove, stool, barrel, and washboard, as well as dozens of other items. Also included is a sheet of old-fashioned labels and advertisements, all in miniature. The accompanying text provides a wealth of background information about the particular setting and its contents.

The guiding intelligence behind these well-researched and superbly thought-out patterns is Bettyanne Twigg, a veteran miniaturist who both lectures on the subject and gives classes in miniature making.

In addition to the country store shown here, Mrs. Twigg offers five other miniature-room patterns: country cottage bedroom, c. 1850; strawberry sweet shop, c. 1890; New England sitting room, late 1700s; Victorian Christmas, c. 1876; and eighteenth-century child's bedroom. These patterns are available directly from Mrs. Twigg through mail order (see Chapter 18).

PIN
BEAD
SEQUINS
WIRE
TOOTHPICK
BEAD
SEQUIN

"TEAPOT" ASSEMBLY: GLUE TOGETHER IN ORDER SHOWN. PAINT WITH GESSO. DRY. PAINT WITH SILVER. ANTIQUE. FINISH SUGAR AND CREAMER THE SAME WAY.

COFFEE GRINDER: CUT MATTBOARD AND ASSEMBLE AS SHOWN. PAINT WITH GESSO. DRY. PAINT RED. PAINT TRIM AND WHEEL EDGE GOLD, AT ᴄᴏᴠᴇʀ AREAS.

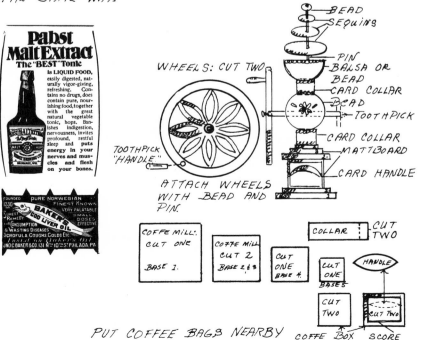

BEAD
SEQUINS
PIN
BALSA OR BEAD
CARD COLLAR
BEAD
TOOTHPICK
CARD COLLAR
MATTBOARD
CARD HANDLE

WHEELS: CUT TWO

TOOTHPICK "HANDLE"

ATTACH WHEELS WITH BEAD AND PIN.

COFFE MILL: CUT ONE BASE 1.

COFFE MILL CUT 2 BASE 2 & 3

CUT ONE BASE 4.

COLLAR — CUT TWO

CUT ONE BASES

HANDLE

CUT TWO

CUT TWO

PUT COFFEE BAGS NEARBY

COFFE BOX SIDES.

SCORE

BUILDING A DOLLHOUSE
FROM PLANS

There is little doubt that the most exciting and satisfying approach to building your own dollhouse is to work from plans, whether they be existing plans, such as the ones we've provided for you in the next chapter, or plans that you create yourself.

The inspiration can come from anywhere: a house in your neighborhood, a photograph in a magazine, a dollhouse you saw somewhere and would like to re-create. Perhaps you've been carrying around in your head an idea of your dream house and would like to construct it in miniature, as Mr. Briggs did ("Mr. Briggs's Dream House" has been displayed at the Museum of the City of New York). Or perhaps you'd like to construct a house you read about in a book, as Stanley Eisenman did when he built a miniature log cabin based on the design and dimensions given in *The Foxfire Book*.

The one thing all custom-made dollhouses have in common is proud owners. But because not everyone is cut out to be a "scratch" dollhouse-builder, it's important to know beforehand just what you're getting yourself into.

Building a dollhouse is a very demanding undertaking. In some respects, it's like building a full-size house. You're the architect, contractor, electrician, carpenter, and painter all in one. So, aside from selecting the size and style of house you want, you should give serious consideration to the amount of time and effort you're willing to devote to the job. Building a dollhouse is a labor of love, but love has a way of turning sour when more demands are made on you than you're prepared to meet.

Try to determine at the outset how long your dollhouse will take to build and then decide if you're up to it. Estimating the construction time isn't easy, and your tendency will be to vastly underestimate it. In practice, once you get going, you will very likely get carried away and lavish on your house unimaginable hours of loving labor. In view of this, a good rule of thumb is to double your best guess. Even then you'll probably err on the low side.

Most of the materials used for detailing (molding, shingles, bricks, etc.) can be bought ready-made (see Chapter 11); and while the cost of these items can add up rather fast, your major expenditure will be time.

In this and the following chapter, you'll find three construction projects of varying degrees of difficulty. The first is a basic miniature room. If you've never built anything before, this is a good project to begin with. You can always hand it down to someone else later on.

The other two projects (see Chapter 14) are dollhouses. They represent two approaches to the same basic house—a Williamsburg Colonial. The first is a simplified version designed for the builder whose time is limited or who simply doesn't require an abundance of detailing. The second version has all the refinements—siding, shingles, dormers, an authentic chimney, wiring, molding, and other time-consuming but highly rewarding features.

We've chosen this particular style because of its widespread appeal as a dollhouse. However, if you have some other style of house in mind that you'd like to build from scratch, don't automatically pass up the next chapter. Some of the construction techniques shown there will be applicable to whatever house you plan to build.

Your skill in carpentry will affect your completion time. If you're an experienced woodworker or model-maker, you are already familiar with the proper tools, and you can get right to work. Otherwise, it would be well to spend a little extra time with Chapter 11—"Tools and Supplies for Making Miniatures and Dollhouses."

An important factor that could affect your end result is whether or not you have a deadline. If you are building the house for yourself, chances are you can control your impatience. But if you're building it for someone else—or for a particular occasion, such as a birthday—this will greatly determine your timetable for completion. Most "clients" are short on patience. Understandably,

Dollhouse built by Fordham W. Briggs in the 1930s.
(Photo courtesy of the Museum of the City of New York.)
Mr. Briggs's dollhouse, interior view.
(Photo courtesy of the Museum of the City of New York.)

your "client" will want the house to be finished as soon as possible so it can be moved into, decorated, and shown off. Consequently, it's a good idea to consider the patience of the person for whom you are building the house.

The amount of time you are willing or able to spend will also affect the degree of realism you can hope to achieve. Realism is a function of close adherence to scale, which requires a great deal of additional research and construction time. Of course, architectural realism is not necessarily the goal of every dollhouse builder. You might prefer a simpler, more stylized approach, or even—at a farther remove from realism—a fantasy house, which might be built to resemble a pumpkin or the stump of a tree. Any approach is valid—it all depends on your personal objectives. If your goal is authenticity, then exact scale is your master; if it is anything less, then you're the master.

If construction time is of little consequence and you want to build a dollhouse that will be greatly admired, you'll want to give much thought to detailing. No matter what style of house you decide upon—Colonial, salt-box, Victorian, castle, fantasy house, whatever—the details are what make the difference. True, a child's dollhouse doesn't need much in the way of detailing. Indeed, the appeal of many early dollhouses (built mainly for children) lies in the folk-art qualities of their simplified architecture. A child's eye isn't fully aware of architectural detail, and such refinements are of little importance in terms of play. To many adults, however, a significant part of the pleasure of building a dollhouse is found in re-creating such details.

The Williamsburg Colonial-type dollhouse described in detail in the next chapter derives much of its appeal from such details as cedar-shake shingles individually applied to the roof and dormers, hand-cut siding applied strip by strip to the front and sides, shutters on all windows, a staircase with lathe-turned balusters, molding along the ceilings, and an electrical system that provides an overhead light in every room except one. These details consume most of the construction time, and they can't be hurried. They require patience and a desire for perfection. Interestingly enough, they demand only a minimal amount of skill. Virtually anyone can do the work; it's mostly a matter of setting your mind to it.

Log cabin built by Stanley Eisenman, based on information given in The Foxfire Book. *Mr. Eisenman worked entirely with native materials found on his property.* (Photo courtesy Stanley Eisenman.)

BUILDING A MINIATURE ROOM

The miniature room described here is of fairly typical dimensions. Before you begin to build it, decide if these dimensions suit the purpose you have in mind. If not, change them to conform to your own needs, keeping in mind that such changes may require more wood and other supplies.

TOOLS AND MATERIALS NEEDED

- 1/2″ plywood, 2′ × 3′
- 1/8″ quarter-round molding, 6′ total length
- 1/8″ basswood, 1/4″ × 6″
- 1/8″ basswood, 3/16″ × 10″
- 1/8″ basswood, 1/8″ × 12″
- 1/2″ veneer tape or 1/32″ wood strips, 1/2″ × 32″
- Saw
- Knife with extra blades
- Hammer
- 1″ wire brads, one dozen
- C-clamps
- Sandpaper (several grades)
- White glue
- Primer/sealer
- Paint and paintbrushes
- Wallpaper
- Wallpaper paste
- Outdoor scene

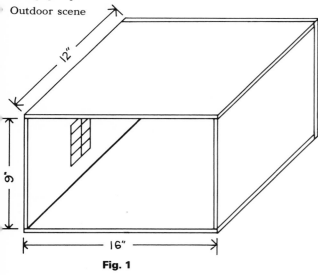

Fig. 1

As you can see in Fig. 1, the room consists of two pieces of plywood 12″ × 16″ (for the top and bottom), two pieces 9″ × 12″ (the sides), and one piece 10″ × 16″ (the back). Start by ruling off these dimensions on your 1/2″ plywood. Then clamp the wood firmly and cut the pieces with your saw. Sand all edges and surfaces until smooth.

The basic decorating is most easily done now, before assembling. Paint or wallpaper the walls, and paint the floor and ceiling as desired. Use primer/sealer before you paint.

If you choose to put in a window with a simulated view, as shown here, cut your basswood pieces to the dimensions given in Fig. 2. Paint or stain the pieces. When they are dry, glue them together; then glue your outdoor scene to the finished window frame. When it is dry, glue the window in place on the wall.

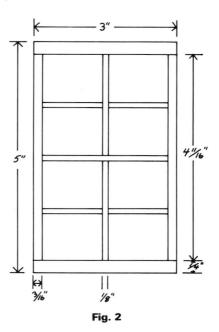

Fig. 2

Assemble the room by gluing the five pieces together. Hammer in several wire brads to hold the pieces firmly in position.

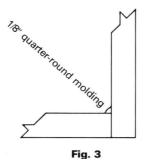

Fig. 3

For baseboard and ceiling trim, use 1/8″ quarter-round molding. First cut the molding to size, then paint or stain. When dry, glue in place. Turn the room upside down when installing the ceiling molding.

Trim the exposed front edges with 1/2″ veneer tape or 1/32″ basswood. Glue in place.

Finish the exterior with paint or stain. If painting, first apply primer/sealer.

Your miniature room is now ready to be furnished.

Exterior view of Williamsburg Colonial dollhouse, for which complete plans are given in this chapter. Shown here is the detailed version of this house, which is covered later in the chapter. The simplified version, covered first, is similar in overall appearance but without many of the details shown here.

CHAPTER 14

COMPLETE DOLLHOUSE PLANS

BUILDING A WILLIAMSBURG COLONIAL DOLLHOUSE— SIMPLIFIED VERSION

The Colonial dollhouse presented here is very ample, measuring 38 1/2″ long × 18 1/2″ deep × 30″ high (not including the chimney). Inside are five rooms, two hallways, and an attic that runs the length of the house. Our room plan has a large living room and a kitchen/dining room combination on the first floor, and two bedrooms and a bathroom on the second floor. However, this configuration can be changed to satisfy your own particular requirements.

If you are new to woodworking, you'll probably feel more comfortable using the dimensions given here. But should you want to modify the design, be sure to consider possible consequent alterations. If, for example, you want a different configuration of rooms and you move the walls to suit your needs, be aware of the changes that will have to be made in the positions of the windows and staircase.

Look over the list of tools and supplies, and make sure you have everything on hand before you start.

TOOLS AND SUPPLIES NEEDED

- Hammer
- Screwdriver
- Sabre saw
- Power drill, 1/4″
- Drill bits: 1/8″, 5/32″, 3/8″
- Countersink
- Chisel, 1/4″
- Knife with extra blades
- Acrylic scoring knife
- Square with level
- 2 large C-clamps
- Pin drill
- Awl

- Small miter box and razor saw
- Dividers
- Ruler
- Pencil
- Sandpaper (assorted)
- White glue
- Duco Cement
- Wood screws
- Nails
- Primer/sealer
- Paint
- Stain
- Wallpaper
- Wallpaper paste
- Roller for wallpaper
- Small hinges for door (pair)
- Doorknob
- Door knocker (optional)
- 1/2″ plywood, 4′ × 6′ (for sides, floors, and roof supports)
- 1/4″ plywood, 4′ × 6′ (for interior walls, façade, roof, and front door)
- 3/4″ pine, 6″ × 30″ (for the aprons, chimney, and front steps)
- 1/8″ quarter-round molding, total of 30′ (for floor and ceiling tracks)
- 8 basswood strips, 1/32″ × 3/8″ × 22″ (for inside window moldings)
- 10 basswood strips, 3/32″ × 1/2″ × 22″ (for corner strips and door frame)
- 13 basswood strips, 3/32″ × 1/4″ × 22″ (for door frame, window frame, and window grid)
- 2 basswood strips, 3/32″ × 3/16″ × 22″ (for window frame)
- 5 basswood strips, 3/32″ × 1/8″ × 22″ (for window grid)
- 2 basswood strips, 1/8″ × 5/8″ × 22″ (for staircase risers)
- 2 basswood strips, 1/8″ × 7/8″ × 22″ (for staircase treads)
- 1 basswood strip, 1/8″ × 2 3/4″ × 22″ (for second-floor railing)
- Basswood post, 3/8″ × 3/8″ × 22″ (for second-floor railing)
- Staircase stringer, two 22″ lengths
- Stair handrail, one 22″ length
- Acrylic plastic, 3/32″ × 12″ × 18″ (for the windows)

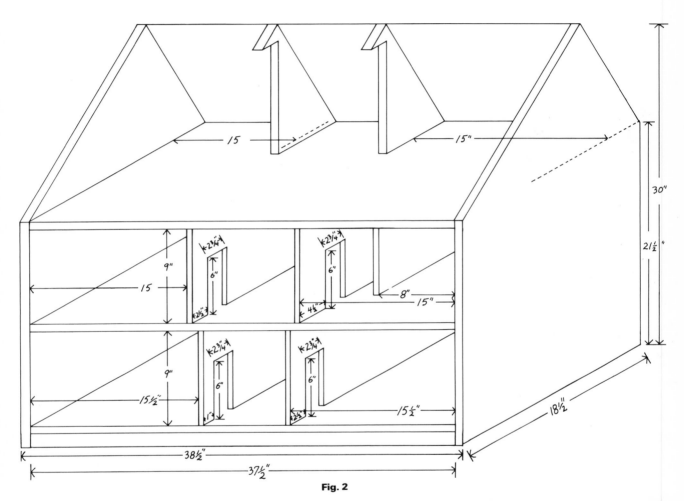

Fig. 2

The supporting structure of the house—the sides, floors, and roof supports—is made of 1/2″ plywood. The interior walls, façade, and roof are made of 1/4″ plywood (Fig. 2).

Start by ruling off and cutting out the pieces shown in Fig. 3 (but don't cut the doorways in the four walls yet). You'll find a power sabre saw to be of great advantage here; with a little practice, you should be able to make nice straight cuts. Make sure you clamp or otherwise hold the wood firmly so that it doesn't shift while you're sawing it. Place a thin piece of wood or cardboard between the clamp and the surface of your work so that the clamp doesn't leave any marks.

After you've cut out all the pieces, sand all of the edges, being careful not to round any of them.

Cutting guide

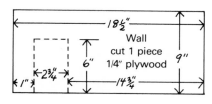

Wall
cut 1 piece
1/4″ plywood

18½″ · 6″ · 9″ · 2¾″ · 1″ · 14¾″

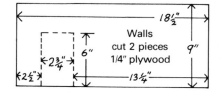

Walls
cut 2 pieces
1/4″ plywood

18½″ · 6″ · 9″ · 2¾″ · 2½″ · 13¼″

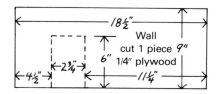

Wall
cut 1 piece
1/4″ plywood

18½″ · 6″ · 9″ · 2¾″ · 4½″ · 11¼″

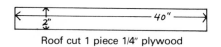

Roof cut 1 piece 1/4″ plywood

2″ · 40″

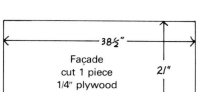

Façade
cut 1 piece
1/4″ plywood

38½″ · 21″

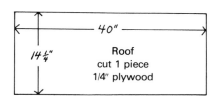

Roof
cut 1 piece
1/4″ plywood

40″ · 14¼″

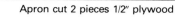

Apron cut 2 pieces 1/2″ plywood

2″ · 37½″

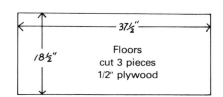

Floors
cut 3 pieces
1/2″ plywood

37½″ · 18½″

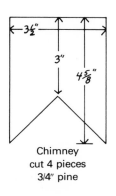

Chimney
cut 4 pieces
3/4″ pine

3½″ · 3″ · 4⅝″

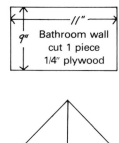

Bathroom wall
cut 1 piece
1/4″ plywood

11″ · 9″

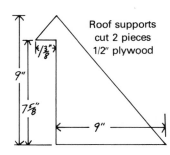

Roof supports
cut 2 pieces
1/2″ plywood

9″ · 3/8″ · 7⅝″ · 9″

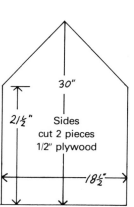

Sides
cut 2 pieces
1/2″ plywood

30″ · 21½″ · 18½″

Fig. 3

165

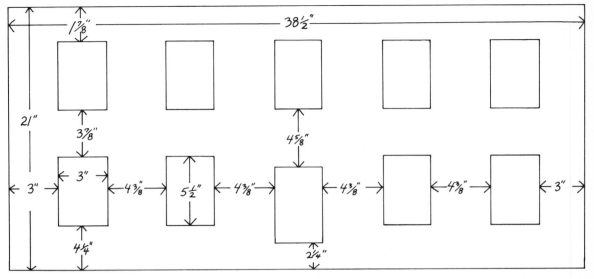

Fig. 7

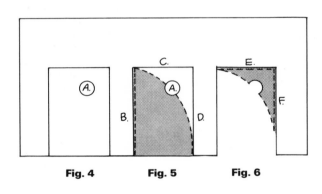

Fig. 4   Fig. 5   Fig. 6

Measure and cut the doorways in the four main interior walls (Fig. 4). The technique of cutting the doorways is as follows: Start with any one of the four walls and, using a hand or power drill, drill a hole (A) in the position shown in Fig. 5 that is large enough to allow your sabre saw blade to pass through (a 3/8″ hole will do). With your sabre saw, make cut B as shown. Now place your sabre saw blade through hole A and cut the arc shown in cut C. Then cut the arc shown in cut D. The shaded portion of the wood will fall out, leaving only the upper right-hand corner, as shown in Fig. 6. Now, starting at the upper left-hand corner, cut along the top line to the upper right-hand corner (cut E). Do the same along the right-hand side, cutting from the bottom to the top along the line (cut F). The corner piece will drop out, leaving a perfect door opening. Lightly sand the inside edges.

Using the same method, measure and cut the doorways in the other three walls.

Now let's apply this same method to cutting the nine windows and the front door of the façade. Take your 1/4″ façade piece and rule off the dimensions, as shown in Fig. 7. Window openings are each 3″ × 5 1/2″. The front door opening measures 3″ × 6 3/4″.

(NOTE: X-Acto makes an accurately detailed working window in kit form (see Chapter 11). If you decide to use the X-Acto windows, alter the size of the window openings shown in Fig. 7 to correspond to the dimensions of the X-Acto windows.)

To cut the window openings, drill two holes diagonally opposite one another, as shown in Fig. 8. Place your sabre saw blade through hole A and make cut C as shown (Fig. 9). Do the same, starting from hole B and cutting toward the top (cut D). Make cuts E and F (Fig. 10). The shaded center piece will fall out, leaving the shape of opening shown in Fig. 11. Place your saw blade in the lower left-hand corner and cut straight up (cut G, Fig. 12). Make cut H along the bottom (Fig. 13), and cut I along the top (Fig. 14). The upper left corner piece will now drop out. Make cut J down the side (Fig. 15) and the lower right corner piece will drop out, leaving the desired window opening. Lightly sand the inside edges.

Repeat this procedure for the other windows and the front door.

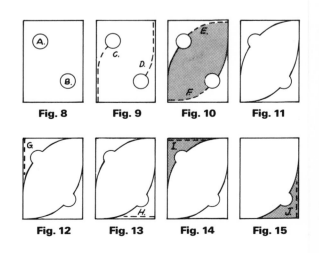

Fig. 8   Fig. 9   Fig. 10   Fig. 11

Fig. 12   Fig. 13   Fig. 14   Fig. 15

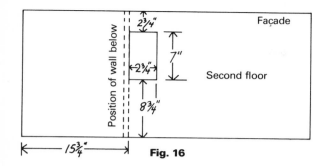

Fig. 16

Use this same technique to make the second-floor staircase opening, ruling off and cutting out an opening with the dimensions indicated in Fig. 16. Then sand the inside edges smooth.

Now, oddly enough, is the time to wallpaper or paint the interior of the house and to finish the floors in whatever way you want. These steps are vastly easier to do when the house is disassembled. After ruling off the outlines of the various rooms on all the interior surfaces, apply wallpaper or paint. If you decide on paint, the raw wood should first be treated with a primer/sealer. While you're at it, prime and paint the apron, the roof supports, and the underside of the roof. The floors can be painted, stained, or papered with a wood-grained or random-plank pattern.

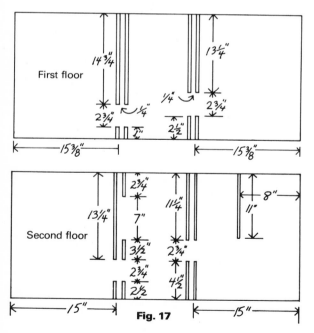

Fig. 17

To hold the interior walls in place, we'll use floor and ceiling tracks made of 1/8" quarter-round molding. Mark the position of each of the walls on the corresponding floors and ceilings. Also indicate the positions of doorways. Measure and cut the molding to size, then stain or paint it as desired. When it is dry, glue the molding in place on either side of your guidelines (Fig. 17). It might help to tack the molding

down with fine brads to hold it in position; use your pin drill to make guide holes for the brads. The molding tracks not only serve as supports for the walls but give a nice finished effect to the floors and walls. They also permit the walls to be removed whenever you want to repaint or rewallpaper.

You are now ready to assemble the main structure of the house, which includes the sides, floors, and walls—everything except the façade, roof, and roof supports. Mark off the position of the floors on the inner surfaces of both sides of the house, as shown in Fig. 18. Mark the position of screws *a, b, c, d, e,* and *f,* about 2 inches in from each side, and drill holes the same size as the diameter of the screws, so they will enter without resistance. Countersink each hole on the outside so that the screw head will be slightly below the surface. To mark the corresponding screw positions on the ends of each of the floors, first lie the pieces on their sides. Line up each floor, in turn, with its corresponding guidelines and, using an awl inserted through the drilled hole, mark the positions of each of the holes. Drill a small guide hole in each of these positions to enable the screw to bite into the wood without splitting it. Now apply glue to the contact points of the floors and sides, and screw the pieces together.

Glue the aprons into position, front and back.

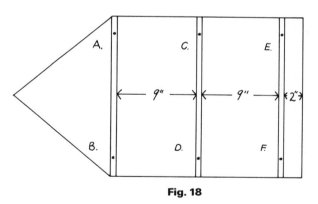

Fig. 18

The windows come next. Our windows consist of clear acrylic, 3" × 5 1/2", to which wood grids that simulate a windowpane effect are attached. Rule off and cut out nine pieces of acrylic, each 3" × 5 1/2". The easiest way to cut acrylic is to score it with an acrylic scoring knife, then snap it along the scored line. You can also saw it with a jeweler's saw or coping saw, but this has to be done very carefully to prevent the acrylic from cracking. Once the windows are cut, insert them into their respective openings to test their fit. If necessary, sand the edges until they fit properly.

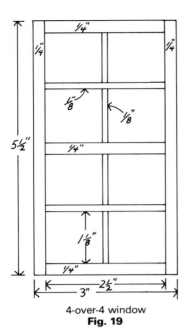

4-over-4 window
Fig. 19

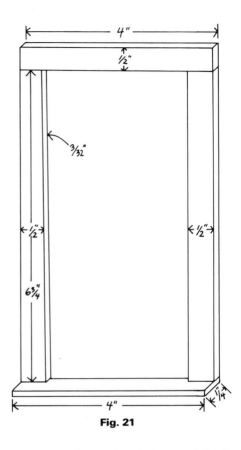

Fig. 21

To make the window grids, first decide on the arrangement of panes you want (4 over 4, 6 over 6, 9 over 9), bearing in mind that the more "panes," the more work (see Fig. 19). Then cut your 3/32" × 1/8" and 3/32" × 1/4" basswood strips to size for the pane arrangement you chose, and glue them at their points of contact. When all of the grids have been made, try them out in the window openings. If necessary, sand them to fit. Then paint all the grids on both sides. We chose to paint ours white.

To attach the grids to the acrylic windows, use a clear adhesive such as Duco Cement. Apply a very light coating to a few pieces of the grid and join the grid to the window, weighting them together until dry.

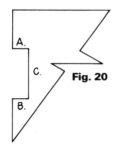

Fig. 20

Now you need a front door. Cut a piece of 1/4" plywood 3" wide by 6 3/4" high. Cut notches for the hinges by using a razor saw to make cuts A and B, Fig. 20. The cuts should be as high as your hinges and just deep enough so that the doubled-over hinge will lie flush with the edge of the door. Use a narrow chisel to make cut C, completing the notch. Sand lightly. To finish the door, prime and paint it, then attach hinges, a doorknob, and a door knocker (if desired). If you'd like to try your hand at a more complex "paneled" door, follow the door-making instructions given in the plans for the detailed version of this dollhouse.

Next, we want to frame the windows and the front door. Let's start with the door. Use 3/32" × 1/2" basswood for the sides and top, and 3/32" × 1/4" basswood for the bottom (doorsill). Cut these pieces as in Fig. 21 and glue them in place around the door opening of the façade.

The framing of the windows is done in the same way. However, instead of fitting flush with the opening, as in the case of the door framing, the window framing will overlap the openings in order to hold the windows in place (see Fig. 22). The bottoms and the tops of the window frames are made with 3/32" basswood, 1/4" wide. The sides are of 3/32" basswood, 3/16" wide. Cut the pieces as in Fig. 22 and glue them into place on all windows.

Now you can prime and paint the entire façade, including the window and door frames. Also prime and paint the sides of the assembled house and the outer surface of the roof.

When the façade is dry, turn it over and insert all of the windows into the window openings. To hold them permanently in place, apply molding made of 1/32" × 3/8" basswood, overlapping the inside of the window openings as on the outside (see Fig. 22). Cut the strips to the length shown, then stain or paint them. When dry, glue them in place.

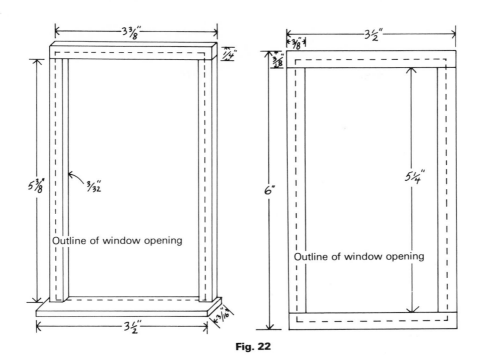

Fig. 22

Now is as good a time as any to attach the front door. Mark the position of the hinges and the screw holes (unless you're gluing the hinges on). Start the hole with an awl or the point of a thin nail and screw the hinges on. Open and close the door to check the fit. If the door rubs in any spot, lightly sand that area until it fits smoothly. Then touch up any paint you may have sanded off.

Risers

5/8"

3/4"

Treads

Pre-cut stringer

Fig. 23

14 steps

9"

Second-floor landing

9"

Fig. 24

The staircase is next. Start with pre-cut stringers, which are either available in 22-inch lengths at miniature shops that sell supplies or can be ordered directly from Northeastern Scale Models. You'll need two lengths to make your staircase. Look at Fig. 24. You'll see that the risers are 5/8" high and that it takes fifteen steps to rise the 9 1/2 inches from floor to floor (the fifteenth step is the second-floor landing itself, so our staircase actually contains fourteen steps). Start by cutting two lengths of stringer, as shown in Fig. 24, and sand lightly. Decide on your staircase width; we chose a width of 2 1/2 inches, corresponding to 2 1/2 feet, the staircase width of many houses of this period. Measure and cut fourteen risers and fourteen

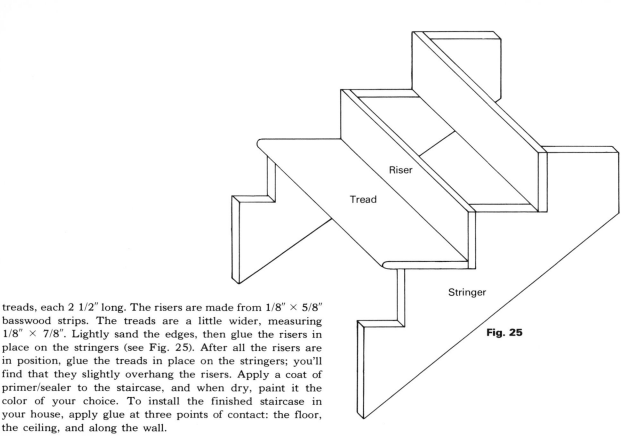

Fig. 25

treads, each 2 1/2″ long. The risers are made from 1/8″ × 5/8″ basswood strips. The treads are a little wider, measuring 1/8″ × 7/8″. Lightly sand the edges, then glue the risers in place on the stringers (see Fig. 25). After all the risers are in position, glue the treads in place on the stringers; you'll find that they slightly overhang the risers. Apply a coat of primer/sealer to the staircase, and when dry, paint it the color of your choice. To install the finished staircase in your house, apply glue at three points of contact: the floor, the ceiling, and along the wall.

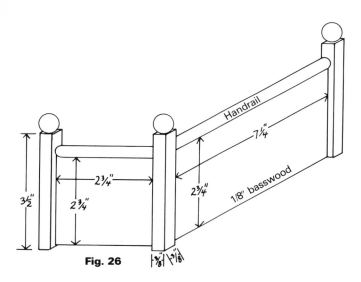

Fig. 26

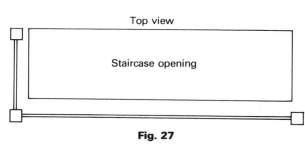

Fig. 27

Fig. 26 shows how to construct the second-floor railing. The three posts, which are made of 3/8″ × 3/8″ basswood, are each 3 1/2″ high and topped by wooden beads or any other decoration. After cutting all pieces to size and sanding the edges, glue the handrail to the 1/8″ × 2 3/4″ basswood siding. Then glue this assembly to the posts. Finally, glue the entire unit into position, using Fig. 27 as a guide.

Fig. 28

Attaching the façade comes next. This is done with a combination of glue and four screws for extra strength. Using your 5/32″ drill bit, drill a hole several inches from each corner of the façade and 1/4″ in from the edge (see Fig. 28). Lay the house on its side and hold the façade in place on the house so that you can mark the position of the four holes. Then, using your 1/8″ drill bit, drill shallow guide holes at each mark. Spread glue on the edges of the sides and the three floors, and attach the façade. Screw in the four screws, and place a weight on the façade in the center to facilitate a strong bond.

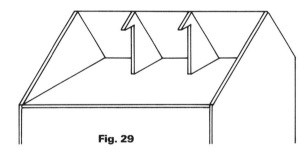

Fig. 29

Now that the façade is attached, it's time to apply the corner strips. Take eight lengths of 3/32″ × 1/2″ basswood to trim the tops of the sides, along the roof line, and the four corners. Cut to size, prime and paint, then glue into place.

Glue the 1/2″ plywood roof supports in place, as shown in Fig. 29, spacing them equally apart from the ends.

Now glue the main section of the roof into place, overlapping the peak by 1/4″. When this section is dry, glue the narrow roof section into place, butting it up against the main section.

To make the chimney, first glue, then nail together the four chimney pieces that you had cut from 3/4″ pine. When the glue is dry, sand the edges smooth. For an interesting effect, paint a black rectangle, 2″ × 2 1/2″, in the center of the chimney to simulate an opening. Then paint the rest of the chimney with a mixture of sand and paint. The gritty texture will hide the laminations and make the chimney appear to have been constructed in one piece.

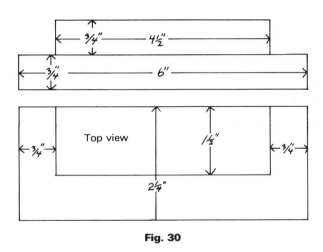

Fig. 30

The front steps are made of 3/4″ pine cut to the dimensions shown in Fig. 30, sanded, glued together, primed and painted, then attached to the house by being glued into position under the front door.

Now that your house is completed, you might want to make a few refinements, such as putting shutters on the windows or trimming off the edges of the open sides with veneer tape. If you're inclined to go further, study the following set of instructions for building a more detailed house. Many of the touches described there can be incorporated into the house you've just built.

BUILDING A WILLIAMSBURG COLONIAL DOLLHOUSE— DETAILED VERSION

This dollhouse, while more complex in its detailing, is almost identical in overall measurements and basic structure to the one just described. Consequently, in guiding you through its construction, we refer back to some of the steps and figures given in the plans for the simplified house rather than repeat them.

Some of the construction techniques employed here are more sophisticated than those used to build the simplified version, and they require some additional tools and materials. Use the list of supplies given at the beginning of this chapter, but add the following:

ADDITIONAL MATERIALS NEEDED

- Dremel Moto-Tool with router attachment, 1/4″ router bit, and protective goggles
- Scriber (for scoring floor to achieve a plank effect)
- Chisel, 3/8″ or wider
- Mallet
- Rasp
- Contact cement
- Electrical supplies:
    Transformer, 12-volt, 1200 milliampere
    2 terminal strips, 6-terminal variety
    Fuse, rated 1500 milliampere
    Fuse holder
    Soldering iron
    Resin core solder
    Silicone cement
    7 bulbs (screw-base or grain-of-wheat) or lighting fixtures
    Tweezers
    Vinyl plastic electrical tape
    3 wall sockets
    Line cord
    #18 stranded wire, 5/64″ diameter (feed wire)
    #32 stranded copper wire, 1/32″ diameter (circuit wire)
    (NOTE: All of the above electrical supplies can be found in the Illinois Hobbycraft catalog.)
- 1/8″ cove molding (for front door)
- 5/32″ cove molding (for ceilings)
- Cedar shingles, 1 1/2″ × 1 5/8″, or irregular
- 1/32″ basswood siding (5/8″ strips, or larger sheets that can be cut into 5/8″ strips)
- Plaster (optional—for making chimney)
- Wood filler
- Wood veneer tape
- Scotch tape
- Handrail, 2 lengths, 22″ long
- 29 turned balusters (or 29 dowels, either 1/8″ or 3/16″ diameter)
- Protractor

Before you begin building the dollhouse proper, we suggest that you first construct the front door. This may seem like a strange way to start a house, but it will do two important things for you. First, it will demonstrate graphically the contribution that detailing makes (in this case, molding); and second, it will give you an enormous feeling of accomplishment from a minimum of effort. Making the front door is a good warm-up exercise and confidence-builder. And with the finished door in your hand, the house can't be far behind.

The front door measures 3″ wide × 6 3/4″ high, so start by cutting a piece of 1/4″ plywood to those dimensions. Sand lightly.

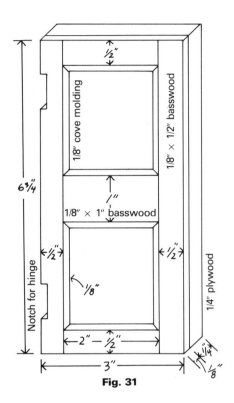

1/2"

1/8" cove molding

1/8" × 1/2" basswood

6 3/4"

1"

1/8" × 1" basswood

Notch for hinge

←1/2→

←1/2→

1/8"

1/4" plywood

←2"—1/2"→

←3"→

1/4"

1/8"

Fig. 31

To finish the door, apply a coat of primer/sealer to seal the grain of the wood so that it will take paint smoothly. When the primer/sealer is dry, sand lightly. Then paint the door. We've had especially good results with Martin Senour's Williamsburg colors, which also happen to be historically accurate and well suited to this Williamsburg-style house. For the finishing touch—and one that will gladden your heart—attach a miniature doorknob and door knocker. These are available at most miniature shops. Now that you're the proud parent of a tiny door, how about a nice house to go along with it?

While this house is similar in overall design to the simplified house described earlier, the dimensions of several comparable pieces vary slightly. The routed slots you'll be making for this more advanced house will be compensated for by making the floor pieces longer and the walls higher. The roof supports also differ because the roof of our advanced house consists of one section rather than two, and this section requires a cut-out notch to allow for the passage of the chimney. The chimney itself is totally different from the simplified one—massive and authentic. These are the principal differences; most of the other dimensions are the same for the two houses.

The paneled effect requires 1/8″ basswood and 1/8″ cove molding. Take your 1/8″ × 1/2″ basswood and cut two 6 3/4″ lengths and two 2″ lengths. Use a razor saw and mitre box to get clean, straight cuts. Next, cut a 2″ length from your 1/8″ × 1″ basswood. Lightly sand the edges, being careful not to round them—wrapping the sandpaper around a block of wood will help. Glue the basswood pieces to the sides, top, bottom, and center of the door, as shown in Fig. 31. Then cut and fit the cove molding along the inside edges of the basswood pieces. A little practice will enable you to cut accurate 45° corners with your knife. Once they are cut, glue the pieces into place. You now have a paneled door.

The next step is to cut notches to recess the hinges. First, decide whether you want the door to open out or in. Most front doors open inward, but we preferred to have our door open outward for easy access to the tiny doorknob. If you decide to have your door open in, simply reverse the position of the hinge.

Mark the height of your hinges on the upper and lower portions of the inside edge of the door. Use your razor saw to make cuts A and B, Fig. 32. Make these cuts just deep enough so that the hinges will lie flush with the door's inside edge. Remove the rest of the wood, using your narrow chisel (cut C), then sand the notches smooth.

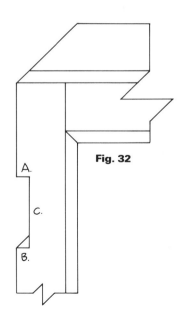

A.

C.

B.

Fig. 32

Cutting guide

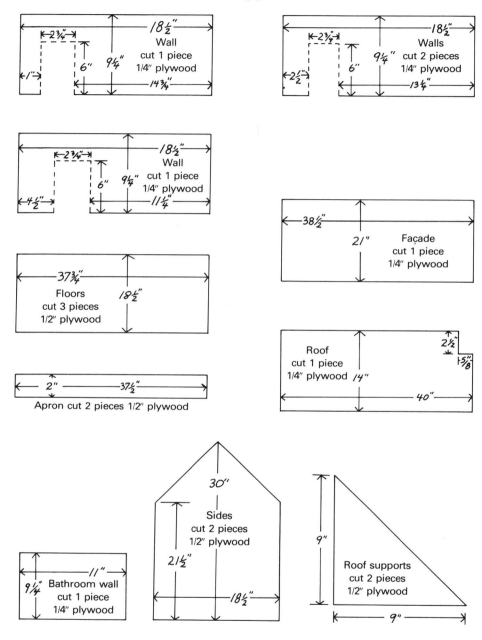

18½"
Wall
cut 1 piece
1/4" plywood
2¾"
6"
9¼"
1"
14¾"

18½"
Walls
cut 2 pieces
1/4" plywood
2¾"
6"
9¼"
2½"
13¼"

18½"
Wall
cut 1 piece
1/4" plywood
2¾"
6"
9¼"
4½"
11¼"

37¾"
Floors
cut 3 pieces
1/2" plywood
18½"

2"   37½"
Apron cut 2 pieces 1/2" plywood

38½"
21"
Façade
cut 1 piece
1/4" plywood

Roof
cut 1 piece
1/4" plywood 14"
2½"
5/8"
40"

11"
9¼"
Bathroom wall
cut 1 piece
1/4" plywood

30"
Sides
cut 2 pieces
1/2" plywood
21½"
18½"

9"
Roof supports
cut 2 pieces
1/2" plywood
9"

Fig. 33

Start by cutting all the main pieces. Follow the cutting guide shown in Fig. 33 (the chimney pieces are not included here but will follow later). When all the pieces have been cut, sand them smooth.

To cut the doorways in the four interior walls, refer to the door-cutting method described for the simplified dollhouse (Figs. 5 and 6).

Next, apply this same technique in cutting the front door and window openings of the façade. Refer to Figs. 8–15 of the simplified-dollhouse plans for details.

Now comes the job of routing—making slots for the floors and walls to fit into. This is an important step for achieving both structural rigidity and a more professional look. The Dremel Company makes an attachment that converts their Moto-Tool into a router. We recommend it for this job. You'll also need a 1/4″ router bit and a pair of protective goggles. If you've never used a router before, follow the instructions that come with the router attachment. Make a few practice slots before you work on the actual piece. You may find that when used freehand, the router has a tendency to pull to one side. This drift can be controlled—and a nice straight cut obtained—by clamping a strip of wood parallel to your cut line to serve as a cutting guide (see Fig. 34).

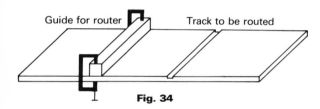

Guide for router   Track to be routed

Fig. 34

There are twenty-six slots to be routed (see Fig. 35). They vary in width from 1/4″ to 1/2″ and in depth from 1/8″ to 1/4″. Because the router blade makes a slot 1/4″ wide, a single pass is all that's necessary to make the 1/4″-wide slots. The 1/2″-wide slots require several passes of the router, and you'll need to move the guide strip each time. To obtain the proper depth of each slot, make several passes, lowering the router blade a bit each time until the correct depth is achieved. If you try to cut the full depth in a single stroke, the resistance of the wood may cause the router to slow down and stop. When all the slots have been cut, sand the routed surfaces with fine sandpaper.

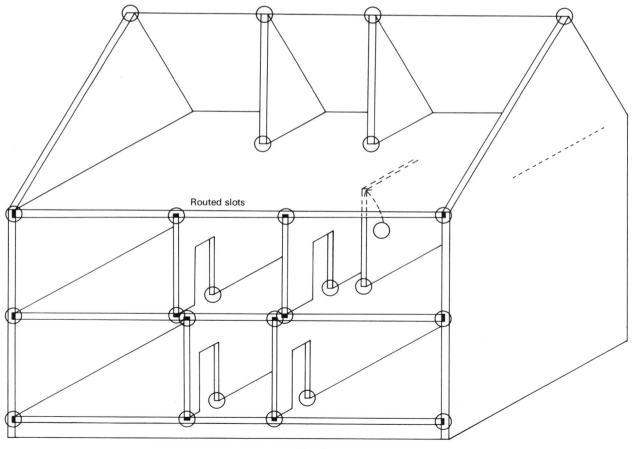

Routed slots

Fig. 35

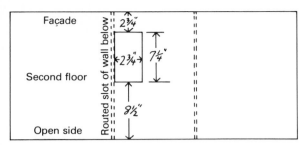

Fig. 36

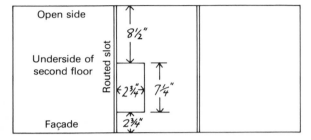

Fig. 37

Now cut the staircase openings for the second floor and the attic. Our attic has a small opening, reached by a ladder placed flat against the wall. Should you prefer a different arrangement, however, decide what type of access to the attic you want before you cut this opening. One side of each of our staircase openings runs along the routed wall-slot of the ceiling below. That's why it was necessary to finish the routing before cutting these openings. Fig. 36 shows what the finished second-floor staircase opening will look like, but because we're using the routed slot for our guide, we have to turn the floor upside down in order to rule the outline of the opening, as shown in Fig. 37. Then follow the window-cutting method described earlier (Figs. 8–15), and cut out the opening. Sand the edges smooth.

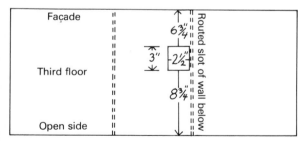

Fig. 38

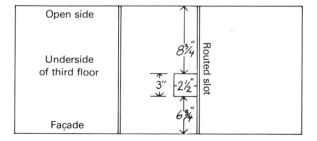

Fig. 39

The attic staircase opening is handled in the same way. Fig. 38 shows the dimensions of the finished opening. Here, too, you'll have to turn the floor over in order to guide yourself by the routed slot. Rule off the opening, as shown in Fig. 39, cut the opening as before, and sand.

This is a good time to wallpaper or paint the interior of the house and to finish the floors—jobs that are much easier to do when the house is disassembled. Rule off the outlines of the various rooms on all the interior surfaces and apply wallpaper or paint. If you're painting, first apply a coat of primer/sealer.

There are many ways to finish floors. We chose to simulate random planking by first priming, then painting the floors with a dark brown latex semi-gloss paint, then scoring lines in the paint with the blade of a screwdriver and a ruler just before the paint was dry.

Once these decorating touches have been completed, you're ready for one of the most satisfying steps of the entire project: assembling the main structure. This includes the sides, floors, and walls—everything except the façade, roof and roof supports, and aprons. Spread a liberal amount of glue on all the routed slots involved and on all the corresponding edges that are to fit into these slots. When joining the pieces, you'll wish you had more than two hands, so try to have someone help you. You'll probably find it easiest to work with the house standing upright, but be sure to use a right-angled triangle or square to make certain the entire structure is standing straight while the glue is drying. A clothesline rope makes a good clamp; wrap it around the outside of the house and knot it securely, first padding the corners to prevent the rope from damaging the house.

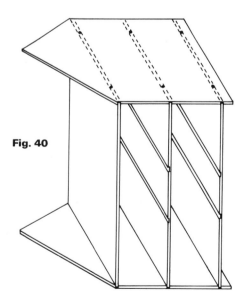

Fig. 40

Once the glue is dry, lay the house on one end and drive a few thin nails into the ends of each of the floors to secure them. If you prefer to use screws, drill small pilot holes first; rub soap on the screws to make them easier to turn. Then turn the house over and secure the other side in the same way.

Glue the aprons into position, front and rear. Do the same for the attic supports (see Fig. 2).

Roof with dimensions of dormer openings

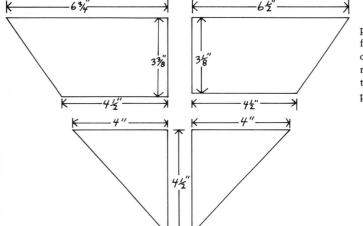

Fig. 41

The dormers are next. The first step is to cut the dormer openings in the roof. Measure and rule off the openings, as shown in Fig. 41. Then cut the openings, using the window-cutting technique described earlier. Sand all edges. You can now prime and paint the underside of the roof.

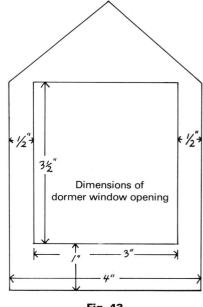

Dimensions of dormer window opening

Fig. 43

To construct the dormers themselves, cut three sets of pieces from 1/4″ plywood, as shown in Fig. 42—a total of fifteen pieces in all. Note that while the two sides of each dormer have identical dimensions, the two sections of each roof do not. One roof section is slightly longer and wider than the other to allow for overlapping. Sand the edges of all the pieces.

Roof opening

Fig. 42

Dormer dimensions

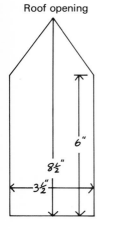

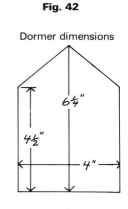

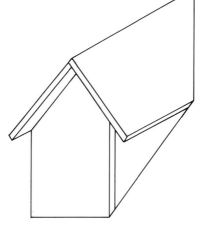

Cut the three dormer window openings to the dimensions shown in Fig. 43, using the window-cutting technique. Clamp the wood firmly and proceed carefully, as the sides of the openings are quite narrow and can easily split. Sand the edges lightly.

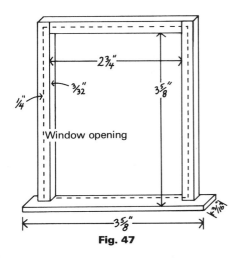

Fig. 47

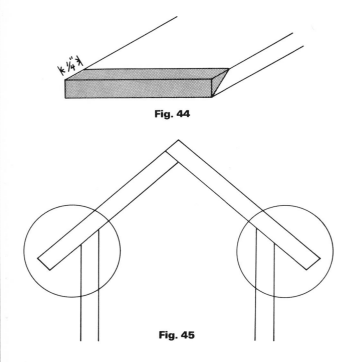

Fig. 44

Fig. 45

The last step prior to assembly of the dormers is to bevel several of the edges. This is done by ruling off the depth of the bevel, then clamping your work firmly and cutting the bevel with a hammer and chisel (see Fig. 44). The bottom edge of the dormer façade and the top edges of the dormer sides each get a 1/4″ bevel (see Fig. 45). Note that the tops of the two sides get beveled in reverse of each other to accommodate the opposite slants of the roof. The rear edges of both of the roof halves each get a 1/8″ bevel. After beveling, sand the chiseled edges to get them reasonably smooth. The dormer pieces are now finished and can be assembled by being glued together.

Next, we want to trim the edges and window frames of the dormers (see Fig. 46). For this we'll use 3/32″ basswood, 1/4″ wide. For the windowsills use 3/32″ basswood, 3/16″ wide. Cut the pieces, as shown in Fig. 47, and glue in place. The window molding overlaps the window opening to create a frame that will hold the window in place. When the trim has been applied to all three dormers, prime them inside and out, then paint them.

Now you're ready to construct all the windows of the house. They consist of clear acrylic to which wood grids are attached, creating the effect of panes. There are two window sizes: 3″ × 5 1/2″ for the first and second floors, and 3″ × 3 1/2″ for the dormers. Window-making instructions are given in the simplified-dollhouse plans (refer to Fig. 19).

After all of the windows have been completed, lay the façade windows aside. We'll be working with the dormer windows first. Insert these windows into the dormer openings. To hold them in place, apply molding around the inside of the windows, following the instructions given in the simplified-dollhouse plans (see Fig. 23).

Now you can attach the dormers to the roof, using an ample amount of white glue.

Before we can attach the dormers, we have to finish off the roof. First, bevel the chimney notch, as shown in Fig. 48, so that the chimney will fit flush against it when installed in position. Then trim the lower edge and both sides of the roof with 3/32″ × 1/4″ basswood strips (see Fig. 49). After that, paint the underside and edges of the roof. When the paint is dry, trim the upper edge of the roof with 1/32″ × 1/4″ basswood strips, stained the same shade you intend to stain the interior molding.

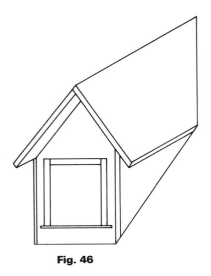

Fig. 46

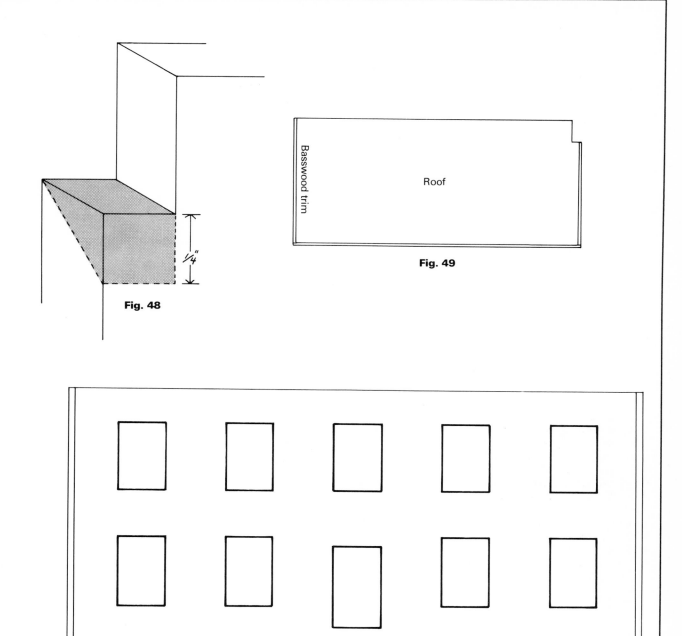

Basswood trim

Roof

Fig. 49

Fig. 48

Fig. 50

We'll be working on the façade next. First, we want to apply corner strips and to frame the front door and windows (Fig. 50). For the corner strips, cut two lengths of basswood 3/32″ × 1/2″ × 21″ long. Glue one to each edge of the façade so that it overlaps by 3/32″ (see Fig. 51). This is to allow for the 3/32″ thickness of the other two corner strips you'll be applying later, which will result in a perfect corner joint.

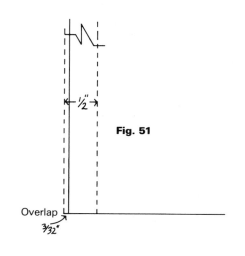

Fig. 51

Overlap
3/32″

For the door frames, use 3/32″ × 1/2″ basswood for the sides and top, and 3/32″ × 1/4″ basswood for the bottom. Cut these pieces to size, as shown in the simplified-dollhouse instructions, and glue them around the door opening (see Fig. 21). Frame the windows in the same way, referring to Fig. 22.

Now comes the siding, which requires both time and patience. You can obtain siding in sheet form, which is a time-saver, or you can cut it and apply it strip by strip, the way we chose to do it. We used sheets of 1/32″ basswood, 4″ wide × 22″ long, cut into strips 5/8″ wide. This width allows for a 1/8″ overlap and 1/2″ of exposed siding. We started siding the house 2 1/4″ up from the ground, level with the bottom of the front door. This gives the house the feeling of having a basement or foundation. The lower 2 1/4″ section can ultimately be bricked or painted a color to resemble stone or masonry.

There are two ways to apply siding to keep the strips perfectly parallel to one another. One method is to rule off 1/2″ guidelines on the façade, from bottom to top, and apply the siding by lining up the top of each siding strip with its guideline. If you choose to follow this method, rule your first line 2 1/4″ from the bottom. Then start your second line 5/8″ up from that. From then on, rule off 1/2″ lines.

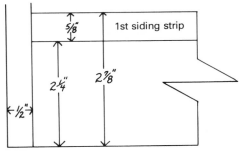

Fig. 52

Fig. 53

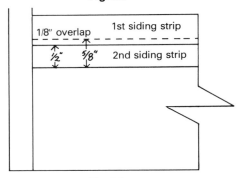

Fig. 54

The other method for applying siding is to line up each strip with the strip below, checking with a ruler from time to time to make sure each strip is the right height from side to side. This method, which we found to be more accurate, requires a compass or dividers. First rule off a line 2 7/8″ up from the bottom of the façade. This will be the top of your first strip of siding (see Fig. 52). Apply a thin coat of contact cement to the back of the siding strip and the corresponding area of the façade. Let the cement dry, then join the strip to the façade. Contact-cemented surfaces bond instantly, so position the strip carefully before attaching it. Then apply cement to the next strip and area of the façade 1/2″ above the top of the first siding strip. Take your compass or dividers and make tiny guide marks 1/2″ up from the bottom edge of the first siding strip (see Fig. 53); this is the guideline for the lower edge of the next siding strip. When the cement is dry, attach the second siding strip, as shown in Fig. 54. This strip will overlap the first one by 1/8″. Handle the entire façade in this way, carefully cutting the strips to fit snugly around windows and doors as you encounter them. Remember, siding requires time and patience, but the gratification you'll receive from viewing your finished work will more than compensate.

After the siding is completed, prime, then paint the façade. When the paint is dry, turn the façade over, lay it flat, and insert all of the windows into the window openings. To hold them permanently in place, apply molding made of basswood strips 1/32″ thick. Refer to the simplified-dollhouse instructions (see Fig. 23).

Now attach the front door. First mark the position of the screw holes. Use an awl or the point of a thin nail to start the hole, then screw the door on. Open and close it to check the fit. If it's too snug in any spot, lightly sand that area until the fit is smooth. Then touch up any paint you may have sanded off.

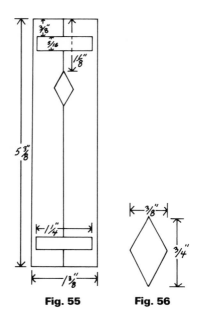

Fig. 55   **Fig. 56**

The last step in completing the façade is to make and attach the shutters. These are made from 3/32″ basswood, 1/16″ wide × 5 3/8″ long (see Fig. 55). Cut thirty-six of these pieces (four for each window) and sand them smooth. The shutters can remain solid, but if you like the appearance of the diamond-shaped openings (as in Fig. 55), cut a template out of thin cardboard or basswood to the dimensions shown in Fig. 56, trace it on each pair of shutters, top and bottom, and cut out the shape with your knife. Join the two halves of each shutter together with a thin coat of white glue applied to the edges. To make the cross pieces, take your 1/32″ basswood and cut thirty-six strips, each 5/16″ × 1 1/4″, and glue them into position, as shown in Fig. 55. When the shutters are finished, prime and paint them. Finally, attach the shutters to the windows by using a light coating of contact cement applied along the sides of the window frames and the corresponding portion of the rear of the shutter.

Your façade is now finished, although you might want to add some decorative touches, such as a simulated lamp on either side of the front door. We'll build the steps leading to the front door at a later stage in the project.

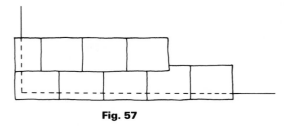

Fig. 57

Shingling the roof is another job that demands patience but delivers big rewards. We used cedar shingles measuring 1 5/8″ × 1 1/2″ and applied them side by side, alternating the rows, as shown in Fig. 57. Start by applying the bottom row of shingles, using contact cement, and overlapping the edge of the roof slightly at the sides and bottom. Now draw guidelines running the length of the roof, at 1″ intervals; these indicate the upper edges of the shingle rows and will result in a 1/2″ overlap of each row. Alternate the rows by starting the second row with a half shingle, as shown. When you encounter the dormers, you'll have to cut the shingles to fit against them.

Once you've finished shingling the roof, shingle the dormers in the same way, starting at the lower edge of each dormer roof section and working up toward the peak. To shingle the peaks of the dormers, cut shingles into 1 1/2″ × 1/2″ pieces, with the grain running lengthwise. Then apply them, as shown in Fig. 58, starting from the front and working back toward the main roof. When the entire roof and dormers are shingled, put the roof aside.

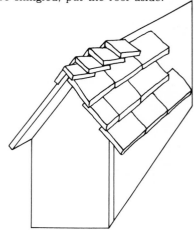

Fig. 58

The next step is to make the chimney. In Williamsburg Colonials, the chimneys were exceptionally large and handsome structures, one of the most distinguishing features of the house. They were frequently set outside, their massive brickwork lending a feeling of great strength and domestic comfort, and enhancing the exterior architecture. On a dollhouse such a chimney adds a great deal of character, especially by comparison with the more familiar "mock" chimney that perches on the peak of the roof. Our chimney is a modification of a Williamsburg design; it retains most of the handsome lines, particularly in its upper part, but we've eliminated some of the complex angles of the lower brickwork.

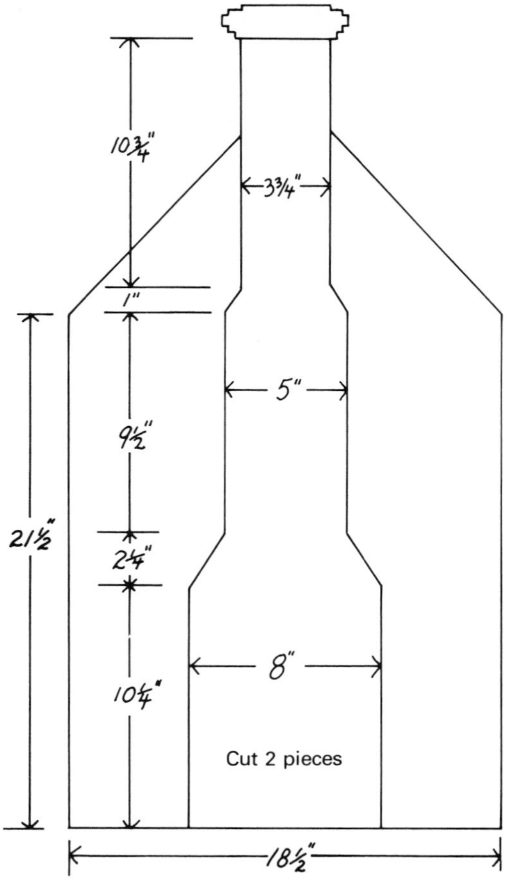

Cut 2 pieces

Fig. 59

A.

B.

C.

D.

E.

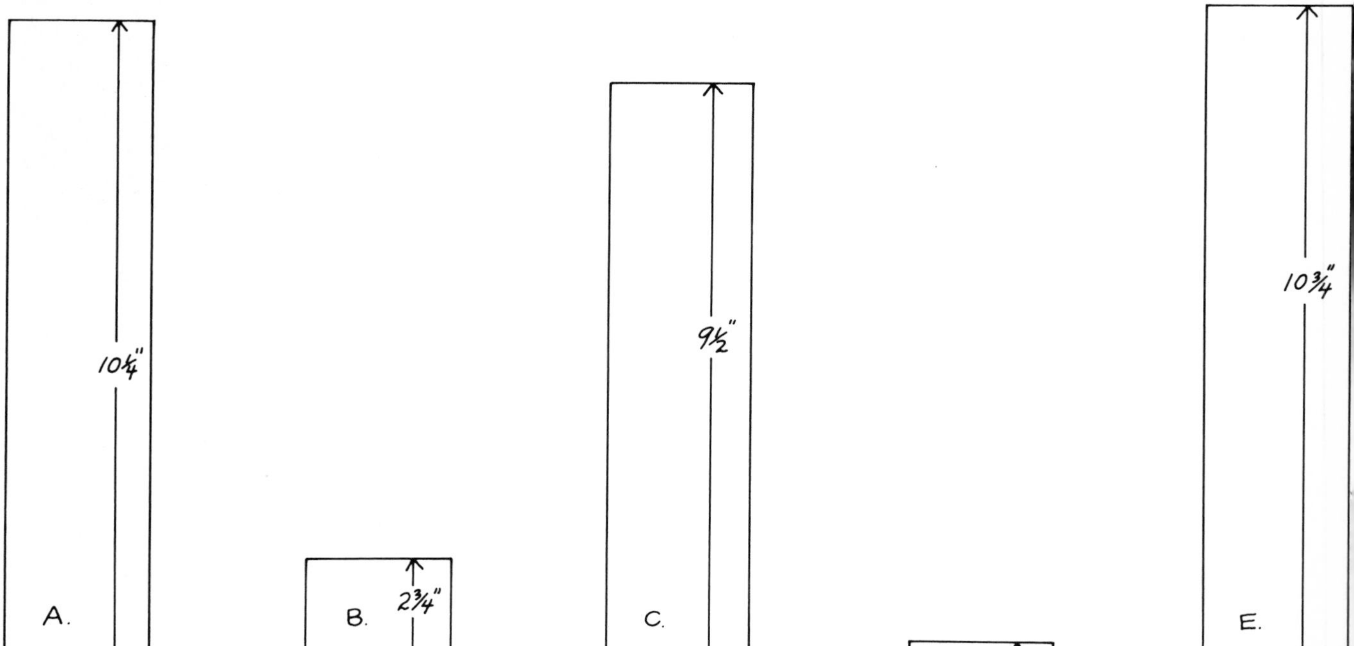

Fig. 60

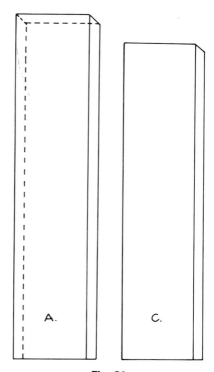

Fig. 61

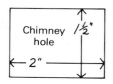

Fig. 63

The chimney is made of 1/4″ and 1/2″ plywood, which [ar]e plastered and painted after assembling; the resulting look [is] most satisfying. To construct the chimney, first cut two [pi]eces of 1/4″ plywood, for the front and back, to the dimen-[si]ons shown in Fig. 59, then sand the edges smooth. For the [si]des, cut two pieces of each of the five shapes shown in Fig. [60]. Bevel the edges of side pieces A and C, as shown in Fig. [6]1. Then glue the chimney pieces together. Large rubber [ba]nds can be used as clamps to hold the pieces together [w]hile drying.

Details of chimney—top section

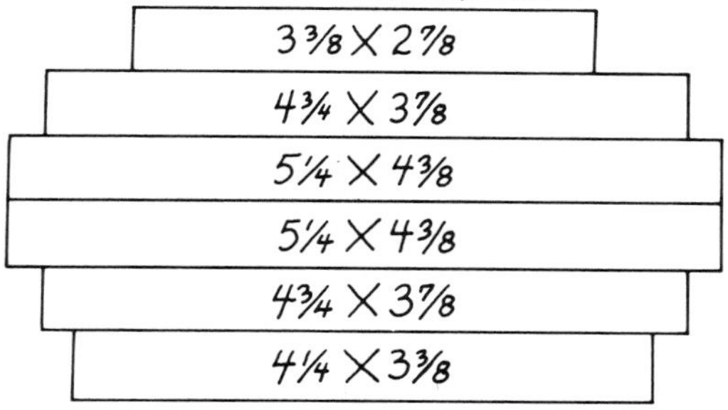

3⅜ × 2⅞
4¾ × 3⅞
5¼ × 4⅜
5¼ × 4⅜
4¾ × 3⅞
4¼ × 3⅜

Fig. 62

To make the chimney top, take your 1/2″ plywood and [cu]t six pieces to the dimensions shown in Fig. 62, then sand [the] edges smooth. If you choose to have an opening in the [ch]imney, rule a rectangle 2″ × 1 1/2″ (see Fig. 63) in the [ce]nter of each of the six pieces, then cut this section out of [ea]ch piece, using the usual window-cutting technique. Glue [th]e pieces together, starting with the two largest pieces in the [mi]ddle, then centering the other pieces (see Fig. 62).

To finish the chimney we applied plaster of Paris to the three exposed sides and the upper portion of the fourth side where it extends above the roof. The plaster fills in some of the irregularities at the corners and imparts an interesting look of its own that gives a feeling of age. When the plaster is dry, sand it smooth. Glue the top section in place, centering it over the main body of the chimney. Lastly, paint the entire chimney brick red.

To attach the chimney, first stand it in place alongside the house and make guidelines by tracing off its shape on the side of the house. Then apply a liberal amount of glue to the chimney and attach it to the house.

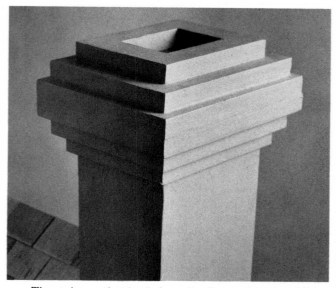

The staircase that leads from the first to the second floor plus the second-floor landing comes next. Follow the stair-case-building instructions given for the simplified dollhouse (see Figs. 23–25), but don't install the staircase after you've built it because first you must build and attach the balus-trade.

To make the balustrade, take the 22″ length of handrail and saw one end at a 54° angle (see Fig. 64), using your protractor to determine the angle. Then measure off 14″ along the top edge of the handrail and saw at a 36° angle. Take your 3/8″ × 3/8″ basswood and saw a piece 3 3/8″ in length for the newel post (see Fig. 65). Next make the balus-ters, which can be either cut from 1/8″ or 3/16″ dowels or bought as handsome, ready-made turnings. If you'll be using dowels, cut thirteen pieces each measuring 2 7/8″ in length; then cut the top end of each dowel at a 54° angle. If you use turned balusters, measure off 2 7/8″ from the bottom and cut off the surplus at the top at a 54° angle (see Fig. 66). Then paint or stain the newel post, handrail, and balusters.

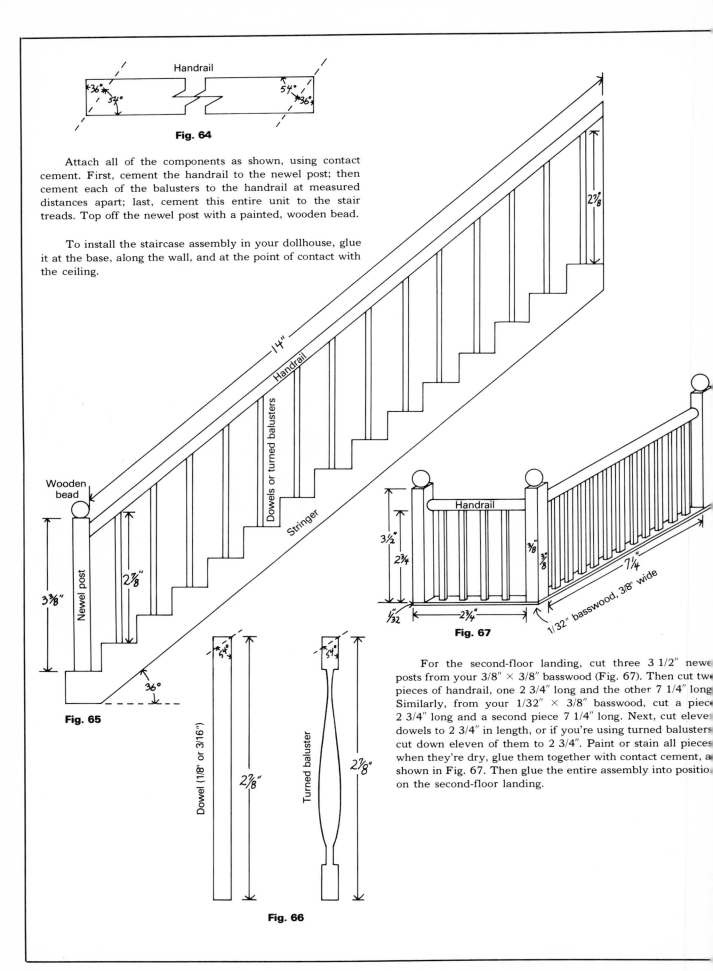

Handrail

Fig. 64

Attach all of the components as shown, using contact cement. First, cement the handrail to the newel post; then cement each of the balusters to the handrail at measured distances apart; last, cement this entire unit to the stair treads. Top off the newel post with a painted, wooden bead.

To install the staircase assembly in your dollhouse, glue it at the base, along the wall, and at the point of contact with the ceiling.

Wooden bead

Newel post

Handrail

Dowels or turned balusters

Stringer

14″

2⅞″

3⅜″

2⅞″

36°

Fig. 65

Handrail

3½″

2¾″

⅜″ ⅜″

7¼″

1/32″ basswood, 3/8″ wide

1/32″

2¾″

Fig. 67

Dowel (1/8″ or 3/16″)

2⅞″

54°

Turned baluster

2⅞″

54°

Fig. 66

For the second-floor landing, cut three 3 1/2″ newel posts from your 3/8″ × 3/8″ basswood (Fig. 67). Then cut two pieces of handrail, one 2 3/4″ long and the other 7 1/4″ long. Similarly, from your 1/32″ × 3/8″ basswood, cut a piece 2 3/4″ long and a second piece 7 1/4″ long. Next, cut eleven dowels to 2 3/4″ in length, or if you're using turned balusters, cut down eleven of them to 2 3/4″. Paint or stain all pieces when they're dry, glue them together with contact cement, as shown in Fig. 67. Then glue the entire assembly into position on the second-floor landing.

We now come to the lighting system—a step that really separates one dollhouse from another. When done carefully and realistically, miniature lighting adds a touch of magic to your dollhouse in a way that nothing else can. Suddenly the house comes to life as if it were inhabited.

There are many ways to wire a dollhouse, but by far the most intelligent and satisfying is the method advocated by Ed Leonard of Illinois Hobbycraft. Our lighting system is based entirely on Mr. Leonard's instructions.

Before you start, you have to make a decision about how many and what kind of ceiling fixtures you intend to have, as well as the number of wall outlets, if any (see Chapter 11). This will determine the size of transformer you'll need. For this house, we chose to have an overhead light in every room except the small, upstairs bedroom—a total of six

fixtures in all. In addition, we installed two wall outlets, one in the living room and the other in the small, upstairs bedroom. To power this many units, we needed a 12-volt, 1200-milliampere transformer. For an extra measure of safety, we connected the transformer to a fuse holder containing a fuse rated at 1500 milliamperes. Laying the house on its side to gain access to the base, we installed these two units—transformer and fuse holder—together with a terminal strip in the hollow base of our dollhouse. A second terminal strip was placed in the attic and was later hidden by a simple window seat that we covered it with.

Placing these components and determining the path of the wiring is easier once you understand the principles of dollhouse wiring. The information that follows, distilled from Ed Leonard's invaluable technical bulletins, with his kind permission, will give you a good education in this area.

LIGHTS AND FIXTURES

Two types of bulbs are available for use in miniature lighting fixtures: screw-base bulbs and grain-of-wheat bulbs. Of these two, the only one which can be applied to fixtures and lamps which are accurately scaled and have a realistic appearance is the grain-of-wheat bulb. Grain-of-wheat bulbs do not screw into sockets but, instead, are equipped with two tails of wire, called "lead wires" or simply "leads", which are connected directly to the transformer or circuit wires. The elimination of bulky sockets allows the fixtures to be more compact and therefore more realistic but inhibits easy replacement of the bulb. It is, therefore, imperative that the miniature electric lamps and fixtures chosen have a voltage rating which will assure the absolute maximum possible life. Illinois Hobbycraft fixtures, when used with an Illinois Hobbycraft transformer, have a minimum guaranteed life of 10,000 hours and a probable life far in excess of that.

WIRE

Two types of wire are available: solid wire and stranded wire. Solid wire is made from a single piece of copper which is extruded to a small diameter and covered with insulation. Stranded wire is made from a number of fine wire strands twisted together to form a larger wire, in much the same way strands of hemp are twisted to make a rope. Either type of wire may be used for dollhouse wiring. However, stranded wire is more flexible than solid wire, is less liable to "kink" during installation and is more resistant to breakage which may result from "knicks" and vibration.

The wiring which is used to connect the bulbs, lamps and other devices to the transformer may be divided into two classes: feed wiring and circuit wiring. Feed wiring is that which supplies or "feeds" electricity from the transformer to several floors of a dollhouse or to a number of circuits. Circuit wiring is the wiring which connects the bulbs, fixtures, wall sockets, etc. to the feed wiring or, sometimes, directly to the transformer. Feed wires are usually heavier (thicker) than the wires used for circuit wiring because they must carry more electricity.

A multi-story dollhouse lighting system necessitates connecting a large number of wires to the power source. One two-story wiring arrangement is shown in the sketch "Two-story Dollhouse Wiring." In this drawing, because of the number of circuit wires involved, feed wires have been extended from the transformer to terminal strips which, in turn, provide for connecting the many circuit wires. The terminal strips simply provide a convenient means for collecting the many circuit wires together and connecting them to the feed wires. They have no electrical effect on the system

(From Illinois Hobbycraft technical bulletin.)

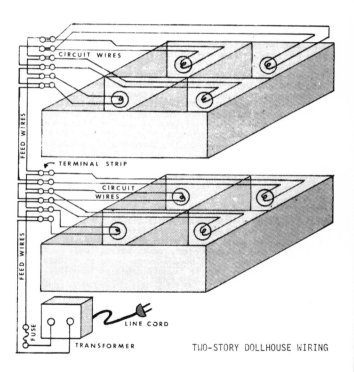

TWO-STORY DOLLHOUSE WIRING

PLANNING THE INSTALLATION

Before beginning the installation of the lamp and power source, it is advisable to determine the locations for both and the route which the wire will take to connect the two. In a miniature room, the transformer or battery pack may be hidden behind the false wall, under a piece of furniture or sometimes, in the ceiling or roof. In a dollhouse, where a transformer is almost always used, the most likely place to hide it is in the attic or under a stairway.

A primary objective in the installation of miniature lighting is to achieve the most realistic appearance possible. This is best accomplished by using the smallest wire obtainable and running that wire in such a way that it is concealed from the casual viewer. 28 gauge (#28) vinyl insulated wire is excellent for this purpose. This wire measures a

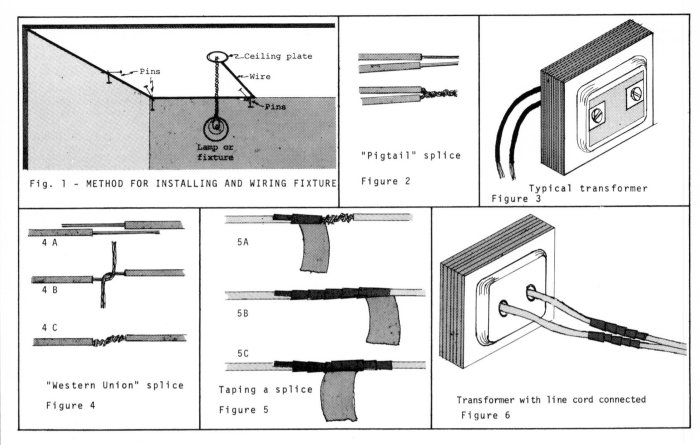

Fig. 1 - METHOD FOR INSTALLING AND WIRING FIXTURE

"Pigtail" splice
Figure 2

Typical transformer
Figure 3

"Western Union" splice
Figure 4

Taping a splice
Figure 5

Transformer with line cord connected
Figure 6

little less than 1/32 inch in diameter and can be effectively hidden from view if it is run in the angle formed by the intersection of a wall and the ceiling or the intersection of two walls. Figure 1 illustrates this method of running the wires.

As shown in Figure 1, the lamp is hung from the ceiling by means of a "ceiling plate". The ceiling plate may be any small, dish shaped disc. Certain jewelry findings are ideal for this purpose. The ceiling plate need only be deep enough to hide the two small "pigtail" splices which will connect your lamp to the feed wires.

PREPARATION FOR INSTALLATION OF THE LAMP

Estimate the length of wire which will be required to reach from your lamp to the power source. Measure and cut two pieces of wire this length. Splice these "feed wires" to the lamp as follows:

(1)   Remove 1/4 to 1/2 inch of insulation from the ends of the lamp wires and the feed wires.
(2)   Slip the ceiling plate over the lamp wires.
(3)   Check to see if the lamp shade will fit over the ceiling plate so that it may be installed at a later time. If t does not fit, install the shade now.
(4)   Hold one lamp wire and one feed wire side-by-side (as shown in Figure 2) so that the ends of the insulation are even. While holding the wires thus, twist the bare ends of the wires tightly together.
(5)   Solder the wires to assure a good mechanical and electrical connection.
(6)   Repeat steps 3, 4 and 5 with the other feed and lamp wires
(7)   Cut off excess wire from the splices to make them as short as possible (about 1/8" long) so that the can be concealed under the ceiling plate later. Be careful not to cut off the entire soldered portion of the splice.
(8)   Insulate the splices. In ordinary electrical work, tape is used to insulate splices. However, in order to keep the over-all size of these low-voltage splices as small as poss-

ible, silicone cement can be used for insulation.

To insulate the wires: squeeze a tube of silicone cement so that the cement is forced up into the neck of the tube. Insert one splice into the neck of the tube until the cement covers the entire splice and part of the insulation. Withdraw the wires slowly. Inspect the splice to see that the bare wires are completely covered with silicone. Repeat the process with the other splice.

Set the spliced wires aside and allow the silicone cement to dry thoroughly.

TRANSFORMER

Feed wires

Line cord

"Pigtail" splices hidden under ceiling plate

Twisted "drop cord"

To other lamps or bulbs if required

115v wall socket

Lamp or Chandelier

Fig. 7 - WIRING DIAGRAM FOR LAMP OR CHANDELIER

CONNECTING THE TRANSFORMER LINE CORD

To connect the transformer to the wall socket of your house, you'll need a "line cord" (Illinois Hobbycraft part #630-001). A vinyl plastic insulated cord, such as may be found at most hardware stores, is easiest to work with. If you can't find a vinyl plastic cord, buy a vinyl plastic extension and cut off the socket (not the plug!).

(From Illinois Hobbycraft technical bulletin.)

Your transformer will probably look like the one illustrated in Figure 3. It may or may not have "feet" for fastening it in place with screws. In either case, it is best to fasten it in place with silicone cement.

The two screws on the front of the transformer are for connecting the feed wires which will run to your lamp or fixture. The large wires coming out of the back of the transformer connect to the line cord which plugs into the 115 volt wall socket in your house.

To connect the cord to your transformer:
(1)   Remove the insulation for a distance of about one inch from the ends of the line cord and the transformer wires.
(2)   If the line cord is to go through the side of your dollhouse or miniature room, drill a hole and put the cord through that hole before starting to connect it to the transformer.
(3)   Hold one wire from the line cord and one wire from the transformer next to each other, as shown in Figure 4A. Twist the wires across each other, as shown in Figure 4B and continue wrapping the wires, as shown in Figure 4C. When you have finished the first pair of wires, splice the other line cord and transformer wires together the same way. Trim off any excess wire which does not fit into the splice area.
(4)   Solder the splices you've just made, to assure a good mechanical and electrical connection. A loose connection can "arc" and might cause a fire.

After soldering, each splice must be individually taped to prevent a "short circuit" or possible shock to the user. Use vinyl plastic electrical tape. Cut off a piece about six to eight inches long. Start wrapping the tape, on top of the insulation, at one end of the splice, as shown in Figure 5A. Continue wrapping until the tape extends over the insulation at the other end of the splice. See Figure 5B. Each wrap of tape should overlap the preceeding wrap by about one half the width of the tape. Be sure to stretch the tape and pull it tight as you wrap.

When the first layer of tape has been applied, continue wrapping the tape back in the opposite direction to apply a second layer to the splice. (Figure 5C) Again, be sure to stretch the tape and pull it tight as you wrap. Continue wrapping the second layer until the tape extends over the insulation.

Tape the second splice in the same manner. When you've finished, your transformer should look like that illustrated in Figure 6. When both splices have been taped, you may wrap a layer of tape over both of them to keep them together and to improve the appearance.

The transformer may now be fastened in place in its proper location.

INSTALLING THE LAMP

After the silicone cement used to insulate the splices has dried completely, slide the ceiling plate out to the end of the lamp wires. Install the shade at this time, if required. Arrange the splices so that they can be concealed under the ceiling plate. Fasten the ceiling plate to the ceiling, being sure that the feed wires are extended in the proper direction. Regardless of the method used to fasten the ceiling plate to the ceiling, it will be accomplished with greater ease if the doll house or room is first turned upside-down. Using nails or screws to fasten the ceiling plate to the ceiling often results in an unsightly appearance. It is recommended that the ceiling plate be fastened with silicone cement. If the room has not been turned upside-down, the ceiling plate will have to be held in position until the cement dries. It is best held in position with a piece of thin wood strip (about 1/16" thick) "bowed" between the ceiling plate and the floor as shown in Figure 8.

Figure 8

Using a bowed stick to hold the ceiling plate in place.

When installing the ceiling plate, be careful that the splices are not crushed between the ceiling plate and the ceiling. After the ceiling plate is securely fastened, test the lamp by connecting the feed wires, temporarily, to the power source. If the lamp fails to light, check to see that the line cord is plugged into the wall. If the power source is plugged in, the cause of failure may be either of two things: (1) One or both of the splices have become disconnected. This is especially likely to happen if you did not solder the splices. (2) The bare wires of both splices are touching each other or are touching the ceiling plate. Either of these will cause a "short circuit" which will prevent the electricity from reaching the bulb.

After the lamp has been tested, the feed wires may be run to the power source via their final route. If the wire is to go through a wall or walls, drill small holes in the proper locations before beginning to run the wire.

To run the wire, stretch the wires from the ceiling plate, along the ceiling, to the rear wall of the room. Insert a straight pin up into the ceiling, close to the wall, for the wire to bend around. Then, insert another pin into the wall, next to the first pin and close to the ceiling, to hold the wire tight against the ceiling. (See Figure 1) Next, stretch the wire to the corner of the room. Insert pins to bend and hold the wire, if required. Continue running and pinning the wire until the power source location is reached. When the power source is reached, connect the wires to the power source to ascertain that the fixture operates properly.

After testing the lamp, check the wires to see that they are taut and held firmly in place along the run. Apply a coat of Sobo craft glue or other transparent glue over the entire length of the wires to hold them in place. This is most easily done with a glue gun. If no glue gun is available, use the flat side of a toothpick to apply and spread the glue. Allow the glue to dry for at least 24 hours before removing the pins.

SAFETY

A dollhouse or miniature room should never be wired so that the tiny bulbs are lighted directly from the 115 volts which is obtained from the wall outlet of your home. Dollhouse and miniature room lighting systems which are to operate from the 115 volt outlet should always be equipped with a suitable transformer to "step the voltage down" to a lower, safe level. The direct use of 115 volts to light miniature bulbs presents a considerable hazard in that it may cause a fire, serious injury or even death. The argument is sometimes advanced that tiny bulbs and fixtures may be safely connected directly to 115 volts if they are "wired in series". This simply is not true. Low voltage bulbs, wire and other components are not designed to withstand the stress of 115 volts and may, as a result, "break down" when connected to that voltage. Furthermore, if a finger or hand is introduced into such a series-wired circuit, its owner may receive a full 115 volt shock.

It must be pointed out that even the best-designed system, incorporating the best and safest components, may become dangerous if it is improperly used or abused. For this reason it is necessary to caution against allowing children to tamper with the fixtures, wiring or cords used in any miniature lighting system.

LIBRARY LAMP.

TECHNICAL BULLETIN 4K11 - SOLDERING

Many persons avoid the use of a soldering iron and put off learning to solder because it is thought to be too difficult. In fact, soldering is easily mastered and, once learned, opens a whole new world of adventure in making metal fixtures and fittings for dollhouses and miniature rooms. All that's needed is a clear understanding of the basics involved and a little practice.

Soldering is a method for bonding two or more pieces of metal together. It is different from glueing in that solder penetrates the surfaces to be joined in such a way that they become practically inseparable. Only certain metals are susceptible to soldering. The easiest to solder are brass, copper and tin. Other metals are either very difficult to solder or can not be soldered by ordinary means.

Solder is a soft metal which is primarily an alloy of tin and lead. It melts at a temperature of about 700 degrees Farenheit. Solder types are referred to by the tin-lead proportions they contain. "60-40" or "63-37" solder is good for ordinary electrical work. Solder is obtainable, in the form of wire, at any hardware store. For miniature work it is best to use the smallest size available: 1/16 inch diameter or smaller. Always use "rosin core" solder. The other kind (acid core) will cause connections to corrode at some later date.

Soldering irons come in many sizes, according to the amount of heat they produce. This heat producing capability is expressed in "watts". For dollhouses and mini-work, the best size is between 25 and 50 watts. The tip of the iron should be about 3/16 inch in diameter. The use of a soldering "gun" is not recommended because operation of a soldering gun requires the use of one hand to squeeze the trigger. A little experience will show that on many occasions it is best to have both hands free when soldering small splices.

Figure 1 illustrates the various parts of a soldering iron. On low-cost irons, the barrel and handle are usually permanently joined. However, the tip should be removeable on any good soldering iron. Since, after some lengthy use, the tip may corrode or oxidize to the point where replacement is necessary, it's a good idea to get a soldering iron with a removeable tip.

The primary purpose of the soldering iron is to heat the "work" which is to be soldered to the temperature at which solder melts. This permits the solder to "flow" onto the surface of the work and make the required bond. In order to pass heat to the work, the soldering iron tip must be shiny or "tinned". Soldering irons which have a nickel-plated tip stay shiny longer so we recommend the purchase of an iron with such a tip.

A collar, such as that shown in Fig. 1, is useful because it permits setting the iron down with the tip elevated off the work surface. This eliminates the need for a stand and places the tip in a good position for soldering small splices.

PREPARATION

Before starting to solder, be sure your soldering iron is in proper condition. The tip of the iron should be shaped like that shown in figure 2. If necessary, file the end of the tip until the pyramidal shape is obtained. During the soldering operation the tip is kept shiny by coating it with solder. When the tip is so coated it is said to be "tinned". Cleaning the tip of a soldering iron and putting on the coating of solder is called "tinning the iron".

While soldering, it will be necessary, from time to time, to wipe off the tip in order to remove the black residue and restore the shiny characteristics. Professionals may use more sophisticated means, but, a pad of old burlap, denim or other such coarse material, about 4" square, is most useful for wiping the tip.

Plug the line cord into the wall outlet and allow the iron to come to full heat. Full heat has been reached when the solder melts easily on the tip of the iron and flows freely.

If you have had to file the tip in order to obtain the correct shape, the tip will require tinning after it has been heated. Apply the solder to the tip of the iron, allowing it to run freely, coating all four sides of the tip. Then, using quick strokes, wipe the tip on the wiping pad. Repeat these operations until a shiny tip is obtained.

IT IS EXTREMELY IMPORTANT THAT THE TIP BE KEPT SHINY AND TINNED DURING SOLDERING OPERATIONS. THE IRON CAN NOT DELIVER HEAT TO THE WORK THROUGH THE SCALE AND CORROSION WHICH FORMS ON THE TIP. IF THE WORK IS NOT HEATED TO THE PROPER TEMPERATURE, A "COLD SOLDER JOINT" WILL RESULT. IF THE SOLDER DOES NOT RUN FREELY ON THE METAL BEING SOLDERED, OR, IF THE SOLDER "LUMPS UP", THE WORK IS NOT BEING HEATED TO A HIGH ENOUGH TEMPERATURE.

SOLDERING

Figure 3 illustrates a method to be used for soldering wires at the bench. Place the soldering iron in a convenient position with the handle facing away from you. Take the twisted wires in your left hand and hold the solder wire in your right hand. Place the bare wire of the splice flat on one side of the pyramidal portion of the tip. Hold the splice in this position just long enough for it to heat up before applying the solder. On small splices this should be about two seconds. Then apply the solder wire at the place where the bare wire is touching the tip, near the middle of the splice. The whole operation must be done very rapidly. If the splice is held on the tip too long, the insulation will shrink back from the splice and leave bare wire exposed. When a splice has been properly soldered, the coating is very thin and the form of the wires can be seen through it. Excess solder does not improve the quality of the splice.

When wires are to be soldered inside of a dollhouse or at some location away from the bench, the same technique is used. In these cases, when the wires are fixed in place by virtue of being attached to a fixture or to the internal wiring, the solder and iron must be moved to the work. For these cases, hold the soldering iron in your right hand and the solder wire in your left. Touch the tip of the iron to the wires to be soldered and hold it there to heat the work. Then, quickly, touch the solder wire to the point where the soldering iron tip and wires meet. Always apply the solder wire on the "high side" so that it will run toward the splice. As soon as the solder has flowed into the splice, remove the solder and the iron.

The use of a "paste flux" can be of great aid in making soldering easier. This material is a brown, greasy looking substance which is sold in hardware stores. In use, a very small amount of flux is applied to the wires of the splice before the splice is heated with the soldering iron. The heat of the soldering iron then causes the flux to "boil" and clean the wires so that they attract the solder better.

Copyright 1974 ILLINOIS HOBBYCRAFT, Inc.

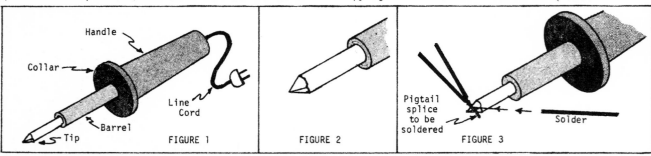

Handle
Collar
Line Cord
Tip
Barrel
FIGURE 1

FIGURE 2

Pigtail splice to be soldered
Solder
FIGURE 3

(From Illinois Hobbycraft technical bulletin.)

Once your house is wired, you can attach the façade. Follow the instructions given in the plans for the simplified dollhouse (see Fig. 28). Then cut and attach the remaining corner strips, using 3/32″ × 1/2″ basswood, and apply strips along the roof line (Fig. 68). Finally, glue the roof supports in place.

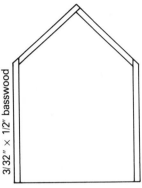

Fig. 68

Your dollhouse is now finished on the outside except for the front steps, which you can build at any time, following the instructions given in the simplified-dollhouse plans (see Fig. 30). The last few touches involve trimming the interior. All trim pieces should be stained or painted before you install them, of course. The first step is to frame the four interior doorways, using 3/32″ × 7/16″ basswood, as shown in Fig. 69. The 7/16″ width will permit the frames to extend 3/32″ past the walls on either side. Next, cut and install the threshold piece in each doorway, as shown in Fig. 69, beveling the front and back edges slightly. Then apply 3/32″ × 3/8″ basswood around the sides and the tops of the door frames on both sides of each doorway, as shown in Fig. 70.

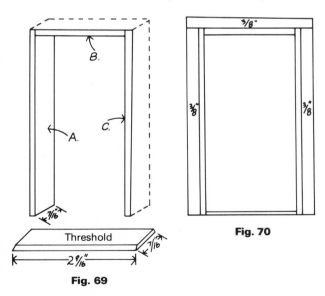

Fig. 69

Fig. 70

You are now ready to apply siding strips to the two sides of the dollhouse. Follow the same technique that you used in siding the façade. When finished, prime, then paint the sides.

Next, attach the roof by gluing it into position on the roof supports.

Once the doors are framed off, you can apply the baseboard molding to all rooms. We used 1/32″ basswood strips, 5/16″ wide. After that, trim all the ceiling intersections and the edges of the attic supports with 5/32″ cove molding. Chair railing and wainscoting can be added to any of the rooms as desired. As a last touch, we trimmed the exposed plywood edges of the walls and floors with basswood strips 1/32″ thick. Veneer tape works equally well.

A final suggestion: You might want to mount the dollhouse on a turntable so that it can be rotated freely from front to back. Turntables can be bought ready-made at many miniature shops, or you can build one yourself from components that can be purchased at hardware stores.

Now step back and admire your work. The dollhouse you've just completed should be the envy of everyone who sees it. In fact, we suggest having a housewarming party to show it off.

Bulletin board with typical announcements of miniature shows.

CHAPTER 15

GETTING DEEPER INTO THE HOBBY

The collecting of miniatures, long a solitary hobby, is today a shared and organized one that allows for participation in a wide range of related activities. Today's miniaturist can subscribe to a host of specialized publications, amass a small library of books on the subject, attend a dizzying number of shows and exhibits, join clubs, attend classes and lectures, and even participate in miniaturist tours of Europe, visiting museums, shops, and private collections there. All of this activity serves to widen the scope of the hobby, making it more interesting and rewarding to a greater number of people than ever before.

SHOWS

Nothing captures the excitement of collecting miniatures as much as a miniature show and sale. Here, in one location, you come face-to-face and elbow-to-elbow with fellow enthusiasts, and only then do you begin to get a faint hint of the high degree of interest in this relatively new hobby. At first exposure, there seems to be something unreal about being surrounded by a vast array of "playthings" with virtually no children around. But you soon become mesmerized by the sheer variety and abundance of miniature objects, and suddenly you've made the transition from spectator to participant.

Attending a miniature show is like shopping in a department store of miniatures, with more objects gathered under one roof than you could possibly see otherwise. Most shows are held in the spring and fall. To find out what's going on in your area, contact your nearest miniature shop. They're sure to know about forthcoming local events.

Miniature show held at the spectacular Lockwood Mathews stone mansion in Norwalk, Connecticut.

PUBLICATIONS

Some are monthly, some are quarterly, one is annual, all are interesting—each of the publications catering to miniaturists has a charm all its own. The following is a brief review of, with subscription information on, the more familiar of these publications. Prices are subject to change, of course, so you might want to drop a note to any publication that interests you in order to confirm its subscription rates.

In addition to the miniaturist publications, we have included several general crafts or hobby periodicals because of the frequent attention they devote to miniatures, and two others that deal with related subject matter.

MINIATURE GAZETTE

This is the largest, handsomest, and most professional of all the regular publications catering to miniaturists—and no wonder, for it is the official publication of the National Association of Miniature Enthusiasts (N.A.M.E.) and draws its material from that organization's many members throughout the country. Credit goes to Editor Robert Von Fliss for turning out a publication that captures all the excitement and variety of the hobby.

Miniature Gazette is the definitive word on what's happening in the world of miniatures. Each issue is filled with information about shows and events, in addition to interesting articles, photographs, and projects. But even if the *Gazette* had none of this, it would be worth subscribing to for the ads alone. Each issue is a virtual directory of suppliers, with many outstanding craftspeople represented among the advertisers.

Miniature Gazette is published quarterly and sent to all members of N.A.M.E. To become a member, send $8.00 to National Association of Miniature Enthusiasts, Box 2621, Brookhurst Center, Anaheim, California 92804.

NUTSHELL NEWS

This diminutive magazine (5 1/2″ × 8 1/2″) embodies all the charm, wit, warmth, and enthusiasm that one could hope for in a hobbyist's publication. *Nutshell News* was founded in 1970 by Catherine B. MacLaren, its editor and publisher, with the objective of informing its readers "all about miniature shops, rooms, furnishings, dealers and craftsmen."

Mrs. MacLaren's style is bouncy and clipped, and takes some getting used to, but that's all part of the fun. She is obviously a woman in love with her subject, and it rubs off on the reader. Contributing columnists supply articles on a wide range of miniature-related subjects, and a calendar of events keeps readers aware of what's happening, and where. Each issue is crammed with interesting ads from craftspeople and dealers, with many brochures to send for. The only shortcoming of *Nutshell News* is that it comes out only quarterly. One wishes it would arrive more often.

Subscription price is $5.00 annually for four issues ($1.00 for a sample copy); $7.50 for overseas. Send check to *Nutshell News,* 1035 Newkirk Drive, La Jolla, California 92037.

THE DOLLHOUSE
AND MINIATURE NEWS

When you subscribe to *The Dollhouse and Miniature News,* buy yourself a looseleaf binder because this publication consists of 8 1/2″ × 11″ pages, three-hole punched, and you're going to want to save each issue.

The Dollhouse and Miniature News is a most informative and highly readable monthly newsletter (not published in July and August)—the work of newspaperwoman and author Marion O'Brien. Along with interesting and well-researched articles, you'll find do-it-yourself projects, tips from experts, the latest news of the field, and many ads.

Subscription price is $7.00 (ten issues). Send check to #3 Orchard Lane, Kirkwood, Missouri 63122.

A.I.M.M. MOTT MINIATURE
WORKSHOP NEWS

This is easily the most ambitious workshop publication in the field, an impressively thick package of projects that comes out once a year and will keep you busy until the next volume arrives. The *Workshop News* is produced by the Mott family in memory of Allegra Mott, whose efforts helped create the National Association of Miniature Enthusiasts.

To give you some idea of the scope of its contents—a recent issue of the *Workshop News* included detailed instructions for building a kitchen range, kitchen cabinet, bedroom dresser, sideboard, icebox, upright piano, piano stool, chairs, and more.

Subscription price is $8.00. Send check to *A.I.M.M. Mott Miniature Workshop News,* P.O. Box 5514, Sunny Hills Station, Fullerton, California 92635.

THE MINIATURE MAGAZINE

Creative Crafts has published a separate magazine devoted entirely to miniatures, called *The Miniature Magazine.* Its 74-page first issue is an absolute "must" for miniaturists, an outstanding collection of articles and projects handled in a thoroughly professional manner, the work of Editor Sybil Harp. At present, *The Miniature Magazine* is an annual publication, but the editor hopes to be able to bring it out more frequently— and we hope so, too.

The Miniature Magazine is available for $1.00. Send to P.O. Box 700, Newton, New Jersey 07860.

THE BERRYHILL NEWS

This cozy little publication has evolved from a newsletter for children into a magazine for a family audience. Published six times a year under the guiding eye of its editor, Elizabeth Berry, *The Berryhill News* has attracted a great many subscribers who are relatively new to miniatures. The magazine nourishes these newcomers by offering background information on the mini-world along with its regular features, which include dollhouse "tours," miniature-making projects, book reviews, general articles, workshop pointers, and more.

Subscription price is $6.00 per year and includes a free gift; $9.00 per year for overseas airmail. Send check to *The Berryhill News,* P.O. Box 1308, Bozeman, Montana 59715.

MINIATURE MAKERS JOURNAL

This small-format quarterly publication is aimed at hobbyists who derive pleasure from creating their own miniatures. Each issue contains plans and photos for a number of different projects. A recent issue gave instructions for building several fireplaces, a porch swing, a Victorian chaise, and a Colonial hutch.

Other regular features are building tips, a review of new products for the miniaturist, a discussion of interesting tools, and a page of classified ads.

Subscription is $6.00 annually; $8.00 for overseas. Single-copy price is $2.00. Send check to *Miniature Makers Journal,* 409 S. First, Evansville, Wisconsin 53536.

FANTASY WORLD

Edited for "Dollers, Miniaturists and Crafters," this chatty, small-format publication contains news, articles, photos of interesting dollhouses, and an ample shopper's guide filled with ads from craftspeople and other suppliers. You'll also find do-it-yourself projects—a recent issue contained instructions for building a cradle and a scoop-candle sconce.

Fantasy World is published monthly. Subscription price is $5.00 per year; $6.00 for overseas. Send check to *Fantasy World,* Cresco, Pennsylvania 18326.

CREATIVE CRAFTS

Creative Crafts is a well-known magazine dedicated to craftspeople in general and covering an unbelievably wide range of interests: sand art, jewelry making, quilting, weaving, basketry, Christmas decorations, doll making—you name it. Although not strictly a miniaturist publication, *Creative Crafts* nevertheless devotes a considerable amount of attention to the subject of miniatures. In a recent issue, more than a third of the magazine pertained to miniatures, and each article was handled with intelligence and thoroughness. Highly readable and useful, it is a credit to its editor, Sybil Harp.

Creative Crafts is published bimonthly. Subscription price is $4.50; $5.00 for overseas. Single copies are 75¢. Send check to Circulation Manager, *Creative Crafts,* P.O. Box 700, Newton, New Jersey 07860.

EARLY AMERICAN LIFE

This magazine has nothing to do with miniatures but everything to do with Colonial life, a subject of considerable interest to most miniaturists. Published by the Early American Society, *Early American Life* is a richly produced bimonthly magazine covering all aspects of American social history, arts, crafts, furnishings, and architecture. The miniature-maker will find here a wealth of information and inspiration for projects.

Early American Life is provided to members of the Society. To join, send $6.00 to Early American Society, 3300 Walnut Street, Boulder, Colorado 80302.

HOBBIES

"The Magazine for Collectors," *Hobbies* is a voluminous (averaging 192 pages) and fascinating monthly magazine, edited by Pearl Ann Reeder. Dealing with a wide range of hobby areas, it covers the subject of miniatures in a regular column entitled "Miniaturia," which dates back to 1941, when O.C. Lightner, the publisher, decided to include a regular section in his publication to serve the growing number of collectors of tiny things, from scale models to oddities.

In 1943 the Lightner Publishing Corporation published a 329-page book entitled *Miniaturia; The World of Tiny Things.* Mr. Lightner was obviously a man of vision.

Subscription price is $6.00 per year; $7.00 in Canada; $7.50 for overseas. Send check to *Hobbies,* 1006 South Michigan Avenue, Chicago, Illinois 60605.

THE OLD-HOUSE JOURNAL

Another publication not specifically aimed at the miniaturist but of potential interest and utility is *The Old-House Journal.* Dollhouse-builders and lovers of domestic architecture will find this well-produced 8 1/2" × 11", three-hole-punched monthly publication a gold mine of useful information.

The Old-House Journal concerns itself with "renovation and maintenance ideas for the antique house." And while the word "house" refers to full-size houses, there's much that can be borrowed by the miniaturist. Carolyn Flaherty, the decorative arts editor, reports that a number of readers have used the decorating ideas from the *Journal* for their dollhouses.

Subscription price is $12.00 per year. Send check to *The Old-House Journal,* 199 Berkeley Place, Brooklyn, New York 11217.

CLUBS

The Cleveland Miniature Society, The Tiny Treasures Society (in Boston), Wichita Miniature Society, Mile High Miniature Club (in Denver)—wherever you live in the United States, there's likely to be a miniature club of some kind nearby. The best way to find out is to inquire at your nearest miniature shop; if there's a club in the neighborhood, they'll know about it.

Whatever local activities you participate in, you'll also want to join the biggest club of them all —the National Association of Miniature Enthusiasts (N.A.M.E.)—which will put you in touch with the world of miniatures on a national basis. Through their publication, *Miniature Gazette,* you'll be kept informed of activities throughout the year. A letter to N.A.M.E. might also help you locate a nearby club to join.

The benefits of participating in clubs are aptly summed up by James Harrell, N.A.M.E. President, in this excerpt from a letter to N.A.M.E. members: "The most important thing is that we who enjoy our hobby are gaining strength by way of our association through N.A.M.E. It has been proven that wherever we can encourage members to form clubs, we may further enjoy our hobby by sharing our mutual interests; and through the added strength of additional clubs, we are able to provide more local and regional events, which add materially to the total enjoyment for all of us who comprise N.A.M.E."

CLASSES AND LECTURES

Opportunities abound for miniaturists to learn more about their hobby by attending classes and lectures on collecting and creating miniatures. Sometimes these are sponsored by clubs, other times by shops and studios.

The Beehive Studio in Deerfield, Illinois, which conducts classes in the techniques of making miniature rooms and furniture, began several years ago as a decoupage shop. "In our continuing search for new dimensions," explains Laura Davis, the owner, "we introduced the use of miniatures into Vue d'Optique. This extension of three-dimensional pictures became so popular that the use of paper was soon discarded in favor of actual walls, floors, furniture, and accessories. Today, the Beehive Studio devotes all of its classes, sales, and creative energy to what we believe is the most fascinating and rewarding outgrowth of decoupage —miniature rooms."

New York City miniaturists are unusually fortunate in being able to benefit from the considerable energies of Kathryn Falk, owner of Mini Mundus. Like an impresario, Ms. Falk has orchestrated a rich program of activities for the interested miniaturist.

In addition to her lecture series, Kathryn Falk has also begun a program of miniature-making classes for hobbyists of all ages. Classes for adults are held in the afternoons and evenings, and special Saturday classes are held for children. My daughter, age twelve, who isn't inclined to volunteer for any more schooling than the law requires, eagerly participated in the Saturday program and came home after her first class ecstatically clutching a very professional-looking miniature hatbox and a trayful of jelly apples that she had made.

Mini Mundus

ANNOUNCING! MINIATURE MAKING CLASSES

TUESDAY AFTERNOONS - 2:00PM-4:00PM
TUESDAY EVENINGS- 6:30 PM-8:30PM
Given by Dorothy Wade- a miniature maker
for fifty years

    Planning a doll house
    Constructing and decorating a doll house
    Colonial decor and furnishings
    Federal and Empire decor and furnishings
    Chippendale decor and furnishings
    Victorian decor and furnishings
    Accessories and specialties

$10.00 per class

FOR CHILDREN: SATURDAY MORNINGS- 10:30PM-12:00PM
             SATURDAY AFTERNOONS- 1:30PM-3:00PM
Given by Linda de Ritter, Judy Faulkner and
Agnes Miri

    Constructing a doll house or shadow box
    Wood furniture and easy upholstery
    Ceramic foods
    Accessories for houses and stores
    Chandeliers, quilts, books
    Christmas accessories

$6.00 per class

    EDWARD ACEVEDO

Thursday afternoons, 4-6.
Thursday evenings, 7:30-9:30.
Woodworking and using power tools.
Creating fine miniature furniture.
$10.00 per class.

OMNIUM GATHERUM

Because we decided <u>not</u> to have a small unassum-
ing catalog, our OMNIUM GATHERUM-VOL.1, a super
32 page illustrated catalog, will be available
in mid-October. It is chock full of historical
notes(we try to date each piece to its proper
origin), dimensions, color choices, and helpful
hints. The cost is $2.00. Not only will you
have approximately 500 items to choose from in
various price ranges, but our descriptive sheets
will also provide you with an unrivaled unique
reference book. There was never before a catalog
like ours.

OPEN

A MINI MUNDUS Lumber Yard and Craft Center- an
assortment of materials for making mini houses
and furnishings.

GREAT COLLECTORS SERIES

Prominent figures in the world of collecting
will appear each month in a series of special
lectures presented by Mini Mundus starting in
October. In addition to the following names,
there will also be lectures given by the great
collectors of dolls, banks and toys, whose
collections are each worth over half a million
dollars. The series can enable you to identify
many valuable pieces.

Robert Lesser
"Comic Art and Memorabilia"

Owner of one of the most outstanding collections anywhere of Buck Rogers, Disney, comic
art and tin wind-up toys, and author of
<u>A Celebration of Comic Art and Memorabilia</u>.

Flora Gill Jacobs
"Antique Dolls' Houses"

Author of <u>Dolls' Houses in America</u>, owner and
curator of the Washington Dolls' House and
Toy Museum.

Lenon Hoyte
"Dolls and Toys"

Owner and curator of Aunt Len's Doll and Toy
Museum, a collection including 2500 antique
dolls and 20 furnished doll houses.

Robert Milne
"Antique Miniatures"

Restorer of antique doll houses, dealer in
antique miniatures, and fabulous collector.

Evelyn and Frank Gerratana
"English and American Miniatures"

A slide show on priceless English miniatures
and exhibit of selected miniature shops from
their private collection. Mrs. Gerratana is
the regional director of the National
Association of Miniature Enthusiasts

For further information on the Great Collectors
Series, write or call MINI MUNDUS- 288-5855.

Dear Collector,

    The goal of these lectures is to bring
you face to face with some of the great
collectors of our day and with the authors who write about them.

    If you have any suggestions on how to
spread the pleasure of Miniature Collecting, please contact us with your
ideas. Perhaps there is someone you
would like to meet.

    Miniature Collectors are a rare breed of
people- and miniatures are a labor of
love. We want everyone to enjoy and share.

             Happy Collecting,

             Kathryn Falk

Mini Mundus newsletter, showing the wide variety of activities offered to the miniaturist.

CHAPTER 16

MUSEUMS
AND EXHIBITS

Many worthwhile exhibits of dollhouses and miniatures can be found throughout the country. New York has the wonderful dollhouse collection of the Museum of the City of New York; California has the incredible Mott's Miniatures exhibit at Knotts' Berry Farm. Some exhibits are tucked away in less familiar places. In Fremont, Ohio, you can see two beautiful and historic dollhouses at the Rutherford B. Hayes Library. The houses belonged to President Hayes's daughter, who played with them when her family occupied the White House. In Rockerville, South Dakota, in the neighborhood of Mount Rushmore, you can visit Stuart Castle, a sixteenth- and seventeenth-century castle in miniature, filled with stately furnishings.

While exhibits of dollhouses and miniatures are widespread, Mecca for the miniaturist is Chicago. Here, at The Art Institute, the legendary Thorne Rooms are on permanent display. And here, at the Museum of Science and Industry, you can visit Coleen Moore's fabulous "Fairy Castle," built at a cost of nearly half a million dollars.

This chapter will guide you through a number of worthwhile exhibits around the country. If you're lucky enough to find one of them nearby, don't hesitate to pay it a visit. You'll be glad you did. We suggest you call before going, however, to make sure the exhibit is open, since visiting days and hours vary.

Doll Museum
Exceptionally large dollhouse, 70" tall, built in Chicago in 1901. The house was originally equipped with running water. Completely furnished, including many sterling silver pieces. (Photo courtesy of Doll Museum.)

Rutherford B. Hayes Library

"1878 Dollhouse," a favorite toy of Fanny Hayes, daughter of President Rutherford B. Hayes, while she was living in the White House. The dollhouse was designed and constructed by George C. Brown of Baltimore, a carpenter-contractor, and was presented to Fanny Hayes on February 13, 1878.

"Christmas Dollhouse," built at the request of President Hayes by M. M. Magruder, a carpenter who had done work at the White House. It was presented to Fanny Hayes on her first Christmas in the White House. The cost of the dollhouse was $15.00. (Photos courtesy of the Rutherford B. Hayes Library.)

Famous Stettheimer dollhouse, c. 1920. (Photo courtesy of Museum of the City of New York.)

Time Was Village Museum
*Four Bliss dollhouses, furnished and
"peopled."* (Photo courtesy Time Was
Village Museum.)

The Toy Cupboard Museum
*German dollhouse, c. 1895, from a large
collection of dollhouses and miniatures.*
(Photo courtesy of The Toy Cupboard
Museum.)

Henry Ford Museum

1940 "Double Town House" dollhouse made by Kathryn B. Booz, Grosse Pointe Farms, Michigan. (Photo courtesy of the Collections of Greenfield Village and the Henry Ford Museum.)

Cooper-Hewitt Museum of Design

Toy Butcher Shop, made in England, c. 1800. (Photo courtesy of Cooper-Hewitt Museum of Design, Smithsonian Institution.)

Amana Home Museum
*Handmade replica of an early Amana
kitchen, mounted on legs.* (Photo courtesy
of Amana Home Museum.)

Stuart Castle
*Princess' bedroom, one of the many
ornately furnished rooms of this
sixteenth-century castle in miniature.*
(Photos courtesy of Rev. Stuart A. Parvin.)

Stuart Manor
*Front view showing the dining room,
music room, main bedroom, and living
room of this fourteen-room Colonial
mansion.*

Mott Miniatures

These dollhouses and shops, each
crammed with miniature furniture,
accessories, and merchandise, are only
part of the vast number of items on
display in this world-famous exhibit. The
entire collection numbers more than
50,000 miniatures and traces its origin
back to the days when Allegra Mott began
collecting Cracker Jack prizes as a girl of eight.

China Shop

Silver Shop

1900 home where Allegra Mott was born and raised

1865 home where Dewitt Mott's father was raised

Doll Shop

1750 Eastern Cabin

**Country Fare
Antique Doll House
and Toy Museum**

*New York Doll House, c. 1870. This
amply proportioned house measures 5'8"
wide, 5' high, 32" deep.* (Photo courtesy
of Country Fare Antique Doll House and
Toy Museum.)

The Hudson River Museum

*"Nuremberg"-type miniature kitchen
with pottery, tin, and pewter implements.
Made in Germany, late nineteenth
century. Gift of Miss Susan Dwight Bliss.*
(Photo courtesy of The Hudson River
Museum.)

206

Interior and exterior views of a dollhouse
and furnishings made in Germany in the
late nineteenth century. The house is
furnished in an appropriately eclectic
Victorian manner with miniatures of the
period. Gift of Miss Susan Dwight Bliss,
1937. (Photos courtesy of The Hudson
River Museum.)

ARIZONA
PHOENIX ART MUSEUM
1625 North Central Avenue
Phoenix, Arizona 85004
Permanent collection of sixteen
Thorne Rooms.

CALIFORNIA
MOTT MINIATURES
Knott's Berry Farm
Buena Park, California 90620
A well-known exhibit of dollhouses,
shops, and more than 150,000
miniatures.

MURIEL'S DOLL HOUSE MUSEUM
33 Canyon Lake Drive
Port Costa, California 94569
Dollhouses and miniatures.

FLORIDA
DOLL MUSEUM
Homosassa, Florida 32646
Very large dollhouse, completely
furnished, plus collection of 1,500
dolls.

ILLINOIS
THE ART INSTITUTE OF CHICAGO
Michigan Avenue at Adams Street
Chicago, Illinois 60603
Permanent collection of sixty-eight
Thorne Rooms.

MUSEUM OF SCIENCE AND INDUSTRY
57th Street and Lake Shore Drive
Chicago, Illinois 60637
The famous "Fairy Castle" of Coleen
Moore.

TIME WAS VILLAGE MUSEUM
Mendota, Illinois 61342
Many dollhouses and miniatures
housed in an eight-building museum
complex.

IOWA
AMANA HOME MUSEUM
Homestead, Iowa 52236
Interesting miniature kitchen.

MASSACHUSETTS
THE CHILDREN'S MUSEUM
The Jamaicaway
Boston, Massachusetts 02130
Furnished dollhouse.

THE TOY CUPBOARD MUSEUM
57 E. George Hill Road
So. Lancaster, Massachusetts 01561
Large collection of dollhouses and
miniatures.

YESTERYEAR'S MUSEUM
Main and River Streets
Sandwich, Massachusetts 02563
Large collection of rare miniatures.

MICHIGAN
HENRY FORD MUSEUM AND
GREENFIELD VILLAGE
Dearborn, Michigan 48121
Furnished dollhouses.

MISSOURI
KINDER MUSEUM
Hermann, Missouri 65041
Completely furnished dollhouse and
toys.

NEW YORK
COOPER-HEWITT MUSEUM OF DESIGN
9 East 90th Street
New York, New York 10028
Antique toy butcher shop.

COUNTRY FARE ANTIQUE DOLL HOUSE
AND TOY MUSEUM
Rt. 82
Stanfordville, New York 12581
More than fifty dollhouses and
numerous miniatures.

THE HUDSON RIVER MUSEUM
511 Warburton Avenue
Trevor Park-on-Hudson
Yonkers, New York 10701
Late-nineteenth-century German
dollhouse and Nuremberg kitchen.

MUSEUM OF THE CITY OF NEW YORK
Fifth Avenue at 104th Street
New York, New York 10029
Outstanding collection of furnished
dollhouses.

ROCHESTER MUSEUM & SCIENCE CENTER
657 East Avenue
Rochester, New York 14603
A small but interesting collection of
dollhouses and miniatures that can be
seen by qualified researchers by
appointment.

THE MARGARET WOODBURY STRONG
COLLECTION
700 Allen Creek Road
Rochester, New York 14618
This vast and world-famous collection
of the late Margaret Woodbury Strong
does not yet have a permanent home.
Interested researchers should apply for
permission to visit the collection by
writing to Mr. Lawrence L. Belles,
Chief Curator of Collections.

OHIO
THE RUTHERFORD B. HAYES LIBRARY
1337 Hayes Avenue
Fremont, Ohio 43420
Dollhouses belonging to Fanny Hayes,
daughter of President Hayes.

PENNSYLVANIA
MARY MERRITT'S DOLL MUSEUM
R.D. 2
Douglasville, Pennsylvania 19518
Dollhouses and miniatures.

SOUTH DAKOTA
STUART CASTLE
Box 54
Rockerville, South Dakota 57701
A sixteenth- and seventeenth-century
castle, completely furnished.

TENNESSEE
DULIN GALLERY OF ART
3100 Kingston Pike
Knoxville, Tennessee 37919
A collection of nine Thorne Rooms
from Mrs. Thorne's first series of
rooms.

VERMONT
SHELBURNE MUSEUM
Shelburne, Vermont 05482
Dollhouses and miniatures.

WASHINGTON
SEATTLE HISTORICAL SOCIETY
MUSEUM OF SCIENCE AND INDUSTRY
2161 East Hamlin Street
Seattle, Washington 98112
Extraordinary Southern Colonial
dollhouse, built at a cost of more than
$30,000 and donated by Mrs. Frederick
Dent Hammons. The house is filled
with furnishings made by world-
famous craftspeople.

WASHINGTON, D.C.
THE WASHINGTON DOLLS' HOUSE
& TOY MUSEUM
5236 44th Street, N.W.
Washington, D.C. 20015
Numerous authentically furnished
houses, shops, schools, churches, and
other miniature buildings.

CHAPTER 17

GOING INTO THE MINIATURE BUSINESS

Once you start making your own miniatures, you may reach a point where you begin to think about selling some of your work, especially if you've become so prolific that your output exceeds your own personal needs as a hobbyist. Unfortunately, some people never get further than toying with the idea because they don't know how to go about marketing their work. This chapter is intended to get you over this hurdle by giving you guidelines and practical information.

The first thing to do is to determine just how marketable your work is. That will depend largely on the appeal of the work itself, the price, and your ability to expose your crafts to potential customers. Let's consider these points in order.

You probably have a feeling about the appeal of your work based on reactions you've had from other people.

How appealing is the price? Try to determine what comparable pieces are selling for. Send for the brochures of other miniaturists and attend as many shows as you can. This will give you an idea of typical prices for a variety of items and a feeling for the marketplace in general.

Once you arrive at the retail price you think you can get for your work, sit down and determine if you can afford to produce it for that price. To do this, figure out the cost of your materials, bearing in mind that if you plan to produce miniatures in quantity, you might be able to buy some of your materials in bulk, thereby reducing the cost of materials per item. Then estimate how long it takes you to make each piece. Last, decide how much you'd like to get paid for your time. Multiply this hourly rate by the number of hours each piece requires, and you'll have the cost of your labor. Add to that the cost of your materials, and you'll have the overall cost of making the piece.

The preceding computation assumes that you're working out of your home. If you're working from a studio or some other location where you have to pay rent, you'll have to factor in the cost of overhead. Figure out, for example, what your rent and utilities are costing you over a given period of time, and apportion this over the number of pieces you can produce in that time.

The cost of making a piece is only part of the equation, however. The cost of selling it is the other part. Here, you have a number of different options, which are discussed further on in this chapter.

Once you have a rough idea of the cost of selling, add that to the cost of making, and you'll have a better idea of what your retail price has to be. How does that figure compare with your original estimate of what you thought the piece could sell for? If your original estimate of the selling price is comparable to or higher than the necessary selling price you've just worked out, then you're in business. The greater the discrepancy between the two prices, the more profit you'll make—which is the equivalent of paying yourself a higher hourly wage. If, however, your necessary selling price is higher than your estimate of what you think you can get for your work, you're in trouble. What the numbers are telling you is that it just might not be practical for you to attempt to sell your work. The problem may be that you need a higher return on your time than your work can command in the marketplace.

In any event, it's a good idea to test the waters before jumping in, and the best way to do that is to proceed on a very limited basis at first. *Creative Crafts* offers this very sound advice taken from its excellent six-part article entitled "Marketing Crafts," written primarily by Loretta Holz, which appeared in the issues of December 1974 and February, April, June, August, October 1975:

"There are many advantages to selling your handicrafts over holding a salaried job. Today there is much emphasis on 'doing your own thing' and being your own boss. In this business you will be just that. Also you do not need to dress for work every day and report there on time. You can set your own hours and make them flexible enough so that you can work whenever you have time, which is particularly important for someone who has duties in the home. You can also choose your projects and set your own goals.

"But before you quit your hourly job and jump into crafting full time, you should be aware of the disadvantages.

"When you get started selling your work, you may find that it is not the very profitable business that you thought it might be. Therefore, before you begin, you should realize that most likely you would be able to earn more on a per hour basis working on a job outside your home. This, of course, depends on your earning potential and the type of job you accept.

"However, if you would like to spend your time with crafts because you enjoy it, rather than doing the work another assigns to you, you will not mind the lower hourly wage. But it is important that you realize the benefits other than monetary and feel they are worthwhile so that you do not feel cheated when your cash receipts are not what you wish they were.

"Once you decide to try to sell your work, your whole lifestyle is likely to change. Your business will have a great impact on how you plan your day, where you go on weekends, how you budget your money, etc. You may be anxious to quit your full-time job, but do not do so immediately. Plan your strategy. Start small and part-time so that

COST OF MAKING
COST OF SELLING
+ PROFIT

= SELLING PRICE

you can develop your product and your market together.

"If you are a mother at home with your children, your problems will be quite different from those of a wage-earner. You will have to try to fit time to do your craftwork between housework and child care. You will have to learn to schedule your activities carefully and conserve time. Try to get your husband's support, and, if the children are old enough, try to get the whole family involved in your project. This way they will be so busy they will not notice that extra layer of dust on the furniture."

You must now turn your attention to the important question of marketing your crafts. There are three main avenues that miniature-makers use to sell their work: through dealers (wholesale), directly by mail, and at miniature shows. The easiest of these is selling to dealers or local shops. This removes the selling effort from your hands, eliminating such time-consuming activities as advertising, answering mail, packing, shipping, and extensive record keeping. You simply sell all your work to the dealer, and he or she takes over the job of retailing it. In some cases, the dealer will buy your entire inventory outright or on a continuing basis. In other cases, he or she may take the work on consignment, which means that it is yours until it is sold. Whichever way you work it, bear in mind that you'll be selling your work at a wholesale rate, which will give you only about half the retail price. You may find that this doesn't yield a sufficient return on your time and effort. If so, consider the alternatives of selling directly by mail order or through shows or both.

Mail-order selling seems to appeal to a great many miniature-makers, particularly part-timers. It multiplies your selling effort by transferring the task of selling from yourself to an advertisement,

which, unlike you, can be in many places at once. Advertising is also a good way to reach out across the country instead of having your efforts confined to your local area. But it also costs money. One way to look at it is to think of the publication in which you advertise as your sales force. The cost of your ad can be equated with the cost of sending this sales force out to contact a certain number of potential customers (the publication's circulation). The size of your ad (which partly determines its cost) and its contents can be likened to the amount of attention the salesman is able to attract on each call.

Miniature-makers who sell their work through mail order don't usually sell specific items through ads, however; rather, they use the ads to promote their brochures and/or price lists. This enables them to present their entire line in as much detail and with as much description as necessary. It also allows them to include a personal letter, which helps establish a friendly relationship. Frequently, photographs of the items being sold are made available at a small charge. A self-addressed stamped envelope (referred to as "SASE") is usually requested in the ad.

If you decide to sell by mail order, make sure that you have your price list, brochure, or whatever follow-up material you plan to send ready and waiting at the time your ad is scheduled to appear. It's poor business to discourage potential customers by making them wait excessively long for a reply.

Chapter 15 lists a number of likely publications in which you should consider advertising. Some of these publications may even be willing to prepare your ad for you. For information about rates, circulation, closing dates, and formal requirements, write directly to the publisher. When replies to your ad start coming in, keep a record of all the names and addresses for future mailings you might want to send out. These names will constitute the core of your mailing list.

The other popular way to go about selling your work is to participate in crafts and miniatures shows. Most shows are really marketplaces for displaying and selling wares. To find out about forthcoming shows in your area, check with local miniature shops; they're usually tuned in to all local events. You might also contact miniature clubs in your vicinity, as most shows are sponsored by such clubs. An inquiry directed to the National Association of Miniature Enthusiasts, Box 2621 Brookhurst Center, Anaheim, California 92804, might also prove to be helpful, inasmuch as N.A.M.E. is in constant touch with clubs all over the country.

With regard to selling your work through shows, *Creative Crafts* offers this helpful advice and information:

"There are advantages as well as disadvantages to selling your work through shows. They are very time-consuming, but if you have the time to go to the show you certainly can make sales and at the same time learn quite a bit about selling your crafts. Shows can be lots of fun and most likely you will enjoy attending them. However, do not expect the shows to make you instantly wealthy—far from it. Going to a show can be a lot of hard work and if you have chosen a poor show then it can be very discouraging.

"One advantage to selling at shows is that you will get exposure for your products and you will begin to make a name for yourself. Also you will receive some excellent feedback from your customers. A show is a good place to try out some new products to see how popular they might be and how much you can charge for them. You can meet people and observe firsthand how they react to your work.

"Another advantage to shows is that you can make some excellent contacts. For example, you may meet shop owners who ask if they can buy wholesale from you for their shops. In addition, shows can offer you a good change of pace if you spend most of your time in your workshop.

"Shows are fun because they give you an opportunity to meet and talk with your fellow craftspeople and most likely make some good friends. Also, seeing the work of other craftspeople and artists may inspire your own creativity.

RATE INCREASE EFFECTIVE JUNE 1st 1975

$3.00
for 1 column inch

Miniature Gazette ADVERTISING

$6.00
2 col. in.

$9.00
3 col. in.

TERMS: Payment must accompany all insertion orders for advertising. Classified ads are 10¢ per word. Display advertising is $3.00 per column inch and may include photos. Special Half-page and Full-page rates are available at $40.00 per Half-page and $75.00 per Full-page ads. We prefer camera-ready copy but will lay out customer's material in our choice of composition if so requested. We reserve the right to edit or alter customer's ad copy in keeping with our over-all theme requirements.

COUNT: Abbreviations, initials, name and address are chargeable words. Zip codes are included free of cost. Hyphenated words count as two words.

AD COPY: Ads submitted should be typed or legibly written. No responsibility is assumed for illegible or poorly prepared ad copy.

NO GUARANTEE: We attempt to protect our readers from ads placed by irresponsible firms or individuals, but it is not possible for us to guarantee the validity of an advertisement. All classified items are subject to prior sale and the Miniature Gazette assumes no responsibilities as to the description or condition of merchandise advertised. We make every effort not to make errors, however we assume no liability for typographical errors except to the extent of rerunning the incorrect portion in the next issue.

DEADLINES: July 31 is closing date for the September issue; October 31 for the December issue; January 31 for the March issue; and April 30 for the June issue.

PHOTOS: Pictures and photographs submitted for display advertising will only be accepted by the Gazette, in the correct size to fit the desired ad space. Reducing or enlarging of photos must be done by customer before they are sent to the Gazette with insertion order.

All advertising insertion orders and inquiries should be directed to:
Advertising Manager; Miniature Gazette,
N.A.M.E., Box 2621, Brookhurst Center, Anaheim, Calif. 92804.

$12.00
4 col. in.

Subscriber's CLASSIFIED AD Blank

WORD COUNT _____   ENCLOSED $_____

"This is all fine and good, you may be thinking, but my main purpose at the show is selling my own products. You will make sales but not always as many as you hoped. At a good show you can do very well. At a fantastic show you can sell out. But at a poor show you may not even cover your booth fee. Every time you go to a show you are actually gambling. You may lose badly if the show is a 'bomb' and costs you money in terms of both time and expenses. Be prepared for this possibility, although you may be lucky enough never to go to such a show.

"The main advantage you might see to attending shows is that you will receive the full retail price of your items directly from the customer. No middleman to take half or all of it, you think. This advantage can be deceptive. Remember, when you do the selling yourself, you must figure the time, effort and expense involved.

"What the show is doing, then, is allowing you to earn the half of your price which is devoted to selling. In that half of your price you must figure your expenses, including the cost of the show, transportation to and from, meals, lodging if necessary, etc. This half of the price is also paying you for your time. A show can be costly in hours, not only the actual hours you sit waiting for customers and helping them, but also the time you spend preparing for the show, traveling to it, setting up your display, taking it down, traveling home and unpacking from the show. Be quite aware of these selling costs, and note that if you were to give yourself a wage from the selling half of the cost of all the items you sold at a very poor show, you may

U.S. SMALL BUSINESS ADMINISTRATION

the starting and managing series
volume 1

3rd edition

starting and managing

a small business of your own

be working for ten cents an hour. Of course at a fantastic show, your selling wage can be quite good.

"If you would like to get started selling your products at shows there are several things you should start doing right away. Before signing up to participate in a show, build up an inventory of items. Try to have more expensive as well as less expensive items if possible. If you plan to attend a three-day show, bring upwards of $500 worth (retail value) of items. For a smaller show you may not need as much.

"As you begin stockpiling your items and before you actually enter your first show, start attending them as a customer to get a feeling for them. If you can find craftspeople there willing to talk with you, then you can learn quite a bit about shows from them. Look at the type of items being sold and the prices being asked. Look at how they are being displayed and notice how craftspeople are handling their customers.

"The first time you attend a show you will have to sit down and carefully make a list of all the items you wish to take along. Packing can be quite a chore, and the more organized you are the easier it will be.

"First you have to pack your merchandise, which can be quite a problem if the items are delicate. As you pack, be sure that each item has a price tag on it so that you do not have to take the time once you have arrived at the show to put the tags on your items. It is a good idea to make a checklist of the items which you are bringing so that you can check off the unsold items when you arrive home and know exactly what you sold.

"You must pack up all of the display equipment you will need and also any tools necessary to set up the equipment or repair it. You also might need items like cellophane tape and scissors to make last minute adjustments.

"In addition bring sales equipment. You will need small bills and coins to make change. Bring your sales pad to write up the sales. If your state requires you to collect sales tax, you will need your sales tax chart. Bring bags in which to put your customers' purchases. If you have business cards, bring these along and most show directors will allow you to leave the cards on your display for customers to pick up.

"If a customer asks to pay with a check, have your answer ready. Decide in advance whether you are willing to take the chance that a check is good or instead lose the sale. Many craftspeople who sell their work on a fulltime basis have Bank-Americard or Master Charge available for customers. They feel that by making credit available they increase their sales by 1/4 at least. Of course using these credit systems costs you money. Check with your local bank if you decide to enroll.

"When the show is over and you have a chance to catch your breath, do a little analysis of what happened at the show so that you can learn by your experience. If you attend a good many shows, write down the information so you will not forget, and keep all of the vital facts in a special folder or file. If you make notes about your sales and keep this information with the show announcement, it will be very helpful to you in deciding whether to attend this particular show again next year.

"Sales is probably your first measure of success, but another consideration is whether you made any good contacts. If you met several shop owners who will be buying your items, most likely you will call the show a success even if your sales were not high.

"If you made a checklist of items you brought, you can check off what did not sell to discover your most popular items and in what price range you had the most sales, so you can plan your production accordingly."

Once you've tested the waters and decided to embark on a course of selling your miniatures, it would be wise to send for the helpful booklet entitled *Starting and Managing a Small Business of Your Own,* prepared by the U.S. Small Business Administration. It can be obtained for $1.35 from the Superintendent of Documents, U.S. Government Printing Office, Washington, D.C. 20402. The booklet number is 4500-00123. Inside you'll find a lot of good, general information about starting in business the right way. You'll learn, for example, the advantages and disadvantages of setting yourself up as a single proprietorship and as a corporation. You'll get some good advice about the all-important chore of record keeping. And you'll be guided as to laws and regulations, taxes, and insurance.

We wish you luck in your new business venture and envy you the satisfaction of watching other people pay money for something you made with your own two hands.

CHAPTER 18

RESOURCES

The following is a comprehensive list of resources for miniatures, dollhouses, tools, and supplies. It includes the names of individual craftspeople who sell via mail order, as well as miniature shops throughout the country. Craftspeople, manufacturers, and mail-order sources are listed alphabetically; shops, geographically. All of the resources mentioned in this book are included here, except for one craftsperson who is so inundated with orders that she requested not to have her address listed.

Catalog offers are indicated, along with their cost, if any. "SASE" means a business-size self-addressed stamped envelope.

When using this resource section, bear in mind that this is a dynamic hobby, in a state of explosive growth; consequently, craftspeople and other suppliers appear and disappear more frequently than with other hobbies that are older and more settled. Many of the men and women who make miniatures do so on a part-time basis, and the press of other commitments sometimes forces a supplier to suspend operations. But the very size of our list, with its numerous alternatives, offers insurance to the searching collector.

Detail of Victorian dollhouse made by Gotfred O. Hoffmann.

CRAFTSPEOPLE, MANUFACTURERS, AND MAIL-ORDER SOURCES OF DOLLHOUSES, MINIATURES, TOOLS, AND SUPPLIES.

Afton Classics
17 Afton Drive
Florham Park, New Jersey 07932
Dollhouse kits. Send SASE for brochure.

Alice's Wonderland
P.O. Box 62
Ramsey, New Jersey 07446
Dollhouse accessories. Send 25¢ and SASE for list.

American Edelstaal, Inc.
1 Atwood Avenue
Tenafly, New Jersey 07670
Unimat precision miniature machine tool. Sold in hardware stores.

Amity Petites
P.O. Box 2882
Lancaster, California 93534
Dollhouses and miniatures. Inquire by mail.

Andrews Miniatures
Patrick and Center Streets
Ashland, Virginia 23005
Miniature furniture, accessories, and dollhouses. Send $2 for catalog.

Hermania Anslinger
320 South Ralph Street
Spokane, Washington 99202
Custom-made miniature furniture and accessories. SASE for list; SASE and $1.50 for photos.

The Appleyards
1444 Shore Road
Linwood, New Jersey 08221
Dollhouses, furniture, and accessories. Send $1 and SASE for catalog.

Architectural Model Supplies, Inc.
P.O. Box 3497
San Rafael, California 94902
Dollhouse building supplies. Send $2.50 for illustrated catalog.

The Ark
4375 Capitola Road
Capitola, California 95010
Dollhouses, miniatures, and dollhouse-making patterns.

Barnstable Originals
50 Harden Avenue
Camden, Maine 04843
Furniture and accessories by Harry W. Smith. Send 50¢ for illustrated catalog.

Berryhill
P.O. Box 1308
Bozeman, Montana 59715
Send $1 for illustrated catalog.

Block House
1107 Broadway
New York, New York 10010
Large distributor of miniature furniture and accessories. Wholesale only.

The Borrower's Press
Route 1
Winterport, Maine 04496
Miniature books, bound in cloth and leather. Send 25¢ and SASE for list.

Milton Breeden
111 North 5th Street
Millville, New Jersey 08332
Miniature glassware and perfume bottles. Send SASE for list.

Broadswords Miniatures
68 Blackburn Road
Summit, New Jersey 07901
Miniature accessories. Send 25¢ in coin and
SASE for list.

Brookstone Company
Brookstone Building
Peterborough, New Hampshire 03458
"Hard-to-find tools." Many items for the
miniaturist. Free catalog.

Brown's Miniatures
P.O. Box 35
Cambridge, New York 12816
Metal miniature accessories. Send 25¢ and SASE
for list.

R. L. Carlisle, Miniatures
703 N. Elm Street
Creston, Iowa 50801
Victorian and turn-of-the-century furniture. Send
25¢ and SASE for printed sheet of photos with
price list.

Chestnut Hill Studio
12 Woodcreek Drive
Taylors, South Carolina 29687
Miniature furniture and accessories of many
periods. Send $2 for large illustrated catalog.

Clare-Bell Brassworks
Queen Street
Southington, Connecticut 06489
Manufacturer of precision brass miniatures.

Colonial Craftsmen Pewter Workshop, Inc.
P.O. Box 337
Cape May, New Jersey 08204
Foremost producer of pewter miniatures. Sold in
numerous shops.

Colvin Originals
30 Walnut Place
Huntington, New York 11743
Kits for making upholstered furniture. Sold at
Mini-Mundus, Miniatures Etc., The Mouse
House, and other shops.

Highly detailed brass bed, made by Norman Nelson.

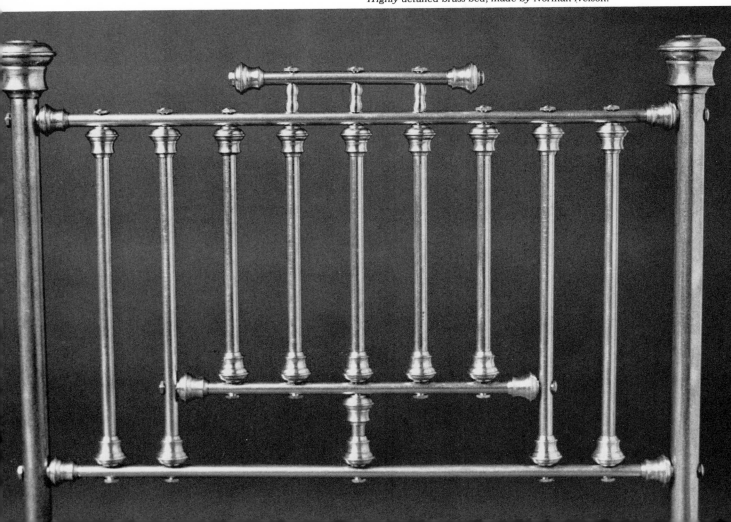

Copper Corner
300 E. Devonia Avenue
Mt. Vernon, New York 10552
Copper miniatures, mostly cookware. Send $1 for
catalog.

Craftsman Wood Service Company
2727 South Mary Street
Chicago, Illinois 60608
Dollhouse building supplies.

Davault Miniature Furniture
422 Livingston
Creston, Iowa 50801
Miniature furniture and furniture-making
patterns. Send 35¢ for illustrated catalog.

Diana, Inc.
9202 Waukegan Road
Morton Grove, Illinois 60059
Wholesale miniature furniture and accessories.

The Dollhouse Factory
Box 456
Lebanon, New Jersey 08833
Dollhouses, miniatures, and supplies. Custom
dollhouses made by Robert Dankanics. Send $1
for illustrated catalog.

The Dollhouse Factory
P.O. Box 2232
Sunnyvale, California 94087
Furniture and accessories larger than 1-inch
scale. Send $1 for illustrated catalog #3000
(allow 60 days).

Dolphin Originals
7302 Hasbrook Avenue
Philadelphia, Pennsylvania 19111
Wicker and other unusual furniture hand-made
by Robert Bernhard. Send SASE for price list.

Dormouse Doll Houses
205 Union Street
Ridgewood, New Jersey 07450
Dollhouses custom-made by Robert Conley.

John Dowling
151 Raymond Street
Darien, Connecticut 06820
Custom-made dollhouses. SASE for information.

*1738 cherry bonnet top highboy, made
by Harry W. Smith, Barnstable Originals.*
(Photo courtesy of Harry W. Smith.)

Down East Construction
Harris Road
Stockton Springs, Maine 04981
Manufacturer of high-quality dollhouses.
Illustrated brochure available.

Dremel Manufacturing Division
Emerson Electric Co.
4915 21st Street
Racine, Wisconsin 53406
Power tools for the miniaturist and dollhouse-
builder. Sold in hardware stores, and hobby, toy,
and miniature shops.

Joan Eastman
9 Johns Road
Setauket, New York 11733
Dollhouse plans.

Elspeth Originals
7404 Helmsdale Road
Bethesda, Maryland 20034
Patterns for making miniature rooms and
accessories.

Enchanted Doll House
Manchester Center, Vermont 05255
Large selection of dollhouses and miniatures.
Send $1.50 for 48-page illustrated catalog.

Fantasy Creations
337 Glenn Avenue
Lawrenceville, New Jersey 08648
Bread dough miniatures. Send 25¢ for catalog.

Favorites from the Past
3492 Nowlin Road
Kennesaw, Georgia 30144
Dollhouses, miniatures, kits, and supplies. Send
$1 for catalog.

Fieldwood Company
P.O. Box 223
Hohokus, New Jersey 07423
Dollhouses, miniatures, and accessories. Send $1
for illustrated catalog.

Floquil-Polly S Color Corporation
Cobbleskill, New York 12043
Paints and stains formulated for miniatures. Send
SASE for information.

Marie Friedman
13200 S. W. Glenn Court
Beaverton, Oregon 97005
Miniature accessories, lighting fixtures, china,
spatterware, and furniture. Custom inquiries
invited.

Madeline Gesser, Inc.
221 Everit Avenue
Hewlett Harbor, New York 11557
Contemporary custom miniatures in stainless
steel, walnut, lucite, and plexiglass. Send $1 and
SASE for brochure and photos.

The Ginger Jar
6133 Wakefield Drive
Sylvania, Ohio 43560
Hand-made furniture and pottery. List and
photos available.

Herbert I. Gory
77 Causeway Street
Hudson, Massachusetts 01749
Custom dollhouses for museums and collectors.

Philip J. Grande—Designer and Cabinetmaker
513 E. Orange Grove Avenue
Burbank, California 91501
Hand-made furniture. Many unusual items. Send
SASE for price list, 60¢ and SASE for photos.

Grandmother Stover's, Inc.
1331 King Avenue
Columbus, Ohio 43212
Manufacturer of dollhouse accessories, widely
sold through miniature shops, gift and card shops,
and toy stores. Send $1 for 28-page catalog.

Green Door Studio
517 E. Annapolis Street
St. Paul, Minnesota 55118
Patterns for making miniature furniture,
accessories, and dollhouses. Send 50¢ for
illustrated catalog.

Hall's Lifetime Toys
2305 E. 28th Street
Chattanooga, Tennessee 37407
Manufacturer of dollhouses and furniture.
Wholesale only.

Handcrafted by Mrs. Anne Ruth Pfister
17 Wickham Avenue
Middletown, New York 10940
Three-sided miniature rooms. Send SASE for list.

Handcrafted Miniatures, Paul E. Rouleau
260 Rock Island Road
Quincy, Massachusetts 02169
Country kitchen and general store pieces. Send
SASE for list.

The Hoffman Collection
16 Valemont Way
Summit, New Jersey 07901
Shaker and other Colonial furniture. Illustrated
catalog available.

Illinois Hobbycraft
12 S. Fifth Street
Geneva, Illinois 60134
Manufacturer, retailer, and wholesaler of
miniature lighting equipment. Also tools, building
supplies, and miniatures. Illustrated catalog
available.

Isn't It? (A Small World)
P.O. Box 218
Bixby, Oklahoma 74008
Miniature furniture and accessories. Send $1.50
for illustrated 28-page catalog.

Joen Ellen Kanze (Mini Contracting Company)
26 Palmer Avenue
North White Plains, New York 10603
Dollhouses made to order. Dollhouse plans.

Miles Kimball Company
41 W. 8th Avenue
Oshkosh, Wisconsin 54901
Mail-order company, some miniatures. Send for
free 196-page catalog containing several pages on
miniatures.

E. J. Kupjack & Associates
1200 South Fairview at Devon
Park Ridge, Illinois 60068
Miniature rooms, by commission.

Le Beau Estate
909 E. McIntosh Road
Griffin, Georgia 30223
Custom-made furniture and accessories. Free
estimates. Send 25¢ and SASE for monthly list.

The Sara Lee
3433 E. 58th Street
Tulsa, Oklahoma 74135
Miniatures and miniature-making kits. Send 25¢
and SASE for catalog.

Leisure Time World
111 Sandstone Drive
Rochester, New York 14616
Mail-order miniatures. Send 50¢ for 80-page
catalog.

Lillie Putt Furniture
One Rowan Road
Chatham, New Jersey 07928
Manufacturer of upholstered furniture kits.

Lilliput House
228 15th Street N.W.
Massillon, Ohio 44646

The Little Red Dollhouse
Westwind Farm R. 2, Box 94
Fennville, Michigan 49408
Miniature accessories. Send SASE for price list.

Interior view of silver shop, from The Enchanted Dollhouse.

Littlestuff
P.O. Box 411
Seymour, Connecticut 06483
Custom-made "museum quality" miniatures.
Newsletter available for $1.35 per year.

Lundby
LL-Bolagen AB, S-443 01
Lerum, Sweden
Manufacturer of furniture, accessories, and
lighting equipment. Distributed by Block House
and sold in many toy and miniature shops.

Paula MacLean, Dollhouse Originals
4228 145th Street S.E.
Bellevue, Washington 98006
Victorian dollhouses. Send 75¢ for color photos.

Jim Marcus
1332 Versailles Avenue
Alameda, California 94501
Victorian dollhouses.

Maritime Miniatures
45 E. 7th Street
New York, New York 10003
Sailing ship models and paintings. Send SASE for
brochure.

Merry Miniature Books
1375 East Fifth Street
Brooklyn, New York 11230
Miniature books, bound in leather. Send 75¢ and
SASE for catalog.

Sonia Messer Imports
527 West Seventh Street, Suite 404
Los Angeles, California 90014
Importer of quality miniatures made in South
America. Available in many miniature shops.

Microbius
4351 N. Springcreek Road
Dayton, Ohio 45405
Miniature ceramics, food, and accessories.
Send $2 for illustrated catalog #4.

Micro-Creations
3708 Winston Churchill Drive
Dayton, Ohio 45432
Manufacturer of miniature shops and display
cabinets. Free catalog.

Milne Miniatures
106 Prince Street
New York, New York 10012
Antique dollhouses, furniture, and accessories.

Min Art Miniatures
7601 Forsyth Boulevard
St. Louis, Missouri 63105
Wholesaler of miniatures, including Mexican
pieces.

Mini Things
5600 East Oxford Avenue
Englewood, Colorado 80110
Miniature ceramics, copper cookware, and
accessories. Send $1 for illustrated catalog.

Mini World of Mrs. La Monica
67 Pomona Avenue
Yonkers, New York 10703
Miniature accessories, general store, and bake-
shop items. Send 60¢ for price list of 600 items.
Send $1 for illustrated catalog of Colombian
furniture.

The Miniature Mart
1807 Octavia Street
San Francisco, California 94109
Furniture and accessories, El-Kru dinnerware.
Send $2 for 50-page illustrated catalog.

Miniature Silver
1200 South Fairview at Devon
Park Ridge, Illinois 60068
Sterling silver replicas of historic museum silver.
Brochure available. Sold in miniature shops.

Miniatures by Elnora
205 Elizabeth Drive
Berrien Springs, Michigan 49103
Furniture and accessories. Send $2 for illustrated
color catalog.

Miniatures by Evelyn Gerratana
24 Chestnut Hill Road
Trumbull, Connecticut 06611
Dollhouse furniture and accessories.
Send SASE for list.

Miniatures by Marty
1857 South Shore Drive
Holland, Michigan 49423
Miniature accessories and food.
Send 10¢ and SASE for brochure.

Miniatures Mansions of Cheshire
P.O. Box 546
Cheshire, Connecticut 06410
Dollhouses and miniature shops.

Morley Miniatures
16752 Cooper Lane
Huntington Beach, California 92647
Victorian furniture. Send $2 for illustrated
catalog.

Bill Muller Wooden Toys, Inc.
87 Commerce Drive
Telford, Pennsylvania 18951
Wholesaler of dollhouses, miniature furniture,
accessories, and decorating supplies.

My Uncle
133 Main Street
Fryeburg, Maine 04037
Dollhouses and dollhouse kits. Brochure
available.

Norm Nielsen, Doll Houses
6678 So. Clayton Street
Littleton, Colorado 80120
Dollhouses and accessories. Send $1.50 for
catalog.

Northeastern Scale Models, Inc.
Box 425
Methuen, Massachusetts 01844
Manufacturer of dollhouse building materials and
moldings of all kinds.

Northford Miniatures
31 Evergreen Road
Northford, Connecticut 06472
Colonial and Shaker furniture. Send 50¢ and
SASE for flyer.

Braxton Payne
60 Fifth Street, N.E.
Atlanta, Georgia 30308
Miniature greenhouses and accessories.
Illustrated brochure available.

P. Pelican Presents
1100 Oak Glen Drive
Santa Ynez, California 93460
Shaker miniatures. Send SASE for flyer.

Posy Patch Originals
P.O. Box 38123
Atlanta, Georgia 30334
Miniature flowers and plants. Send $2 for
illustrated catalog.

Mell Prescott
P.O. Box 177
Warrenville, Connecticut 06278
Miniature furniture. Send SASE for list.

Marion Rahrer
63 Glenholme Drive
Saulte Ste. Marie
Ontario, Canada
Dollhouse furniture. Send 10¢ for brochure and
photo.

Robin's Roost
P.O. Box 186
Grayslake, Illinois 60030
Petite Princess furniture and other miniatures
and dollhouses. Send SASE with two stamps for
list.

Betty Rockoff
1031 East Magnolia Boulevard
Burbank, California 91501
Miniature foods, including whole dinners. Send
SASE for list.

Paul A. Ruddell
4701 Queensbury Road
Riverdale, Maryland 20840
Mail-order book business devoted to miniature
and doll collectors. Over 1100 items. Free
catalog.

Scientific Models, Inc.
340 Snyder Avenue
Berkeley Heights, New Jersey 07922
Manufacturer of Realife Miniatures dollhouse
furniture kits. Sold at hobby, craft, toy, and
miniature stores, or direct from Scientific Models.
Send 25¢ for color catalog.

Victorian furniture in the style of John Henry Belter, hand-carved by Hermania Anslinger. (Photo by the Commercial Photographers, Spokane, Washington.)

Shaker Miniatures
2913 Huntington Road
Cleveland, Ohio 44120
Shaker and general-store furniture and accessories. Send 50¢ and double stamped envelope for brochure.

Doreen Sinnett Designs
418 Santa Ana Avenue
Newport Beach, California 92663
Bricks, shingles, and wallpapers. Also "Mini-Hooker" for rug making. Send SASE for rug price list; $1.50 for catalog.

Sally W. Smith
86 Church Street
Hudson, Ohio 44236
Hooked rugs. Send SASE for price list.

Something Different Miniatures
P.O. Box 1628 F.D.R. Station
New York, New York 10022
Colonial painted tinware and mirrors. Send 50¢ and SASE for list.

Tahitian Tikis Imports
1785 Vistazo West
Tiburon, California 94920
Bakery and other food items, plus accessories. Send 25¢ for sheet of pictures and price list.

Teri's Mini Workshop
Box 469
Belmont, Massachusetts 02178
Miniature sporting goods, pool tables, nursery items, and schoolroom supplies. Send 25¢ and SASE for catalog.

Noel Thomas—Open House
P.O. Box 213
Seaview, Washington 98644
Highly detailed dollhouses.

Jean Townsend Miniatures
415 Manzano N.E.
Albuquerque, New Mexico 87108
Miniature accessories, blue spatterware, and southwestern designs. Send $1 for illustrated catalog.

The Toymakers
4021 Burning Tree Lane
Garland, Texas 75042
Furniture, accessories, and dollhouses. Send SASE for catalog.

Village Miniatures
RT. 3, Box 326
Chesterfield, Missouri 63107
General stores and other shops, plus miniature shop items. Send $1.50 for catalog.

The Village Smithy
R.D. #5, Hemlock Trail
Carmel, New York 10512
Wrought-iron miniatures.
Send $3 for large, illustrated catalog.

Wickersham & Sons
1740 White Oak Way
San Carlos, California 94070
Mini accessories: tennis rackets, pencils, and
hand tools. Send SASE for catalog.

Windfall
Main Street
Sharon Springs, New York 13459
Hard-to-get miniatures. Free catalog.

Woody's Miniatures
Peterson Road, P.O. Box 207
Sturgeon Bay, Wisconsin 54235
Furniture, circus wagons, stagecoaches, and
cannons. Send $2 for catalog.

The Workshop
424 North Broadview
Wichita, Kansas 67208
Building supplies for making dollhouses and
miniatures. Send $1 for illustrated catalog.

The World in Miniature
1780 Newell Drive
Walnut Creek, California 94595
Furniture and accessories. Send $1 for illustrated
catalog.

X-acto
45-35 Van Dam Street
Long Island City, New York 11101
Manufacturer of tools for model making. Also
"House of Miniatures" kits for making
authentically reproduced miniature furniture.
Available at craft, hobby, and miniature shops.

Yield House, Inc.
Box 1000
North Conway, New Hampshire 03860
Manufacturer and retailer of gift, accessory, and
home furnishing items. Also miniature furniture
and dollhouses. Large, illustrated catalog free.

D. E. Ziegler, Art Craft Supply, Inc.
2318 Admiral Blvd.
Tulsa, Oklahoma 74150
Manufacturer and distributor of supplies for
making miniature artwork (frames, canvas, easels,
and shadowbox frames). Send $1 for color
catalog.

Wrought iron miniatures made by Al Atkins, "The Village Smithy."

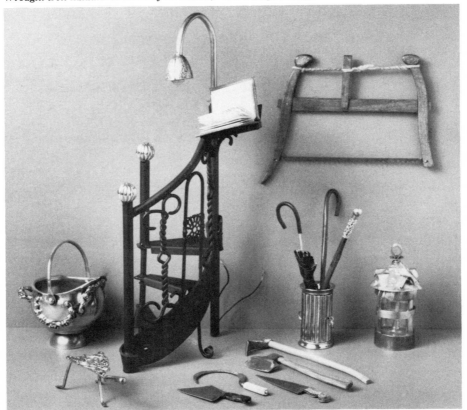

INDEX

A

Adhesives, 131
Advertising, 213–214
Afton Classics, 220
 dollhouse kit, 154
A.I.M.M. Mott's Miniature Workshop News, 9, 194
Alice's Wonderland, 220
Amana Home Museum, 200, 208
American Edelstaal, Inc., 220
Amity Petites, 91, 220
Amy Vanderbilt's Complete Book of Etiquette, 67
Andrews Miniatures, 220
Anslinger, Hermania, 40–41, 220
Antique miniatures, 18, 76, 107–119
 dealers in, 110, 113, 118
 dollhouses, 27, 74, 107, 113
Antiques, 10, 35
Appleyards, The, 220
Architectural Model Supplies, Inc., 220
Architectural realism, 24–25, 160
 pattern for dollhouses, 155
Ark, The, 220
Art Craft Supply, Inc., 228
Art Institute of Chicago, 8, 198, 208
Ash, Suzanne, 42
Atkins, Alfred L., 11, 43
Auctions, 113

B

BankAmericard, 217
"Barbi" scale, 18
Barnstable Originals, 62, 220
Bavaria, Duke of, 3
Bay Window Ltd., The, 229
Beehive Studio, Inc., The, 196, 229
Beerbohm, Max, 3
Belloc, Hilaire, 3
Bench, plans for, 148

Benson, A.C., 2, 3
Bernhard, Robert, 44
Berry, Elizabeth, 194
Berryhill, 220
Berryhill News, The, 194
Block House, 9, 67, 220, 225
Book of the Queen's Dolls' House, The (Benson),
 2, 3, 21
Bookshelf arrangement, 75
Borrower's Press, The, 220
Breeden, Milton, 220
Briggs, Mr., 15, 158
British Bouquet (Chamberlain), 5–6
Broadswords Miniatures, 221
Brookstone Company, 221
Brown, Iris, 113, 118
Brown, Susan, 77
Brown's Miniatures, 221
Building a dollhouse, xi–xii, 121, 152–189
 complete plans for, 163–189
 from a kit, 152, 154
 from patterns, 74, 152, 155
 from plans, 75, 152, 155–156, 158–160
 supplies and tools for, 120–139

C

Carlisle, Robert L., 45
Castle-style dollhouse, 160, 198, 200, 209
Catalogs, xii, 9, 11
Chamberlain, Samuel, 5–6
Chesterton, G. K., 3
Chestnut Hill Studio, 11, 35–37, 221
Chicago World's Fair, 8
Children's Museum, The, 208
Chillon, castle of, 6
Chippendale, Thomas, 17
Chippendale furnishings, 17, 27
Chrysnbon, 64, 67

Clare-Bell Brass Works, 55, 221
Classes, 196
Cleveland Miniature Society, The, 196
Clubs, xii, 9, 196
Cochran, Mary Frances, 46
Colonial Craftsmen Pewter Workshop, Inc.,
    64, 68–69, 221
Colonial furnishings, 64, 194
Colonial-style dollhouse, 158, 160, 163–189
Colvin Originals, 141, 221
Conley, Robert and Carolyn, 105
Conrad, Joseph, 3
Consignment, 213
Conventions, 9
Cooper-Hewitt Museum of Design, 203, 208
Copper Corner, 55, 222
Country Fare Antique Doll House and Toy Museum,
    204, 208
Country Stuff and Dollhouses, 230
Cowles, Arthur and Mary-Dudley, 35
Craftsman Wood Service Company, 222
Craftspeople, 11, 21, 35, 64, 67, 195, 214, 217
    list of, 219–230
Creative Crafts, 194, 195, 212, 214
Custom-made dollhouses, 75, 100–105, 140, 158

D

Dana's of Rochester, 230
Dankanics, Robert, 10, 101–103
Davis, Laura, 196
Decorative Supply House, 230
Decoupage, 9
Devault Miniature Furniture, 222
Diana, Inc., 222
Dioramas, 15
Display cases, 74, 77
Doll Houses, 226
Doll Museum (Chicago), 199, 208
Dollhouse, The, 229
Dollhouse Factory, The, xi–xii, 10, 101–103, 222, 230
Dollhouse and Miniature News, The, 9, 194
Dollhouse Originals, 225
Dollhouses:
    antique, 27, 74, 107, 113
    building, xi–xii, 121, 152–189
    complete plans for, 163–189
    custom-made, 75, 100–105, 140, 158
    factors in selecting, 79–80
    fantasy, 74
    finish-it-yourself, 75
    introduction to, 72–81
    list of resources for, 219–230
    museum and exhibits, xii, 198–209

patterns, 74, 152, 155
from plans, xii, 75, 152, 155–156, 158–160
prices, 79, 82–99
Queen Mary's, 3–5
range of dimensions, 83
ready-made, 75, 82–99
scale in, 14–17, 21
shopping for, 82–99
tools and supplies for, 120–139
Dollomites, 21–24
Dolphin Originals, 44, 222
Doormouse Dollhouses, 105, 222
Doreen Sinnett Designs, 227
Dowling, John, 222
Down East Construction, 222
Doyle, Sir Arthur Conan, 3
Drafting supplies, 121, 122–123
Dremel Manufacturing Division (Emerson Electric
    Company), 11, 222
Dremel Moto-Shop, 128
Drill-Press Stand, 129
Dulac, Edmund, 5
Dulin Gallery of Art (Knoxville), 8, 209
Duz Soap, 67

E

Eagle's Nest Antiques, 230
Early American Life, 195
Early American Society, 195
Eastman, Joan, 222
    plan for dollhouse, 155
Ecology boxes, 9, 10
"Effect of Size on the Equipment of the Queen's
    Dolls' House, The" (O'Gorman), 21–24
Egypt (ancient), 1, 2
Eisenman, Stanley, 158
Electrical supplies, 136–138
Ellen's Toy Chest, 230
Elspeth Originals, 222
    miniature patterns by, 157
Empire furnishings, 27
Encyclopaedia Britannica, 110
Encyclopedia International, 110
Enchanted Dollhouse, 83, 223, 230
Enchanted Toyshop, 230
Exhibits and museums, xii, 107, 110, 198-209

F

"Fairy Castle," 198
Falk, Kathryn, 196
Fantasy Creations, 223
Fantasy-style dollhouses, 74, 160
Fantasy World, 195

Favorites from the Past, 223, 229
Fieldwood Company, 223
Finishing supplies, 139
Finish-it-yourself dollhouse, 75
Flaherty, Carolyn, 195
Flint, Russell, 5
Floquil-Polly S Color Corporation, 223
Foxfire Book, The, 158
French furnishings, 64
Friedman, Marie, 47, 223
Frog Pond, 230

G
Galsworthy, John, 3
Georgian architecture, 88
Ginger Jar, The, 51, 223
Gingerbread Man, The, 92–93
Gory, Herbert I., 223
Grande, Philip J., 48, 223
Grandmother Stover's, Inc., 9–10, 67, 70–71, 223
Granny's Attic, 230
Green Door Studio, 145, 223
    dollhouse plans, 156

H
Hall's Lifetime Toys, 223
Hand tools, 124–127
Handcrafted Miniatures, 223
Handcrafted by Mrs. Anne Ruth Pfister, 223
Happy Things, 229
Hardy, Thomas, 3
Harp, Sybil, 194, 195
Harrell, James, 196
Hayes, Rutherford B., 198
Henry Ford Museum and Greenfield
    Village, 203, 208
Heppelwhite and Sheraton furnishings, 27
Herb Farm Store, The, 229
High Button Shoe Originals, 229
Historical miniatures, 1–5
Hobbies (publication), 195
Hobby shops, xi
Hoffman, Gotfred O., 94–96
Hoffman Collection, The, 49, 223
Holz, Loretta, 212
Housman, A. E., 3
Hudson River Museum, The, 204–205, 209

I
Illinois Hobbycraft, 223
Inflation, antiques as a hedge against, 118
Inventory, 217
Iris Brown Antiques, 230

Isn't It? (A Small World), 224, 230
It's a Small World, 229
Ivory soap, 67

J
Jacobs, Flora Gill, 107
Jacobs, Judy, 50
Jaina Island, 2
Jarque, Jack, 50
Jean Townsend Miniatures, 227
Johnson, Arthur Le Roy, 35
Johnson, Mary T., 230
Johnson, Rita Cowles, 35

K
Kanze, Joen Ellen, 104, 140–143, 224
Kellogg's Corn Flakes, 67
Kinder Museum, 208
Kipling, Rudyard, 3
Kirkwood, Jean, 51
Kitchen Parlor and Doll House, 229
Kits:
    dollhouse, 152, 154
    for miniatures, 140, 141–142, 144–145, 226
Kleenex, 67
Knotts' Berry Farm, 198
Kupjack, E. J., 39, 52–54
Kupjack & Associates (E. J.), 224

L
Le Beau Estate, 224
Lectures, 196
Leisure Time World, 224
Library of the Queen's Dolls' House, The (Benson), 3
Lightner, O.C., 195
Lightner Publishing Corporation, 195
Lillie Putt Furniture, 224
    kits by, 141
Lilliput House, 224
Little Red Dollhouse, The, 224
Littlestuff, 225
Littwin, Harry, 55
Lundby, 67, 225
Lutyens, Sir Edward, 3

M
MacLaren, Catherine B., 193
MacLean, Paula, 89, 225
Madeline Gesser, Inc., 223
Madurodam (miniature village), 6
Mail-order selling, 213–214
    list of sources, 219–230
Manufacturers, list of, 219–230

Marcus, Jim, 92–93, 225
Mare, Walter de la, 3
Margaret Woodbury Strong Collection, The, 209
Marinaccio, Mary Anne, 230
Maritime Miniatures, 50, 225
"Marketing Crafts" (Holz), 212
Marketing miniatures, 213–217
Mary, Queen of England, 3
Mary Merritt's Doll Museum, 209
Master Charge, 217
Mayan pottery figures, 2
Meket Re figures, 2
Memorabilia boxes, 10
Merry Miniature Books, 50, 225
Microbius, 225
Micro-Creations, 77, 225
Mile High Miniature Club (Denver), 196
Miles Kimball Company, 224
Milne, Robert, 18, 110, 113
Milne Miniatures, 225
Min Art Miniatures, 225
Mini Contracting Company, 224
Mini Mundus, 67, 196, 221, 230
Mini Things, 225
Mini World of Mrs. La Monica, 225
Miniature Gazette, The, 9, 193, 196
Miniature Magazine, The, 194
Miniature Makers Journal, 194
Miniature Mansions of Cheshire, 94–96, 226
Miniature Mart, The, 11, 225
Miniature room, see Shadow box
Miniature Silver, 225
Miniature Vignettes (Brown), 77
Miniatures:
    antique, 18, 76, 107–119
    classes and lectures, 196
    clubs, xii, 9, 196
    distinction between toys and, 14, 18
    fascination of, 1–7, 8
    going into business of, 210–217
    growth of popularity, 8–11
    historical, 1–5
    introduction to, 26–37
    list of resources for, 219–230
    making yourself, 140–151
    museums and exhibits, xii, 107, 110, 198–209
    outstanding makers of, 39–63
    patterns for, 157
    popular furniture and accessories, 64–71
    publications, xii, 193–195
    scale, 12–25, 140
    shows, xii, 9, 76, 107, 110, 113, 191, 213, 214–217
    tools and supplies for, 120–139
    villages, 5–6
    ways of housing, 72–81
    See also Dollhouses
Miniatures, as a business, 210–217
    advantages and disadvantages of, 212–213
    inventory, 217
    labor and pricing considerations, 210–212
    marketing, 213–217
Miniatures by Elnora, 225
Miniatures Etc., 221, 230
Miniatures by Evelyn Gerratana, 225
Miniatures by Marty, 226
"Miniaturia" (column), 195
Miniaturia; The World of Tiny Things, 195
Minikin Fantasy, 229
Moore, Coleen, 198
Morley, Franklin J., 56–57
Morley Miniatures, 56–57, 226
Mostly Miniatures, 229
Moto-Lathe, 120
Moto-Saw, 129
Moto-Tool, 129
Mott, Allegra, 8, 194
Mott family, 194
Mott's Miniature Workshop News, 9, 194
Mott's Miniatures, 198, 201, 208
Mount Rushmore, 198
Mouse House, The, 221, 230
"Mr. Briggs' Dream House," 15, 158
Muirhead, David, 5
Muller, Bill, 226
Muriel's Doll House Museum, 208
Museum of the City of New York, xi, 15, 158, 198, 207, 209
Museum of Science and Industry (Chicago), 198, 208
Museums and exhibits, xii, 107, 110, 198–209
My Dollhouse, 229
My Uncle, 90, 226
    dollhouse kit, 154
Myers Florist and Antiques, 229

N
Nash, John, 5
National Association of Miniature Enthusiasts (N.A.M.E.), 8, 193, 194, 196, 214
New York Times, The, 67
New York World's Fair, 8
Nicholson, Sir William, 5
Nielsen, Norm, 226
Noble, John, 15–18
Northeastern Scale Models, Inc., 226

Northford Miniatures, 226
Nutshell News, 9, 193

O
O'Brien, Marion, 194
O'Gorman, Col. Mervyn, 21–24
Old Curiousity Shop, The, 229
Old New Inn (Bourton-on-the-Water), 5
Old-House Journal, The, 195
One-inch scale, 13, 18–21, 140
Open House, 97–99, 227

P
P. Pelican Presents, 226
Patterns:
    dollhouses, 74, 152, 155
    miniatures, 157
Payne, Braxton, 59, 226
Payne, Mary, 58
Pearson, Eric, 39
Phoenix Art Museum, 8, 208
Plans, 194
    for bench, 148
    detailed Williamsburg dollhouse, 172–189
    for dollhouses, xii, 75, 152, 155–156, 158–160
    making your own, 140
    for shadow box, 161
    simplified Williamsburg dollhouse, 163–171
    for stone fireplace, 149–151
    for trestle table, 146–147
Posy Patch Originals, 58, 226
Power tools, 121, 128–129
Prescott, Mell, 60, 226
Prices:
    dollhouse, 79, 82–99
    lists, 11, 213
    setting, 210–212
Publications, xii, 193–195

Q
Queen Anne furnishings, 25, 27, 64
Queen's Dolls' House, 3–5

R
R. L. Carlisle, Miniatures, 221
Rahrer, Marion, 226
Railroad, model, 5, 8
Ready-made dollhouse, 75, 82–99
Realife Miniatures, 142, 226
Realism, 24–25, 160
Reeder, Pearl Ann, 195

Resources, 219–230
Revere, Paul, 35
Robin's Roost, 226
Rochester Museum & Science Center, 209
Rockoff, Betty, 60, 226
Rouleau, Paul E., 223
Router attachment, 120
Rowley, Anthony, 230
Ruddell, Paul A., 226
Rutherford B. Hayes Library, 198, 206, 209
Rutherston, Albert, 5

S
St. Pierre Cathedral (Geneva), 6
Salem House, 230
Salt-box style dollhouse, 160
San Francisco World's Fair, 8
Sara Lee, The, 224
Scale, 12–25
    in antique miniatures, 113
    "Barbi," 18
    difficulties of adhering to, 21–24
    importance of, 14–17
    one-inch, 13, 18–21, 140
    realism and, 24–25
Schramm, Mrs. Jean, 83
Scientific Models, Inc., 226
Seattle Historical Society Museum of Science
        and Industry, 209
Shadow boxes, 9, 10, 25, 27, 73
    advantages of, 73–76
    building, 158
    plan for, 161
Shaker furnishings, 27
Shaker Miniatures, 227
Shelburne Museum, 209
Shop, miniature, 74
Shoppe Full of Dolls, 230
Short, Sir Frank, 5
Shows, xii, 9, 76, 107, 110, 113, 191
    selling at, 213, 214–217
Simone, Constance, 61
Smallness, fascination of, 1–7, 8
Smith, Harry W., 62
Smith, Sally W., 227
Something Different Miniatures, 61, 227
Sonia Messer Imports, 64, 65–66, 67, 225
Sotheby Parke Bernet, 113
Stamp collecting, 5
Starting and Managing a Small Business of Your Own,
    217
Stokes, Adrian, 5

Stone fireplace, plans for, 149–151
Stover, John, 9
Stuart Castle, 198, 200, 209
Stuart Manor, 200
Supplies, 120–139
 adhesives, 131
 building, 132–135
 component parts, 130
 drafting, 121, 122–123
 electrical, 136–138
 finishing, 139
 hand tools, 124–127
 list of resources for, 219–230
 power tools, 121, 128–129
Swissminiatur (miniature village), 6

T
Tahitian Tikis Imports, 227
Television, 9
Teri's Mini Workshop, 227
Thomas, Noel, 97–99, 227
Thorne, Mrs. James Ward, 8, 17
Thorne Rooms, 8, 15–17, 27–35, 39, 198
Time Was Village Museum, 202, 208
Tiny Treasures Society, The (Boston), 196
Tools, see Supplies
Toy Cupboard Museum, The, 202, 208
Toymakers, The, 227
Toys, distinction between miniatures and, 14, 18
Trestle Table, plans for, 146–147

U
U.S. Small Business Administration, 217
U.S. Tariff Act of 1930, 110

V
Victorian furnishings, 27, 64, 118, 194
Victorian-style dollhouse, 88, 160
Vignettes, 9, 73, 74, 77
Village Miniatures, 227

Village Smithy, The, 43, 228
Village Smithy, The (Atkins), 11
Village Toys & Hobbies, 229
Villages, miniature, 5–6
Vitrine, 74
Von Fliss, Robert, 193

W
Walpole, Hugh, 3
Washington Dolls' House & Toy Museum, The, 209
Watties' Decorative Arts, 229
Webster's Dictionary, 67
Wee "C" Shop, 229
Wee Little Studio, 230
White House, 198
Wholesale dealers, 213, 214
Wichita Miniature Society, 196
Wickersham & Sons, 228
William and Mary furnishings, 27
Williamsburg Colonial-style dollhouse, xii, 158, 160
 detailed plans for, 172–189
 simplified plans for, 163–171
Windfall, 228
Wooden Toys, Inc., 226
Woody's Miniatures, 228
Workshop, The, 228
World in Miniatures, The, 228
World War II, 110

X
X-Acto, 144, 228

Y
Yesteryear's Museum, 208
Yield House, Inc., 228

Z
Ziegler, D.E., 228
Zorn, Betsy, 51